DAILY LIFE IN

IMPERIAL RUSSIA

Recent Titles in the
Greenwood Press "Daily Life through History" Series

The Revolutionary War
Charles P. Neimeyer

The American Army in Transition, 1865–1898
Michael L. Tate

Civilians in Wartime Europe, 1618–1900
Linda S. Frey and Marsha L. Frey, editors

The Vietnam War
James E. Westheider

World War II
G. Kurt Piehler

Immigrant America, 1870–1920
June Granatir Alexander

Along the Mississippi
George S. Pabis

Immigrant America, 1820–1870
James M. Bergquist

Pre-Columbian Native America
Clarissa W. Confer

Post-Cold War
Stephen A. Bourque

The New Testament
James W. Ermatinger

The Hellenistic Age: From Alexander to Cleopatra
James Allan Evans

DAILY LIFE IN

IMPERIAL RUSSIA

GRETA BUCHER

947
B919d

Library of Congress Cataloging-in-Publication Data

Bucher, Greta.
  Daily life in Imperial Russia / Greta Bucher.
      p. cm. — (Greenwood press "daily life through history" series, ISSN 1080–4749)
  Includes bibliographical references and index.
  ISBN 978–0–313–34122–9 (alk. paper)
1. Russia—History. 2. Russia—Social life and customs. 3. Kievan
Rus—History. 4. Kievan Rus—Social life and customs. I. Title.
  DK40.B83   2008
  947—dc22   2008002111

British Library Cataloguing in Publication Data is available.

Library of Congress Catalog Card Number: 2008002111
ISBN: 978–0–313–34122–9
ISSN: 1080–4749

First published in 2008

Greenwood Press, 88 Post Road West, Westport, CT 06881
An imprint of Greenwood Publishing Group, Inc.
www.greenwood.com

Printed in the United States of America

The paper used in this book complies with the
Permanent Paper Standard issued by the National
Information Standards Organization (Z39.48–1984).

10 9 8 7 6 5 4 3 2 1

For Will, Rebecca, and John

Contents

Acknowledgments

I would like to thank many people for their help in writing this book. The interest my students have shown over the years in everyday life in early and imperial Russia inspired me to embark on this topic, which is somewhat outside my usual area of research. Linda and Marsha Frey made this project possible by putting me in touch with my editor at Greenwood, Mariah Gumpert, whose help was invaluable in completing this book, particularly in finding and obtaining appropriate images. My superiors at the department of history at West Point were generous in helping me arrange my schedule in such a way that I had time to read and reread the rich literature in Russian social history that informed my own writing. Finally, my husband and children endured many weekends and most of a summer without me, while I locked myself away to write. Without their forbearance and patience, this book would not exist.

Chronology

1722	Table of Ranks
	Law of Succession establishes emperor's right to choose heir
1722–1723	Persian War
1724	Poll tax first collected
1725–1727	Empress Catherine I
1727–1730	Emperor Peter II
1730–1740	Empress Anna
1733–1736	War of Polish Succession
1735–1739	Russo-Turkish War
1740–1741	Emperor Ivan VI
1740–1748	War of Austrian Succession
1741–1762	Empress Elizabeth
1756	Diplomatic Revolution in Europe
1756–1763	Seven Years' War
1762	Emperor Peter III
	Emancipation of the nobility
1762–1796	Empress Catherine II "The Great"
1764	Smol'nyi Institute established
1767	Catherine's *Instructions*
1767–1768	Legislative Commission
1768	Smallpox vaccine introduced to Russia
1768–1774	First Turkish War
1770–1772	Plague in Moscow
1772	First Partition of Poland
1773–1774	Pugachev revolt
1774	Treaty of Kuchuk Kainarji ends Turkish War
1775	Provincial reforms
1782	Educational reforms
	Police Statute
1783	Academy of Sciences founded
1785	Charters to the Nobility and Towns

1786	Charter on National Schools
1787–1792	Second Turkish War
1789	French Revolution
1790	Radishchev's *A Journey from St. Petersburg to Moscow* published
1792	Treaty of Jassy ends Turkish War
1792–1795	Russo-Swedish War
1792–1797	First Coalition against France
1793	Second Partition of Poland
1795	Third Partition of Poland
1796	Law on Succession establishes primogeniture
1796–1801	Emperor Paul
1798–1799	Second Coalition against France
1799–1837	Alexander Pushkin
1801–1825	Emperor Alexander I
1802	Senate and ministry reforms
1803	Law on Free Agriculturalists
1805–1807	Third Coalition against France
1807	Treaty of Tilsit
1807–1812	Continental System
1807–1813	Wars with Sweden, Turkey, and Georgia
1812	Napoleon invades Russia
1813	Battle of Nations
1815	Congress of Vienna
1816–1831	Military colonies
1820	Holy Alliance
1821	Greek Revolt
1825	Decembrist Revolt
1825–1855	Emperor Nicholas I
1830	Polish revolt
1833	Law Code
1840	Potato riots

1843	Prostitution legalized
1848	Revolutions of 1848
	Cholera epidemic
	Communist Manifesto published
1849	Hungarian campaign
1853–1855	Crimean War
1855–1881	Emperor Alexander II "The Great Reformer"
1856	Treaty of Paris ends Crimean War
1861	Emancipation of the serfs
1863	University Statute
	Polish rebellion
	Chernyshevsky's *What Is to Be Done?* published
1864	Zemstvo Reform
	Public School Statute
	Judicial Reform
1867	Alaska sold to United States
1869–1886	Alarchinskii and Liubianskii courses for women
1870	Unification of Germany
1872	Guerrier courses for women established
1874	Military reforms
	"Go to the People" movement
1876–1887	Women's medical courses
1877–1878	War with Turkey
1878	Treaty of San Stefano ends wars
	Congress of Berlin revises Treaty of San Stefano
	Vera Zasulich shoots Governor-General Trepov
	Bestuzhev courses for women established
1881	Alexander II assassinated by the People's Will
	Okhrana (secret police) created
1881–1894	Emperor Alexander III
	Russification intensifies

1881–1905	Temporary Regulations
	Prime Minister Pobedonostsev
1884	University Statute sharply curtails universities' autonomy
1887–1890	Reinsurance Treaty with Germany
1889	*Zemskii Nachal'nik* (Land Captain) instituted
1890	Zemstvo Law places zemstvo more firmly under noble control
1892–1903	Finance Minister Witte's reforms
	Industrialization develops rapidly
1894	Franco-Russian Alliance
1894–1917	Emperor Nicholas II
1897, 1898, 1901	Famine
1898	Social Democratic Workers' Party Founded
1901	Socialist Revolutionary Party established
1903	Social Democratic Party splits into Bolsheviks and Mensheviks
1904–1905	Russo-Japanese War
1905	Treaty of Portsmouth ends Russo-Japanese War
	January Bloody Sunday
	Potemkin mutiny
	October general strike
	October Manifesto
1906	The Fundamental Laws
	The first Duma
1906–1907	Second Duma
1907–1911	Prime Minister Stolypin
	Wager on the Strong and Sober
	Third Duma
1911–1917	Fourth Duma
1912	Maternity leave mandated
1912–1913	Balkan War

1

Introduction: Early History through Peter the Great

This book discusses daily life in Imperial Russia. We look at the way the nobility, serfs/peasants, townspeople, and clergy lived—their work, leisure activities, rituals, celebrations, religious life—and the way their lives changed as Russia dealt with the challenges of modernity. Imperial Russia began with the reign of Peter the Great, who turned Russia from a rather remote kingdom on the edge of Europe into an empire that became heavily engaged in European affairs. Imperial Russia ended with the Bolshevik revolution that was precipitated by World War I, so this book concentrates primarily on the period from 1700 to 1914.

Daily life in Russia was deeply affected by the political and economic changes of an expanding country; in order to help readers understand these changes, the first two chapters focus on the Russia's political development. This introduction begins with Kiev and ends with Peter I; we begin with Kiev because Peter's great reforms, which had a significant impact on the daily lives of all of his subjects, did not occur in a vacuum. He built on the structures that his predecessors had created and on the traditions of Russian culture. Peter is often credited with "westernizing" Russia, but this is both an overstatement and an oversimplification of the facts. Rulers before Peter had imported Western ideas, technologies, and experts, and Russia after Peter remained very different from the western European cultures that he so admired. In order to make sense of Peter's changes, we begin by looking at the roots of the society in which he grew up and hoped to change.

KIEVAN RUS (900–1240)

The study of Russian history usually begins with Kievan Rus. The city of Kiev grew up along the Dnieper River as a convenient location to engage in trade among the Slavs in the area, the Varangians (Vikings) of the north, and Byzantium to the south. Among these groups of peoples, one was known as the Rus, but it is not clear exactly where that term began or to which group it refers, although most historians agree that the Rus were either partially or entirely of Varangian heritage. The unlikely legend in the Russian *Primary Chronicle,* written several hundred years after the event, claims that the Slavic tribes tired of constant warfare among themselves and begged the Varangians to come to rule over them. Three brothers came, and each ruled a city—the eldest, Rurik, taking Novgorod. His descendants eventually took Kiev, which emerged as the center of power and an important urban and trading hub around 900 B.C.E. The society in Kiev became dominated by Rus warriors (possibly of both Scandinavian and Slavic extraction) who controlled the largely agricultural Slavic population. Eventually, the Rus intermingled with the numerically dominant Slavs, and by 960, the Slavic language had become established among the ruling class as well. The leaders of Kiev did not rule a unified state but placed sons (as polygamists, they often had many sons) and other relatives as rulers in other cities along the trade routes. These cities sometimes cooperated in trade and sometimes went to war with one another as their rulers fought to dominate trade and each other. Kiev also warred with the steppe peoples in the area and with Byzantium. The rulers consistently attempted to gain control over the areas surrounding the Volga River because the river was the key to trade. By the end of the tenth century, the early rulers had managed to gain control over the Volga and unite all the East Slavs in the area.

RELIGION AND LAW

Vladimir, ruler of Kiev (980–1015), adopted Byzantine Christianity in 988 as the official religion of the Rus. We look more closely at the conversion later in the text, but suffice it to say here that the adoption of Christianity was an attempt to unite the Rus under one religion with Kiev as its religious center. It also gave Kiev more prestige in Christian Europe: Vladimir made a deal to help the Byzantine emperor in a civil war and adopt Christianity; in return Vladimir was given the emperor's sister in marriage and named her his only legal wife. This relationship with the emperor of Byzantium placed Vladimir on almost equal footing with Europe's most powerful leader and established Kiev as the most important city of the Rus.

The rulers of Kievan Rus also developed a law code throughout the period. Kievan law levied a fine for most offenses, including murder and theft, and the fine was divided among the sheriff, the Church, and the prince. The fines depended on the victim's status, with those closest to the prince being worth the most and peasant women the least. The bloodwite (fine for murder) of a woman was half that of a man. The prince even had bloodwite collectors who traveled around the country to collect fines, living off the local population in each area they visited. Judges, sheriffs, scribes, and officials who specialized in torture also collected fees associated with their jobs. The Church had jurisdiction over what we would today call family law—marriage, divorce, and rights of inheritance—as well as matters of rape and incest. The Church also focused on stamping out vestiges of pagan practice. Although the law and Christianity could be seen as attempts to unify the area under a central government, Vladimir and his heirs did not try to create a unified state. Vladimir had 12 sons whom he sent to rule the other major cities in his realm. He did not create a central bureaucracy or a unified army. Kievan Rus was ruled as a federation of city-states, unified by family ties, trade, and religion. Each city-state and its surrounding farmlands were ruled by a Rurikid (of the line of Rurik) prince, aided by the local elites. In addition, each city had a *veche*, or an assembly of all freemen, about which little is known. The *veche* has sometimes been described as a proto-democratic institution, but most references to it in documents occur only during times of crisis when the people of the city gathered to protest a particular policy or to demand action in a time of trouble. There is no indication that it had any administrative or legislative function.[1] Kievan Rus continued to exist as a powerful political entity until the end of the reign of Iaroslav the Wise in 1054. After that point, the growth in size and importance of other towns led to more civil wars and continued jockeying for position among the Rurikid princes until 1240, when Kiev was destroyed by the Mongols.

Kievan Rus was a large, thriving state for several hundred years. By 1200, the Kievan princes had lost control of their territory in the northern Black Sea steppe, and civil wars occurred more frequently, but Kievan Rus remained the largest state in Europe; only Constantinople was larger and more magnificent than the city of Kiev. This all ended suddenly in 1240 with the Mongol invasion.

MONGOL PERIOD (1240–1480)

The Mongols get blamed for a lot in Russian history. The traditional view of the "Tatar yoke" is that it prevented Russia from developing in the same way that western Europe developed, cut off trade, prevented a Renaissance (and by extension a Reformation or an Enlightenment), and basically kept Russia isolated, poor, and backward. Mongols are frequently blamed for Russia's autocratic nature, the seclusion of elite women in the *terem*, Russian leaders' apparent unconcern for human life or individual rights, and her "oriental" despotism. For the most part, these notions of the Mongol impact on Russia are false. In fact, the Mongols did not cut Russia off from the West, did not discourage trade, and were completely unconcerned about whether or not Russia experienced a Renaissance or any other intellectual reorientation, as long as it did not interfere with paying the Mongol tribute or lead to rebellion. Russia had never developed in imitation of western Europe and had long been oriented toward Byzantium and the steppe peoples rather than toward the West. The Mongols did not change that, nor did they institute any new restrictions on Russian contact with other peoples. In terms of trade, the Mongol period is sometimes known as the "Pax Mongolica" because the Mongols kept roads clear and free of bandits in order to protect their own ability to trade, collect tribute, and travel quickly to put down any signs of rebellion. The Mongols encouraged trade because trade led to revenue. The institution of the terem (women's section of the home, discussed later) certainly did not come from the Mongols, given that the Mongols had no such tradition themselves. This does not mean that the Mongols did not have an impact on Russia, but that impact is often misinterpreted and is a matter of serious historical debate. The Mongol impact on daily life, our primary interest here, is very difficult to determine because we have so little information on the experience of common people during this period. We can, however, draw a few general conclusions based on the existing research and the ongoing scholarly argument over the impact of the Mongols in the development of Russian history: in Russia, the Mongols were largely absentee rulers who had limited interaction with the common people, but whose rule was instrumental in destroying the power of Kiev, shaking up the political and landholding structure, and eventually leading to the rise of Moscow as the most important urban center in Russia.

MONGOL BACKGROUND

First, it is important to know who the Mongols were. The Mongols appeared on the Central Asian steppe in the early thirteenth century. The Rus had long dealt with Turkic nomadic peoples in this area, both by trading with them and by fighting with them. The lifestyle of the steppe nomads was vastly different than that of the Rus: The Rus were farmers and traders who lived in settled villages, towns, and cities; the steppe peoples were nomadic herders and warriors who lived in tents and moved seasonally to find grazing for their herds. In general, the steppe peoples were organized by clan—in other words, everything depended on family ties of blood. The women and children took care of the herds, moving from summer to winter pastures, while the men engaged in warfare. Boys began to train as mounted warriors at a young age, and their clan fought as a unit under the clan elder. They warred with other clans over grazing rights, politics, or personal feuds. When one clan defeated another, it assimilated the survivors into the clan, inventing a history of blood ties to legitimize the union. But because the steppe peoples were nomads, they could not effectively conquer and control the settled civilizations around them any more than those civilizations could effectively conquer and control the nomads. The nomadic tribes might raid the Rus farmlands for slaves or, during hard times, for food. On the other hand, nomadic tribes could be persuaded to assist a Rus prince in a war against another Rus prince or against a common enemy—another nomadic tribe, for example. Both of the cultures benefited from trade.

The Mongols came from Inner Asia and conquered the nomads in Central Asia. The Mongol lifestyle was similar to that of the Turkic nomads, focused on family ties, herding, and warfare. Their religion was shamanist (they would later convert to Tibetan Buddhism), and they worshipped a variety of nature gods. They began with the typical fragmented clan structure but developed a different type of organization that proved to be extremely efficient and deadly before appearing on the Central Asian steppe.

The Mongol leader who united the tribes of Inner Asia, Chingis Khan,[2] believed that he had a divine mission from the god of the Great Blue Sky to rule over all people in felt tents (nomads). After uniting all of the nomads in Inner Asia, he proceeded to change the organization of his troops and acquire new technologies in order to conquer sedentary peoples as well. To this end, he adopted siege warfare and technology, drafting Chinese and Muslim experts, and began his conquest of the world with an army that combined the highly disciplined and rapid warfare of the nomads with a very effective and extremely large siege-warfare machine. The combination proved unbeatable so long as the Mongols (actually by this time a conglomeration of several different nomadic tribes and siege-warfare experts from settled cultures) were united by a strong and capable leader. Although Chingis died in 1227 and divided his armies among his four sons, one became the Great Khan, overlord of all the others, and the conquest continued successfully until his death. Batu led the western campaigns and subdued Russia—in the only successful winter invasion of that land in history—and went on to Poland and Hungary. Once they began conquering lands, they continued: China, Korea, all of Inner Asia and the Central Asian steppe, the Caucasus, Russia, Persia, Mesopotamia, and Syria. At its height, the Mongol Empire stretched from Poland and the Balkans to the Pacific and from the Arctic Ocean to Turkey, the Persian Gulf, and southern China. They stopped only because the Great Khan died, causing an upheaval in Mongol internal politics. Batu withdrew from his westernmost lands (Hungary and Poland) and settled at Old Sarai on the lower Volga; this became the capital of the Mongol domain known as the Golden Horde or the Kipchak Khanate, which included all the western Mongol territory down to the Caucasus Mountains and the northern Caspian Sea as well as Siberia as far east as Mongolia. To the southwest the Golden Horde was bounded by the Il-Khanid Khanate, in the southeast by the Chagatai Khanate, and in the northeast by the Great Khanate. These four Khanates remained united under the Great Khan until 1368, when the Mongol Yuan Dynasty in China fell, and each of the Khanates became fully independent, although all still related through their Chingisid heritage.[3]

MONGOL CONQUEST OF KIEVAN RUS

Batu's conquest of Kievan Rus was devastating. Most of the Rus princes chose to protect their own territory rather than banding together against the onslaught, and Batu was able to pick them off one by one. Mongol tactics were brutal—they destroyed everyone and everything in their path, besieging cities using the siege weapons of the Chinese and the Muslims along with battering rams and catapults. When the Mongols attacked a city, they besieged it until it surrendered and then often razed and burned it, killing or capturing everyone inside. The stories of Mongol attacks spread panic and terror, encouraging many to surrender without a fight—Novgorod in northern Russia simply accepted the Mongol Khan as overlord and pledged tribute to him, thus escaping the attack. Terror also ensured that no rebellion rose against the Mongols in their wake. In addition to destroying cities, Mongols burned peasant villages and crops and scattered livestock. Among the survivors, those with useful artisanal skills were carried off to work in other parts of the Mongol empire, and others were taken as slaves. Kiev and the surrounding regions were destroyed and depopulated. The destruction of Kiev and virtually all of the cities along the river trade routes meant that the southern trade was stopped, but the destruction of crops and all other resources left nothing to trade anyway. Even villages and towns that escaped attack felt the economic repercussions of the huge loss of population, production, and trade caused by the Mongol onslaught. There are no accurate demographic records from this period, but the fact that historians have speculated that parts of Ukraine were utterly depopulated attests to the magnitude of the destruction. Even after the area was under Mongol control, war parties were occasionally sent back to keep the area subdued. In addition to the massive loss of life and property, the Mongols exacted a heavy tribute that one historian has calculated at between five and seven thousand rubles a year—a staggering sum for such a devastated area.[4]

MONGOL RULE

Initially, the Mongols had a direct and ruinous impact on Russia, but the overall effect of two centuries of Mongol control was complicated and depended a great deal on location and social status. After the conquest, most of the Mongols withdrew except for a few governors who remained to see that submission continued and that the tribute was collected. As the remaining population began to reconstruct their lives, they had to adapt to the losses around them, but the level of destruction varied according to location. The northern part of the region recovered and even prospered quickly after the Mongol invasion. Novgorod and its surrounding lands continued to trade and farm in much the same way they had before the invasion because Novgorod had surrendered before being attacked. The loss of many of the towns along the river routes slowed trade initially and forced Novgorodian merchants to turn their attention to the north and west rather than the south and east for a time. Here we have a clear indication that the Mongols had no interest in cutting Russia off from the West; the Mongols encouraged this relationship by extending tax exemptions to the Hanseatic merchants who entered Russia through Novgorod. The Mongols also protected the Baltic and Volga trade routes. Furthermore, the Mongols levied a 5 percent tax throughout their lands on all trade that did not involve grain. In 1270 the Khan of the Golden Horde guaranteed protection of trade throughout his domain: "Whoever comes to me with arms, them I will deal with myself; but the merchant has unhindered passage through my domain."[5]

Still, the destruction in much of the rest of Russia halted trade for many years, and the pattern of recovery in the south seems to have moved the economy more into the realm of agriculture than a revival of the earlier robust trade. As the princes in Moscow extended their power over more territory, they claimed ownership of all the land under their control. They gave this land freely to servitors or to the Church, and this conferred upon the new owner the right to collect rents and fees from any peasants already farming the land. The new owners also had the responsibility of governing the peasants living on the land they received. The elite competed among themselves for power and prestige, which became increasingly associated with the favor of Moscow. Although the Rurikid family continued to dominate the princely lines in Russia, the family had grown large and spawned many branches; some were wealthy, and others were not. The new elite centered at the court in Moscow around the grand prince and was composed of *boyars* who put their military retinues at the disposal of the grand prince and formed his advisory council. This new government would evolve from a combination of steppe and Byzantine influences into a unique political system.

For approximately the first hundred years, the Mongols sent governors to various regions of Russia to oversee the administration, but after that, they relied on native Russian princes to collect the tribute and keep order. Throughout the Mongol period, the various lines of the royal family, the Rurikovichi, continued to struggle with one another for power and prestige, but now they had to obtain the patent of the Great Khan to wield power. This meant that the various contenders for power had to demonstrate their ability to fulfill the Mongols' demands for tribute and for an acquiescent Russia.

As different branches of the family vied for power in the form of the title of grand prince and the right to collect the Mongol tribute, the center of power moved from one city to another, beginning in Vladimir, moving briefly to Moscow, then to Tver, and eventually, back to Moscow.

There were numerous advantages to holding the office of grand prince. The princes could manipulate the taxes to profit themselves. If other princes objected, the grand prince could request a Mongol horde to destroy the recalcitrant city, as Iurii Dolgorukii of Moscow did to the city of Tver. The most successful grand princes were the princes of Moscow. Generally, the grand prince would exempt his own lands from contributing to the tax and would levy proportionally higher taxes on the lands held by other nobles. Because the Mongols did not care who paid or how much was paid as long as they received their designated portion, the wily grand prince could collect more than the allotted tribute and keep the profits for himself and his domain. In this way, the princes of Moscow grew wealthy and powerful while impoverishing those around them. As the lords in the adjacent lands lost revenue, they cut deals with the Muscovite prince and thus came under his control in exchange for a reduction in taxes. The Muscovite princes further collected lands through purchase, marriage, and annexation. As the Muscovite princes brought more lords under their control, their reach extended further afield as they gathered more and more lands under their dominion and added revenue to their treasury. The Metropolitan, the highest official of the Orthodox Church in Russia, finally moved to Moscow as well, reinforcing Moscow's claim to be the most important city in all of the Russian lands. The Mongols respected all religions and exempted them from taxes in exchange for prayers for the Great Khan. The Orthodox Church was no exception, and as a result, it became very wealthy under the Mongols and acquired enormous estates, which were willed to it by boyars in order to avoid taxes or to ensure that prayers were said for their souls. As a result, the grand princes and the Church constructed many churches and monasteries during the last one hundred years of Mongol rule, many in and around Moscow.

THE RISE OF MOSCOW

Moscow rose as a prominent city in Russia partially as a result of her privileged position with the Mongols, but also because she had extraordinarily capable rulers who made good use of the benefits of their office and the support of the Church. The state that eventually emerged had been shaped by Byzantine and Mongol influence on the native Kievan political culture to create a uniquely Russian style of government. The society that this state governed was not molded by outside forces but instead emerged as a response to the challenges and opportunities presented by Mongol rule from a tradition firmly rooted in the Kievan culture of the medieval period. The ascension of the Muscovite princes to uncontested power over their fellow Rurikid contenders took over two hundred years and was extremely tumultuous. Although the princes made good use of the power of the Khan, the Church, the Byzantine connection, their wealth, and their family ties, the entire period from the beginning of Iurii Dolgorukii's reign in 1304 to the end of Vasilii III's reign in 1533 was full of political intrigue, wars with other Rurikid princes and with foreign powers, upheavals in the Church leadership, Mongol attacks, and natural disasters (the Black Plague, for example).[6]

Moscow eventually emerged as the most powerful city because her princes made good use of the power of the title grand prince to expand and consolidate their power. The Muscovite princes also appreciated and harnessed the power of the Orthodox Church. In 1325, before Ivan I attained the title of grand prince, the Metropolitan of the Church moved to Moscow. The princes used marriage to forge alliances with the other powerful families and with the other branches of the Rurikid line. They used their position as tribute collectors to add to their own coffers and created incentives for wealthy landowners to join with them by granting exemptions from taxes to those who placed their lands under the grand prince's domain. The growing wealth of Moscow was also attractive to noble families in cities that were less well off or cities that had come under recent Mongol attack—Ivan I of Moscow, for example, was able to convince many of the nobles from Tver to transfer their allegiance to him after that city was sacked in 1327. Ivan also broke the Kievan tradition of lateral inheritance (to the brother instead of the son) of the office of grand prince. Furthermore, the Muscovite family managed not to squander its lands among many sons. The custom among the princely families had always been to divide inheritance among all legitimate sons. Over a few generations, this practice often reduced the family domains to small estates that were no longer capable of maintaining a military force. Although the Muscovite princes followed this practice, the sons managed to cooperate with one another and with the grand prince, so that the Muscovite wealth and power could be effectively harnessed to pursue a united policy. Other branches of the family, particularly in Tver, the Muscovites' chief rivals, did not get along as well and wasted resources arguing and warring among themselves. In addition, in 1353 the Black Plague struck the Muscovite family, killing all but two of the heirs, which reunited all of the branch's lands back under Ivan II.[7]

THE GATHERING OF THE LANDS

Most historians credit Ivan III (1462–1605) with finally consolidating the power of Moscow over the other princes. He was, in the words of one historian, a "master politician."[8] His father, Vasilii II, had, through civil war and clever management, done much to quell opposition to the Muscovite ascendancy. Ivan III was the first grand prince successfully to assume the title without asking permission from the Great Khan. Ivan managed to subdue Novgorod and Tver and finally brought those cities and their huge territory firmly under Moscow's control. Partially as a result of these victories, Ivan instituted a new system of landholding known as *pomestie*, which, as will be discussed further, had profound consequences for the future social, political, and economic structure of Russia. Vasilii III (1505–1533), Ivan's son, completed the annexation of troubling territories by adding Pskov and Riazan to the new kingdom. In addition, much of the eastern part of the Lithuanian grand duchy was added during their reigns.

ESTABLISHING LEGITIMACY

Gathering territory was not the only way that Ivan and Vasilii consolidated power. Ivan in particular was very aware of the importance of words and symbols in establishing his house supreme in the region. He began to use the title *Tsar*, which had previously been used for both the Byzantine emperor, or Caesar, and the Mongol khan. The title tsar clearly indicated a ruler who was sovereign—vassal to no one. These rulers not only used the title themselves but, by Vasilii III's reign, had even convinced other ruling houses, most notably the Habsburg Holy Roman Emperor, to acknowledge their right to claim it. In addition to the new title, Ivan began using the double-headed eagle, symbol of the Byzantine and then the Habsburg emperors, as the symbol of his house as well. In the 1520s, an Orthodox monk articulated a new concept known as the "Third Rome." According to this theory, the first Rome, which was the city of Rome where the Christian Church was founded, was lost to the true faith in the schism between the Orthodox and Catholic churches in 1054. The second Rome, which was Constantinople, where the Byzantine emperor headed the Orthodox Church, fell when the Muslim Turks defeated Byzantium in 1453. Moscow was the Third Rome, last bastion of the only true faith, Orthodoxy; to fail in protecting the faith would bring on the apocalypse because there would be no fourth Rome. The political ideology of the Third Rome clearly raised the importance of Moscow and her princes and strengthened the idea that Moscow was the heir to the Byzantine Empire. To reinforce this connection, Ivan III married the niece of the last Byzantine emperor. Perhaps the most important symbol of Ivan III's reign was the Battle of the Ugra River in 1480, when Ivan's armies faced the armies of Khan Ahmed across the river. After much negotiation, Khan Ahmed withdrew with very little loss of blood on either side. Although the "battle" did not really affect the relationship between the Mongols and Moscow, the Russians have designated this date as the end of the "Tatar yoke." The Russian tsars continued to pay tribute to various khans on a sporadic basis until 1699, but their status as independent, sovereign rulers was clearly established.

MUSCOVITE SOCIAL STRUCTURE: *POMESHCHIKI* AND *MESTNICHESTVO*

The consolidation of power under the tsars in Moscow had profound consequences for the social structure of Russia. The newly expanded kingdom meant that the rulers had several new challenges to overcome. They had to establish some sort of administration to rule over this much larger territory; they had to figure out what to do with all of the new elites that had come under their control; they had to decide how much cultural variety was acceptable, particularly in terms of laws and religious practices; finally, they had to come up with a military able to defend their much expanded borders. Ivan III began the process with the acquisition of Novgorod and its territories. In order to assure himself of the loyalty of that fiercely independent city, Ivan confiscated the lands of those nobles who had most vigorously opposed Muscovite domination as well as many of the local church lands. These he gave to his own loyal servitors or to local men he chose to become the new nobility of Novgorod. The practice of giving land to loyal men was not new, but these lands carried new stipulations with them. All of those who received these grants, known as pomestie, agreed to serve the tsar for life; these lands were not heritable, but returned to the tsar upon the landholder's death. This system placed men loyal to Ivan in control of the Novgorod province because any who proved not loyal would lose their lands. It enabled Ivan to reward those among his own retinue and those already in Novgorod who had shown loyalty to him throughout the struggle. It also dispossessed all of the old elites who had opposed Ivan's efforts to extend his control over the territory. This system worked so well that it became the standard method of integrating new territories into the kingdom, creating a much larger group of nobles who owed everything to the tsar and who could be called on at any time to serve in the tsar's armies. Pomestie thus became the social and economic foundation of the tsar's rapidly growing army because a servitor given a pomestie could be expected to feed and equip himself for regular cavalry service, and this helped to solve the problem of securing the borders. These new nobles, called *pomeshchiki,* also presented a social challenge to the older hereditary nobility both in Moscow and in the new territories. The old princely and boyar families found their positions undermined by these newly created or newly enriched elites who could be relied on to support the tsar with far fewer questions than the older nobles, who were not so completely reliant on the tsar for their wealth and power.

In order to integrate the various new elites who entered the service of Moscow, a new hierarchy known as *mestnichestvo* was created. Mestnichestvo was an elaborate ranking system of the elite families based on birth; individuals were ranked by clan, place within the clan, and length of service to the tsar. Originally mestnichestvo determined social precedence—where one was seated at a dinner, for example—but eventually, this highly complicated and elaborate system was extended to determine status and rank in all areas, to include military assignments; no one could be asked to serve beneath anyone with a lower standing. For example, if boyar A served under boyar B in a campaign, boyar B's son could not serve under boyar A's son in a future battle. Some of the problems in such a system are immediately apparent: What if boyar B's son was an idiot, and boyar A's son a military genius? Could boyar B's youngest son serve under boyar A's oldest son? As time went on, and the elite families became more and more connected by marriage, figuring out the relative status of various descendants became extremely difficult and led to protracted arguments and wrangling at court that could delay important decisions. Elite families sought to improve their mestnichestvo standing through marriage into higher-ranking clans, convoluting the process further. Ultimately, the system served to increase the aristocracy's dependence on the tsar, who, by granting posts or not granting them, could increase a family's status in the system or refuse to do so. The system fostered competition within the aristocracy as well, pitting them against each other in the struggle for the tsar's favor and preventing them from developing any kind of corporate cohesion that might have inspired them to look for institutional enhancement of their political power; rather than trying to increase the political power of the nobility as a whole through some kind of parliament that could limit or challenge the tsar's authority, they each tried to enhance their own power through personal connection to the tsar. This is not to say that the tsar's power did not have traditional or practical limitations—the tsar had to have a certain measure of cooperation from the nobility in order to implement policies—but the tsar's claim to supreme and absolute authority remained intact without any institutional challenges. Despite the system's usefulness to the tsar in maintaining his authority and integrating the elites during the periods of rapid expansion, it proved to be a huge headache for future tsars who sought to circumvent cumbersome constraints of birth in their military and administrative appointments. For example, Tsar Ivan IV asserted his right to ignore claims of mestnichestvo in times of war. Despite its drawbacks, mestnichestvo continued to operate as the organizing principle for the elite for the next two centuries and was not fully displaced until Peter the Great instituted his Table of Ranks in 1722.

To rule the new regions, Ivan created the post of provincial governor. These governors were appointed from the elite at court and were sent to various parts of the kingdom to see that the local infrastructure and defense were maintained and to dispense justice. Although this was a very difficult job, given that laws and customs varied from place to place, it could also be a lucrative position because the governor charged fees for his services, living off the local people in order to fulfill his obligations. Many of these positions were in small and poor areas, but the governor of Novgorod, for example, had a very profitable position. These governors were the mechanism through which the tsars administered their growing territories and kept watch on potentially volatile areas of the kingdom. The governors kept order and imposed some central authority on the region. These positions usually lasted only a year or two before they rotated to a new man. The duties were heavy, and it was not a popular position with the local population, but in the absence of a bureaucracy or proper government administration, the position served to bring some order to the realm and offered opportunities for advancement and wealth that the courtiers in Moscow coveted.

CONSOLIDATING POWER

To further integrate his new territories, Ivan III issued a new law code in 1497 that laid out the judicial system, establishing officers of the court, their responsibilities, their fees, and defining the punishments they could impose. It prohibited judges from soliciting or accepting bribes and established the grand prince as the supreme lawmaker and judge for all of the lands controlled by Moscow. All of the lands now came under a uniform system of laws, punishments, and fines, although the Church did not fall under the jurisdiction of the code. This law also restricted peasant movement to the two weeks surrounding St. George's Day in November, although it did not create serfdom. By the end of Vasilii III's reign, the Muscovite tsars seemed to have successfully consolidated power in their own hands. They had developed a large, centrally commanded army supported by a new system of landholding; they had unified all of their lands under a centralized law code; they had gained the firm support of the Orthodox Church as the only legitimate rulers of the Russian Orthodox people; they had begun to develop a rudimentary administrative system that allowed them to keep an eye on their far-flung lands and ensure that taxes and fees were paid and laws were followed; they had acquired titles, prestige, and control of a substantial treasury and had turned the city of Moscow from a provincial backwater into an impressive capital with lofty churches and palaces designed to awe all who saw them. They had not, however, established a firm law of succession. While the Muscovite family had managed to shift the inheritance of their throne from their brothers to their sons, they had not completely stamped out the old practice, nor had they a clear plan for how to handle succession in the absence of an adult son.

IVAN THE TERRIBLE (1533–1584)

Vasilii III died without an adult heir. His son, Ivan IV, later known as Ivan the Terrible, was only three years old. Ivan's mother, Elena Glinskaia, served as regent, quite competently, until her early death when Ivan was eight. This left the young prince to the mercies of the noble factions at court, which some historians have cited as one of the reasons behind his later peculiar and violent behavior. The boyars spent the nine years of Ivan's minority murdering and exiling one another until Ivan came of age. It is important to note that these families did not seek to undermine the power of the tsar; rather, each family sought to wield it for themselves, once again demonstrating the lack of cohesion among the noble families in Moscow. Ivan IV was the first Muscovite prince to be ceremonially crowned tsar by the Metropolitan of Moscow in 1547. His coronation was a very lavish affair that consciously pulled traditions from Byzantium as well as the ancient Rus customs. He was invested with a jeweled cross, a ceremonial collar, and the cap of Monomakh—a crown with a fictitious history of having been granted by the Byzantine emperor to Vladimir Monomakh of Kiev in the eleventh century. Although Vasilii III and Ivan III had both used the title tsar, neither had claimed it as openly and with such fanfare as Ivan IV. The grand prince was clearly gone, replaced by the all-powerful, God-appointed tsar of all the Russias.

Ivan's reign is perhaps the most notorious of all Russian rulers. Stories about him abound, ranging from his enjoyment of torturing small animals as a child to his blinding the architects who created St. Basil's Cathedral, to the wholesale slaughter of his opponents. Although all of these stories are more or less true, they provide only a distorted view of Ivan's reign in which he continued the consolidation of power into the hands of the tsar. One historian has described him as a "Renaissance Prince," and there is much to recommend this theory, keeping in mind that Ivan was a product of his time.[9] In the fifteenth and sixteenth centuries there were many violent and ruthless rulers in other parts of Europe as well—Vlad the Impaler in Transylvania, Bloody Mary in England, and Catherine de Medici in France, to name only the most notorious. During Ivan's life, western Europe became engulfed in the various wars of religion generated by the Reformation and the violence that attended the emergence of national monarchies. Ivan was also engaged in creating a national monarchy, but his reputation as a nation-builder is lost in the disasters that followed his reign. Although many of his early policies helped to rationalize and centralize the tsar's authority, the consequences of his excesses contributed to the catastrophic period that followed his reign, the Time of Troubles.

IVAN'S EARLY YEARS: GOVERNMENT, CHURCH, AND MILITARY REFORMS

The early years of Ivan's reign were marked by continued intrigue at court as the noble families tried to gain ascendancy over the tsar.

For our purposes, the most important change was that Ivan chose to marry a woman from a minor noble family, Anastasia Romanova, which immediately elevated some of her male relatives to boyar status and gave the family new influence at court. Ivan's early years are widely recognized as some of the most productive in terms of consolidating not only the tsar's power but also Russia's position vis-à-vis the other emerging monarchies of the region. Ivan's activities at the beginning of his reign institutionalized the ad hoc government system that he inherited. He called the first *zemskii sobor,* or meeting of the lands, apparently to get advice from the leading families of his kingdom and to gather their support for the changes he intended to make in the administration of the government and the military. He issued a new law code targeting corruption in government and strengthening the position of the provincial governors. He also called a Church council in 1550 to weed out corruption and problems in Church administration. Finally, he organized the administration itself into departments, known as *prikazy,* each with a separate jurisdiction and with a single chief. The *prikazy* continued to grow and to be the institutions that governed Russia until Peter I reorganized the government in the eighteenth century.

Ivan also reorganized the army in preparation for his conquest of Kazan. The backbone of the army had long been the cavalry, composed of nobles and pomeshchiki. Because most of their foes were steppe nomads, it made sense that the Russian army continued to emphasize mounted warriors over the new musket firearms, which were expensive, cumbersome, difficult, and slow to deploy to the borders and largely ineffective against mounted nomads on the open terrain of the steppe (this would change later when firearms and firearm techniques became more sophisticated). The cavalry, however, was plagued by disputes over precedence that often hampered military campaigns as officers argued over who could take orders from whom. Ivan issued a new law that allowed him to appoint men of his own choosing to lead regiments and the overall army (consisting of five regiments) and stipulated that the chain of command among the commanders would depend not on mestnichestvo but on the position each held in the army. For example, the regimental commanders had to obey the army commander no matter what their relationship in the mestnichestvo system was. This helped but did not wholly resolve the problem as the men involved sometimes continued to argue over such points. He also created six companies of musketeers known as *streltsy* to complement the cavalry. The streltsy did not receive estates; instead they drew a salary from the royal treasury. They gained increasing importance in the tsar's army because they were primarily responsible for besieging fortresses and were often used as garrison troops in newly taken territory. With his freshly strengthened army, Ivan finally defeated Kazan and added considerable territory to Russia.

THE OPRICHNINA

Although Ivan continued the consolidation policies of his forebears, his reign is most widely remembered for the disasters. After his victory against Kazan, Ivan embarked on a long and ultimately fruitless struggle against his western neighbor, Livonia, costing his kingdom dearly in both lives and treasure. His creation of the *oprichnina* was even more costly. In 1565 Ivan removed himself, his family, and his treasury to a monastery outside Moscow and announced that he was abdicating the throne because of the disloyalty of the boyars and nobility. His conditions for returning to the throne (and bringing back the treasury) were that he would create a separate kingdom ruled exclusively and directly by Ivan himself called the oprichnina. The rest of the kingdom would be ruled by the Boyar Council, which would bring only the most important issues to Ivan. To administer his new lands, he created a new army, also known as the oprichnina, whose members had to take a written oath to Ivan. He clothed his new army in black robes, like monks, and made their symbols a dog's head and a broom, signs that their job was to bite like dog and then sweep the land clean. He then embarked on a series of purges that involved all from the highest princely families to their retainers and peasants. Several waves of treason accusations, torture, and execution or exile followed. The victims of these attacks included very powerful men who Ivan may have believed threatened his power, but the victims also included common merchants and artisans. A conviction of treason did not result in the death of only the accused, but also most of his family, often his retainers and servants, and sometimes even the peasants on his estate. Tens of thousands of people were killed or displaced in the final 20 years of Ivan's reign. In 1570 Ivan set up his court in Novgorod, which his grandfather had subdued and placed under the control of Moscow courtiers, and killed over 2,000 people under torture and execution. His oprichnina spent months ravaging the city and the surrounding countryside, looting, burning, raping, and killing all in their paths, sending the number of victims much higher. This seems particularly incomprehensible given that Novgorod had long been a valuable source of taxation for the princes in Muscovy; Ivan's purge destroyed the city's economy. Novgorod was the most extreme victim of Ivan's strange wrath, but other parts of the kingdom suffered similar fates as the oprichnina sought out victims, destroying them and the areas they passed through on their hunt. The economic devastation was enormous, and the repercussions would be felt for several generations.

Ivan also engaged in highly confusing behavior in other ways. In 1575 he announced a new tsar in the person of Simon Bekbulatovich, a descendent of the khans, and moved himself to another part of Moscow, calling himself Ivan of Moscow. The pretense did not last long but certainly added to the general confusion of Ivan's final years. On the other hand, not all of Ivan's actions were so bizarre; he supported the pomeshchiki, the backbone of his regular army, by protecting them from income loss when he issued temporary decrees that forbade peasants from leaving their landlords. The years that peasants were forced to stay put were known as the Forbidden Years and were a precursor to full enserfment. Although the Forbidden Years were certainly very hard on the peasants, they protected Ivan's most valuable servitors from losing labor to large noble landholders and the Church, one of the largest landholders in Russia. The combination of highly expensive, protracted wars and the devastation caused by the oprichnina left the Russian economy in a shambles and left the Russian people confused at the vindictive actions of the tsar. To make matters worse, toward the end of his life, Ivan accidentally killed his oldest son and heir, Ivan, in a fit of rage. This left his son Fedor, a weak man who had limited mental abilities, as the only direct heir to Ivan's throne.

THE IMPACT OF IVAN THE TERRIBLE

Ivan's reign had profound consequences for all of his people. The princes, boyars, and nobility could find themselves under attack at any moment, causing much upheaval among the elite. Some families were wiped out entirely, others eclipsed for a time only to regain prominence either later in Ivan's reign or after. New families rose to prominence. Some survived; others did not. Ivan succeeded in removing most of the oldest and most powerful families from their traditional sources of power—nearly 60 percent of the nobles listed in court records were moved from their familial districts to new districts over the last half of the sixteenth century.[10] This resulted in curtailing the power of the affected families; however, Ivan did not succeed in breaking the power of the elite in Russian politics. None of Ivan's actions attacked the system of government that placed the tsar in the middle of the web of noble and near-noble families at court. Although the members of the elite changed during Ivan's reign, the role of the elite did not. Ivan succeeded better in destroying the economy, not only of the elite but of Russia as a whole. His *oprichniki* looted at will and simply took whatever they wanted, not only from the victims that Ivan identified, but from anyone else as well. People were afraid to stand up to the oprichniki. In addition, the destruction of so many people and so much property was devastating for the tsar's treasury. The tsar confiscated a lot of land from his victims, but he also distributed considerable amounts of land both to those he elevated to power and to the Church. The constant displacement of elite landowners meant that they were no longer interested in long-term agricultural development and wanted only to squeeze as much out of their lands and peasants as they could. The loss of revenue from destroyed villages and cities, in addition to hurting the royal treasury, hurt the economy as a whole, resulting in famine and peasant flight, which led to further dislocation and deterioration of the economy. High taxes to pursue his wars contributed to the decline in the peasant economy, as did a series of natural disasters. Peasants entered into slavery (slaves paid no taxes) or simply fled. This in turn hurt the lesser nobles and pomeshchiki in particular, and they sometimes abandoned their estates. These problems not only cost the government tax revenue but also weakened the cavalry because of the loss of pomeshchiki. In addition, the crisis of leadership that followed Ivan's reign prompted Poland, Lithuania, and Sweden to move in and try to grab parts of Russia and even the Muscovite throne. The combination of all of these events culminated in a 30-year period of civil war, foreign invasion, famine, and near collapse known as the Time of Troubles.

TIME OF TROUBLES (1585–1613)

The Time of Troubles was one of the most turbulent times in Russian history. A combination of factors contributed to the disasters of this period, among them famine, a succession crisis, an economic crisis, peasant flight, and foreign invasion. These problems were exacerbated by civil war among various boyar factions desiring to gain the throne for themselves. Although we have moved quickly through the political developments thus far, we next look more closely at this short period of time because the instability of this time period firmly established the tsar as supreme autocrat, cemented the position of the nobility in Russia, and led directly to the establishment of serfdom and consequently had profound consequences for the daily lives of all segments of the population.

BORIS GODUNOV (1584–1605)

After Ivan IV died, his only surviving legitimate son, Fedor (1584–1598), took the throne. Fedor has been described as weak both physically and mentally and had to be guided by a strong advisor. The man who occupied this position was Fedor's brother-in-law, Boris Godunov, who had risen from obscurity through the oprichnina to prominence in Ivan's court. Boris was a very capable ruler who tried to mitigate the problems caused by Ivan IV; he was hated by the more prominent families at court who believed that they had a better right to advise Fedor and then to succeed him after he died childless in 1598. Fedor's death without an heir ended the clear succession from father to son that the Muscovite princes had enjoyed since they emerged from obscurity in the beginning of the fourteenth century. Rumors also circulated that Boris had murdered yet another claimant to the throne in 1591—Dmitrii, Ivan IV's son from his seventh, uncanonical wife. The story of Dmitrii's murder at the hands of the evil usurper Boris Godunov has gone down as legend in Russian history and has even been memorialized in the famous opera, *Boris Godunov.* At the time, an investigative committee, headed by Vasilii Shuisky (one of Boris's rivals for power at court), found that Dmitrii had experienced an epileptic fit while playing with a knife and had stabbed himself during his seizure. Historians have since concluded that the investigative committee was probably right—there were few reasons for Boris to bother to kill Dmitrii in 1591. Dmitrii was not a strong claimant for the throne, considering that, as the son of a seventh marriage not sanctioned by the Church, he was illegitimate; he had also been exiled with his mother to an estate at Uglich, far from the center of power. Perhaps more importantly, there was no reason to think in 1591 that Fedor would not produce an heir of his own for the throne. Finally, even in the absence of another direct heir, there were plenty of other people with better claims to be Fedor's heir than Boris or Dmitrii. Murdering Dmitrii did not put Boris any closer to the throne than he already was. However, many of his contemporaries rejected the verdict and continued to whisper that Boris had murdered Dmitrii.

Murder of Dmitrii, son of Ivan IV (the Terrible). North Wind Picture Archives.

The problems of dynastic succession and legitimacy were at the heart of the Time of Troubles. When Fedor died, Boris managed to get the throne through a series of intelligent political maneuvers and because the boyars could not agree which among them should lead the next dynasty and eventually had to acknowledge Boris as the next tsar of Russia. Boris was crowned in 1598. One could make the argument that Boris had more authority while he was Fedor's advisor because after he was crowned, he could not command the same kind of loyalty from the Russian people that the Rurikid dynasty had claimed. The problem of legitimacy would plague not only the reign of Boris but also the succeeding rulers. As long as legitimacy was in doubt, various factions had a rallying cry for rebellion in the name of the "rightful" tsar. And with all of the problems that Russia experienced under Boris and after he died, there were plenty of disgruntled people eager to find an excuse for the calamities that Russia experienced during these years.

FAMINE AND REBELLION

All of Europe experienced a cold snap at the turn of the century. In Russia this resulted in lost crops in 1601 and 1602. Boris's government tried valiantly to help the people of Russia during the famine but simply could not provide enough food to enough places to stave off starvation. Thousands of starving peasants roamed the countryside looking for food and causing trouble. Boris put down several small rebellions in the north of his realm, but the greater threat came from the south, where the Cossacks lived and attracted discontented peasants. In 1604 a pretender named Grishka Otrepev, claiming to be Ivan IV's dead son Dmitrii, arrived in southern Russia with Polish backing. This "False Dmitrii," as he came to be called, claimed that he had escaped Boris's plans to kill him and was now back to reclaim his right to the throne. False Dmitrii presented the perfect opportunity for discontented Russians to revolt against Boris, and False Dmitrii found backing not only from the discontented peasantry but also from noble families who resented Boris's rise to power—most notably, the Romanovs. False Dmitrii also gained support from Cossack bands that had been stirred up by the fugitive peasants who had recently arrived from Russia. He eventually created a formidable army and challenged Boris's right to the throne. In seventeenth-century Russia, this was about the only way that large-scale rebellion could be formed. Few peasants would openly rebel against their tsar, but the False Dmitrii's claims allowed them to rebel in the name of the "rightful" tsar to take the usurper Boris off the throne. The famine that preceded False Dmitrii's arrival confirmed in the minds of many that Boris did not have a legitimate claim to the throne—his sin in killing (or now, trying to kill) Dmitrii and his usurpation of the throne were seen as the catalyst for God's punishment of Russia with the famine. The only way to rectify the situation was to put the right man on the throne; rebellion was the duty of every Orthodox. Of course, not everyone involved in the rebellion needed an excuse to rebel, but the situation made it easier for those who believed themselves to be loyal to the autocracy to join, and it made wonderful propaganda as the rebellion spread to new territories. False Dmitrii's troops swelled to the thousands and included Cossacks, peasants, townsmen, Poles, and nobles, especially the Romanovs.

Over the course of 1604, False Dmitrii's forces moved toward Moscow. In April of 1605, Boris suddenly died, his supporters abruptly went over to the rebels, and the False Dmitrii was crowned Tsar Dmitrii. The violence might have ended there except that Dmitrii had spent much of his life in Poland and adopted Polish ways, including becoming a Catholic. He did not do a good job of concealing his religious leanings, and to make matters worse, he married a Polish Catholic. Although Dmitrii was publicly accepted as Ivan's son and was even "recognized" by the real Dmitrii's mother, who was released from her convent in order to legitimize her "son," many at court secretly rejected his claims—most notably, Vasilii Shuiskii, who was descended from the Rurikid line and who had led the investigative committee that had pronounced Dmitrii's death an accident. As Tsar Dmitrii grew less popular, a boyar faction led by Shuiskii led an uprising in 1606, in which Dmitrii was killed. To reinforce the idea that Dmitrii was a pretender and that he was defeated, Shuiskii had Dmitrii's naked corpse dragged around Moscow by its genitals, the body burned, and the ashes shot from a canon toward Poland; he was proclaimed a satanic sorcerer. An angry mob ravaged the city for two days, killing about 2,000 foreigners. Shuiskii was then proclaimed tsar.

TSAR VASILII SHUISKII

One of Shuiskii's first acts upon assuming the throne was to have the corpse of the real Dmitrii dug up and brought to Moscow. He then had Dmitrii canonized in an attempt to convince everyone that Dmitrii had died 15 years earlier at Uglich. Unfortunately for Shuiskii, Dmitrii's remains had decayed (the bodies of saints do not decay), and it was difficult to convince people that Tsar Dmitrii had truly been a pretender. Tsar Vasilii Shuiskii was condemned by the people of Moscow as an aristocratic pawn, ready to serve the elites rather than the townsmen and peasants. Other noble families, again led by the Romanovs, believed that their claims to the throne were as good as Shuiskii's and continued to plot against him. The south, where the rebellion that put False Dmitrii on the throne had begun, refused to acknowledge Shuiskii as tsar, and another rebellion quickly began that swelled into a significant military threat by the end of the year. The leader, a former slave named Bolotnikov, issued manifestos calling for slaves to kill their masters and for peasants to burn manor houses. Such speeches eventually alienated his noble and upper-class followers, who switched sides and took their troops to support Shuiskii, who finally won in the fall of 1607.

After defeating the uprising, Shuiskii attempted to stabilize his kingdom by forbidding peasants and townsmen from moving. Nobles were given the right to track down peasants who had fled, and local officials were responsible for checking up on all newcomers to make sure that they were permitted to move around. Shuiskii desperately needed for people to stay put, not only to improve the economy and collect taxes, but also just so that he could know where they were. The years of famine and rebellion had encouraged people to move around, and the government no longer had any clear idea of who or where its population was. The government, however, had no ability to enforce these decrees except immediately around Moscow. Particularly in the south, where both major rebellions had begun, the tsar had no control at all. But although these decrees were impossible to enforce, they did have the effect of angering the lower-class population, who resented losing their ability to move and certainly resented being forced to stay in the areas that had been devastated by the fighting and where it was difficult to survive. Although the long-term economic benefits of a stable agricultural population were obvious, in the short term, life was very difficult for the peasants who did not think they should be forced to stay in the hungry regions of the kingdom. Thus, the policy created less stability than ever—on the one hand, because it was not enforceable, it did not stabilize the economy or the population or help the elites that it was supposed to bolster; on the other hand, it served to ignite even more lower-class discontent and to show the elite that Shuiskii's government could not create the stability it needed in order to prosper.

THE SECOND FALSE DMITRII

Very soon after the Bolotnikov rebellion was defeated, a new rebel force formed in the south, led by yet another man pretending to be Dmitrii. The "Second False Dmitrii," as he is, of course, known, claimed to be both the original Dmitrii and the First False Dmitrii. He and his forces made it all the way to the gates of Moscow by 1608 but could not take the city and so withdrew to Tushino, a few miles away, to set up a rival court. Dmitrii's mother was once again produced to recognize her son, and the First False Dmitrii's wife also recognized her husband. The Second False Dmitrii was clearly neither of these people—he looked nothing like the First False Dmitrii and was obviously from the lower classes. Still, being the wife or mother of a potential tsar was infinitely preferable to exile in a convent, so they both accepted him, and his "wife" quickly became pregnant. Shuiskii had to take desperate measures to combat this new threat and even turned to Poland and Sweden, concluding treaties with both so that they had to withdraw their support from the Tushino government; Sweden even sent troops to help the Moscow court. In addition to the foreign troops on Russian soil, there were several elite families who now had nothing to lose by joining with the foreigners—the Romanov family had supported the Second False Dmitrii and understood that Shuiskii could not safely allow them back into his good graces. Filaret Romanov, an ambitious man who had been forced to go into a monastery for his attempts to take the throne, threw his lot in with the Poles. In 1610 False Dmitrii made another bid for power supported by Poland. Shuiskii was defeated and forced to enter a monastery. No tsar sat on the throne, and no clear candidate existed. The elite families could not agree on a new tsar.

THE INTERREGNUM AND THE THIRD FALSE DMITRII

In the absence of a tsar, seven boyars formed a council as a stop-gap measure to save Russia from the Swedes advancing from the north and the Poles advancing from the south. For a while, they seriously considered inviting the Polish prince to rule Russia on condition that he would convert to Orthodoxy. A delegation, including Filaret Romanov and the former Tsar Vasilii Shuiskii, went to Warsaw to finalize the deal with the Polish king, who rejected the terms of the agreement and demanded to be made king of Russia himself with plans to convert the region to Catholicism. The delegation refused and was promptly arrested. The Second False Dmitrii was murdered, and Moscow remained in the hands of the Poles while the Cossack forces found a new pretender—the four-year-old son of the Second False Dmitrii and his Polish wife, known as the "Baby Brigand." Once again, Russian forces were divided and at war with themselves. Patriarch Hermogen called for Orthodox unity, and a new army was formed whose leaders wanted to oust the Poles and the pretender and to select a new tsar from among those with blood ties to the Rurikid dynasty. To this end, they called a *zemskii sobor* to choose the new tsar even as they fought against the Poles. As they approached Moscow, some of the Cossack troops joined their cause, and in the fall of 1612, Moscow was liberated from the Poles, and the Baby Brigand and his mother were captured and eventually executed—the four-year-old boy was hanged. At that point, the leaders insisted that the *zemskii sobor* meet as soon as possible to bring political unity to the kingdom.

THE ROMANOV DYNASTY

In January 1613 the *zemskii sobor* met with representatives from all groups of free men—nobles, clergy, townsmen, and peasants. They eventually decided on Mikhail Romanov as a good compromise for the new tsar: The Romanov family was tied to the Rurikids through Anastasia's marriage to Ivan IV. They had been active supporters of the Second False Dmitrii, which made them acceptable to the lower classes, but Mikhail himself was only 16 and not seen as a threat to the other powerful families who might have balked at the installation of his father, Filaret—who was under arrest in Poland during the *sobor* anyway—as a threat to the safety of the other clans. Mikhail had no personal involvement in the skirmishing that had been going on among the elite families both before and during the Time of Troubles and could be expected to deal more gently with his family's rivals than the older men who had been personally involved in the disputes. He was crowned tsar in the summer of 1613 and faced an incredibly difficult task—Russia had been devastated by the Time of Troubles. The almost constant warfare had destroyed crops and towns and forced people of all classes to abandon their homes, fields and businesses. The government was totally bankrupt and faced formidable enemies in Poland, in Sweden, and among the Cossacks to the south. In addition to the physical and economic problems, the Russian people were exhausted and demoralized. God's punishment for their sins had been severe, and it would take decades for them to recover. From these inauspicious beginnings, the Romanov dynasty created one of the most powerful autocracies in Europe.

THE EARLY ROMANOVS

The turmoil of the rise of Moscow and the Time of Troubles created a very difficult situation for young Mikhail Romanov (1613–1645). Mikhail attempted to redress the fiscal problem by levying seven special taxes between 1613 and 1618 and by raising the tax on alcohol. More importantly, he responded to the pleas from his pomeshchiki by extending the time limit to recover fugitive peasants to 9 and then 15 years, thus acknowledging the central place that these servitors played in his army and government and further reducing peasant freedom. Mikhail's reign was not spectacular, but given the condition of Russia at his ascension, the fact that he managed to keep Russia united and sovereign, expand the army and border fortification, and hold his own against the Poles argues for very able and adroit leadership. Mikhail's son, Alexei (1645–1676), assumed the throne upon the death of his father and began to expand his kingdom. He also rationalized the administration of government, making procedures across the government more regular and less personal. Despite these advances, Alexei had a tumultuous reign plagued by revolts as he continued to try to get his government out of debt through high taxes and debasing the coinage. In 1649 Alexei published a new law code that further enhanced the position of the pomeshchiki and finally enserfed the peasants.

Mikhail and Alexei began developing a more professional army, moving toward paid cavalry units. The expanding government and army, the new law code, and the schism in the Church, however, did not change life for most people very much except for the increased burdens of taxation and conscription. High-ranking townsmen and nobles were exempt from taxes, but peasants and lower-level townsmen paid taxes based, in theory, on what they should be able to pay. For peasants, this ability was judged by surveys of land and analysis of its quality, but these surveys were few and far between. In addition to their usual taxes, tsars levied special taxes whenever the fiscal situation became desperate, a frequent occurrence because of the wars that Russia continued to fight. In addition to higher taxes, the lower classes were also subject to occasional conscription for the tsar's wars. The changes in warfare that occurred over the course of the seventeenth century increased the size of the army from about 34,500 soldiers in 1630 to more than 200,000 in the 1680s.[11] Most of these soldiers were now gunpowder units; the traditional pomeshchik cavalry units virtually disappeared. Unlike the western European practice of hiring mercenaries, the tsars preferred to conscript soldiers whenever they needed to enlarge their forces; for example, in 1654 the draft took one man from every twenty households.[12]

All in all, the early Romanovs successfully reunited and stabilized Russia. In the 63 years that Mikhail and Alexei ruled, Russia's borders were secured, and the Romanov control of the throne was unchallenged. The nobility was secure in its position under the control of the tsars, and the peasantry was firmly entrenched in serfdom. By the time Peter I assumed the throne, Russia was stable enough to endure the upheavals that his reign would cause and emerge as one of the great powers of Europe.

PETER THE GREAT (1682–1725)

Without question, Peter I, better known as Peter the Great, had a profound impact on the development of Russia. He transformed Russia from an obscure kingdom on the edge of Europe into one of the major powers in European diplomacy. He forced the upper classes to abandon their traditional notions of honor, piety, and

Tsar Peter the Great, 1775. Erich Lessing / Art Resource, NY.

custom and embrace European morality as well as European dress and titles while leaving the peasants to their traditional ways and miring them even deeper into serfdom. He opened up new industries in Russia and encouraged increased trade with the West, although his wars and grand construction projects drastically increased the tax and conscription burden on the lower classes. He created the first Russian navy, restructured the government, opened military schools, encouraged technical education, and insisted on loyal and constant service to the state from all Russians regardless of rank or traditional privileges. Building on the foundations laid by his Rurikid and Romanov forebears, Peter I created Imperial Russia.

PETER'S EARLY YEARS

Peter was born to Tsar Alexei's second wife, Natalia Naryshkina. It seemed unlikely that he would ever become tsar given that Alexei already had two sons, Fedor and Ivan, by his first wife, Maria Miloslavskaia. Indeed, upon Alexei's death, Fedor III assumed the throne and ruled for six years but then died without an heir. The next logical person in line for the throne was Ivan, who was handicapped, although it is not clear how. Most descriptions of Ivan stress that he had "an affliction of the eyes," and others mention a variety of other problems: a stutter, inability to speak, and inability to move without help, among other problems.[13] When Fedor died, a hastily called assembly elected Peter to the throne, but a struggle broke out almost immediately between the Miloslavskiis and the Naryshkins over this decision. The streltsy took advantage of the turmoil to begin a revolt on their own account, largely over the way they had been treated by their commanders rather than over the question of the heir to the throne. After some very bloody fighting, a compromise was reached in which both Peter and Ivan V (1682–1696) were crowned co-tsars, with Ivan's older sister Sophia as regent. This rather odd arrangement worked very well for a while. Peter took part in many of the ceremonies at court that were required of the tsar, but particularly during the later years of Sophia's regency, Peter spent much of his time at an estate outside Moscow with his mother while Ivan V performed most of the ceremonial duties of tsar.

TOY SOLDIERS AND WESTERN INFLUENCE

Peter seemed happy to escape the tedious life of court ceremony. He spent much of his time playing with his "toy soldiers," young men that Peter gathered from the surrounding country and his own household, supplemented by soldiers requisitioned from army units and foreign experts, and formed into two regiments; the Preobrazhenskoe and Semenovskoe regiments had Western-style uniforms, ranks, and training and, by 1685, their own wooden fortress. Peter insisted that all of the recruits, including himself, work their way up through the ranks. He also spent much of his time in the "German Quarter" of Moscow, the section of the city set apart for foreign residents. There he found the more open atmosphere much more congenial to his tastes, and he learned many skills from the craftsmen in the quarter. In 1689, after a struggle between his supporters and Sophia's streltsy, Peter and Ivan ruled without a regent until Ivan's death in 1889. Peter continued to pursue his interests in the German Quarter, learning about ships (his true passion) and training with his regiments, and left much of the monotony of court life to Ivan. Peter led a campaign against the Ottomans to take Azov on the Black Sea in 1694–1695, which failed, resulting in his determination not only to remake the Russian army but also to create a navy; one of the major reasons for his loss at Azov was that the Ottomans had been able to supply themselves from the sea because Peter had no navy with which to stop them. In 1696 Peter again attacked the fortress at Azov with the support of 69,000 troops and a Russian flotilla that cut off Turkish reinforcements. This time, he was victorious, taking Azov in less than two months and proving, at least in his own mind, the value of his navy.[14]

Peter then embarked on his famous Grand Embassy to Europe in hopes of reviving the Holy League and beginning a crusade against the Ottomans. In addition to visiting the most important rulers, Peter endeavored to learn how to build and use the best technology available and spent a few months studying shipbuilding in England. Peter's trip was cut short by another revolt by the streltsy. Peter dashed back to Moscow and ruthlessly suppressed the rebellion, torturing thousands of streltsy in an unsuccessful attempt to prove that Sophia had instigated the rebellion and eventually executing more than 1,100 streltsy. It seems unlikely that Sophia took an active role in the rebellion, but it is clear that the streltsy, who had many grievances about ill treatment under Peter's government and who feared that they were being replaced in the army by the new infantry regiments, hoped to put Sophia on the throne. After the executions, Peter had more than 200 of their heads mounted near Sophia's convent window as a warning against future plots. As a result, the streltsy were banned from the capital and from

Russian palace guards, or Streltsi, of the 1600s. North Wind
Picture Archives.

then on continued to be a source of discontent throughout Russia.
Sophia died in 1704 in her convent, ending her days isolated from
all contact with her female relatives and friends.

PETER BEGINS TO RULE

After the 1698 Revolt, Peter began to rule Russia in earnest.
No aspect of life was untouched by Peter's reforms; he changed
Russia's military, its government structure, the tax system, the
economy, the elite social structure, and the culture. He changed
Russia's borders and built a new capital in addition to modernizing

Russia's infrastructure. Peter's reforms affected every aspect of life for all Russians—he even changed the way that Russians counted days; Russia had not moved with the rest of Christian Europe to the Julian calendar that calculated years from the birth of Christ. Their calendar counted time from their religious identification of the beginning of the world and began new years in September. On January 1, 1700 (7209 by the Orthodox calendar), Peter put Russia on the Julian calendar. Peter deeply believed that it was everyone's duty to serve the state and referred to himself as the servant of the state. In theory, creating a well-ordered state, served by a loyal and dedicated populace, would also serve the common good, but in all cases, individual needs were subordinate to state needs. He frequently referred to the fact that he served the state, that he sacrificed himself to the state, and that he had no interests other than state interests, and it is hard to find evidence to the contrary; he even sacrificed his only son on the alter of Russian greatness, and he expected all of his subjects to serve with equal zeal. This, in part, explains how Peter was able to make such sweeping changes during his reign—he worked tirelessly toward his goal of making Russia into a great European power, and he insisted that everyone around him do the same.

MILITARY CHANGES

Peter's reforms were driven by his desire to make Russia a great power, and to this end, he spent almost his entire reign at war. The Great Northern War with Sweden (and involving Poland and Denmark) lasted from 1700 to 1721, and Peter was at war with Turkey in 1695–1696 and 1710–1713 and with Persia in 1722–1723. He had to deal with various large-scale rebellions of the streltsy in 1698, the Astrakhan revolt in 1705–1706, and the Bulavin Cossack revolt in 1707–1708. One can readily see why military matters concerned the tsar so much. Although Peter's reforms were certainly wide-ranging and changed the Russian military machine significantly, he built on the foundations laid by his predecessors. Both Mikhail and Alexei Romanov had begun to create the more modern infantry units that were beginning to emerge in all European armies—in fact, these units had become important enough by the mid-seventeenth century for the pomeshchiki to feel threatened by them. By that time, the Russian army included regiments based on the "new model," which included infantry and lancer and dragoon units trained and led by foreign officers as well as two select infantry units. Nor were

Peter's armies the largest that Russia ever fielded—Ivan IV fielded an army of 150,000 in his war with Kazan.[15] Peter's changes were significant not because they transformed a medieval army into a modern army or because they were systematically planned and carried out, but because they spread a lifetime-service obligation throughout the population, instituted regular training of all troops, and relied on a professional officer corps composed of foreigners and eventually Russians trained in Peter's military academies. They also necessitated a variety of reforms in the government and economy that are discussed later.

RECRUITMENT

The changes in recruitment are important to our discussion because they had a profound impact on the way people lived. In the past, noblemen had been called to service in the cavalry for specific campaigns, after which they were permitted to return to their civilian duties either on their estates or at court. They received a commission for their service, but only while the campaign lasted; their real reward was their noble status and the privileges that conferred, particularly the right to own populated estates. When called, nobles were also told how many armed men to bring with them to fill out the units. There were problems with this system that became more pronounced as warfare changed. The shift to infantry and gunpowder weapons meant that more recruits were needed than the noble class could provide, which was exacerbated by the fact that men often simply did not show up when they were called. To create new cavalry units (or any kind of unit) under this system would expand the landowning class. As one historian has succinctly put it, "The relationship between land ownership, military obligation, and status had an inhibiting effect on flexible recruitment."[16] Peter dealt with this by making service to the state a lifelong obligation for all nobles. Those who did not serve lost their rank and their estates. Those who served had to move up through the ranks and were paid a salary rather than given automatic rank or more grants of land. This meant that the state had to come up with the money to pay the military, but it did not have to create new nobles in order to fill its officer corps, as earlier tsars had had to do. It also meant that in order to keep the estates they already possessed, nobles had to devote their entire lives to state service and could not limit their service to specific campaigns. This change provided a more reliable pool of officers, but noblemen did not constitute the bulk of

Peter's armies. Most of his soldiers were simple infantrymen who were recruited in a variety of ways. Special levies offered attractive salaries and board to any freeman who would join the army. Special conscriptions forced "superfluous men," sons of clergymen and low-level government clerks, to join the army. Joining the army conferred freedom upon serfs, but serfs could volunteer only with their masters' permission. The vast majority of recruits came from forced conscription levies. Usually, 1 man from every 20 households had to be given up for the army, although additional special conscriptions sometimes changed that ratio. Conscripting soldiers was not a new practice, but Peter did it far more frequently and on a larger scale than previous tsars had done.

REGULATING THE ARMY

In the army itself, Peter worked hard to establish standard procedures, regulations, and punishments as well as to regularize salaries and provisions for all of his troops. He did not succeed so well in these areas because provisioning and paying such large armies was difficult given Russia's poor infrastructure and lack of resources. Peter wrote that officers should care for their men as a father would; he pointed out that soldiers who were underfed and overtaxed could not perform well on the battlefield and stated that officers should make every effort to ensure that their soldiers received their allotted provisions and pay. Furthermore, despite his lengthy Military Statute, published in 1716, he admonished officers that they were responsible men who should use their judgment rather than hiding behind regulations—soldiers who were exhausted from battle or from marches, for example, should not pull ceremonial guard duty simply to satisfy a regulation; an officer who treated his soldiers badly and hid behind the regulations was subject to the tsar's disapproval. That said, Peter was a stickler for discipline, and his regulations went on to state that soldiers must not complain about their situation or their officers even if they were not receiving their promised pay and provisions. Soldiers who deserted were subject to a variety of punishments including hard labor, having their nostrils slit, flogging, and hanging. Corporal punishment was used freely in the Russian army, and it was widely believed that the life of a soldier was worse than the life of a serf—Russian soldiers endured long marches as they moved from campaign to campaign, and they might pull any kind of duty, from fighting in a battle to digging trenches, to manning a garrison, to ship duty. Leave was rare, and even injured and disabled soldiers were often kept in the army as trainers rather than discharged. Russia's armies were poorly fed and very poorly clothed—Peter was the first tsar to create uniforms for all of his units, and this was a long process. Peter's letters indicate that he was well aware that his troops were very poorly dressed, to the point that they were sometimes in real danger of freezing to death. All in all, the life of a soldier did not change much under Peter, but the constant need for so many soldiers not only to fight his many wars but also to garrison his increasing border fortifications meant that more men were soldiers, and resources were stretched even farther than they had been in the past.[17]

THE NAVY

Of course, Peter's most celebrated military reform was the creation of a navy. Peter's navy is the most famous and the most romanticized aspect of his attempt to modernize the Russian military. Many of Peter's contemporaries believed that the navy was a very expensive and dangerous whim. Others pointed out that naval power was essential to compete with the great powers of Europe, and Russia's first Azov campaign demonstrated the dangers of fighting against an enemy who had naval capabilities that Russia could not counteract. The navy was certainly expensive and, as it turns out, not terribly important in most of Peter's battles, although in a few cases, the navy proved important to victory. Although it was difficult to train serfs to be effective soldiers, it proved even more difficult to train Russians to be effective sailors. The frustration that Peter suffered over training his navy often obscures the fact that Russians were not strangers to the water. Kievan Rus, we remember, was built on river trade. Even the Muscovite grand princes had made effective use of river ways and river trade to build their power. Tsar Alexei, Peter's father, had begun to build a small flotilla, but the first and only ship was unfortunately destroyed during a rebellion. It is true, of course, that Russians had not been involved in ocean voyages and that the revolutionary changes that had occurred in Europe since the fifteenth century in oceanic navigation and naval warfare had bypassed Russia completely. Despite these hindrances, Peter pushed his navy forward with his customary forcefulness and insisted that it be manned with whatever recruits could be persuaded or forced to learn the skills. The navy was and still is the symbol of the emerging Russian empire.

GOVERNMENT REFORMS

The government that Peter inherited has been aptly described as "proto-modern or semi-modern" presiding over a "decidedly medieval society and economy."[18] Peter and his subjects viewed Russia—the land, resources, institutions, and people—as Peter's inheritance, his personal property. Although previous tsars had each added to the bureaucracy in an attempt to make it work better, there was no institutional framework for the state other than the tsar—in other words, the tsar was the only absolute constant in the system. The way to power within the system was always and only through proximity to the tsar, whether by birth, ingenuity, or connections. Although some men did rise to prominence through their abilities, ability alone was very rarely enough to make a career; networking through marriage, intrigue, and political alliance was necessary to gain or maintain access to power. Because the system relied on personal contact and influence rather than efficiency and merit, government business was subordinate to personal interest; it was unlikely that nobles or clerks would view their primary function as carrying out their government duties efficiently; rather, their most important duty was to use their government position to improve the welfare and position of their families, resulting in a government rife with bribery and favoritism. The Russian government was not run by professionals; its machinery moved exceedingly slowly when it moved at all and was ill-equipped to deal with a rapidly growing military machine and the challenges that this machine presented to the state.

THE SERVICE STATE

The changes in the military and the addition of the navy necessitated government reform. In order to obtain and coordinate the additional equipment, experts, and manpower, the bureaucracy had to expand. In order to pay for the expanded military and the expanded government, the state needed more revenue. In order for any of these things to happen, Peter needed a government that ran efficiently and professional servitors who would not subordinate their state responsibilities to their families' interests. There is no evidence that Peter had a master plan for reorganizing the state, although it is clear that he recognized that there were fundamental problems in the structure of the bureaucracy and the attitudes of its staff. Peter frequently admonished his servitors to be efficient and to work hard; he often wished for an orderly, efficient state that worked like a well-oiled machine, a police state in the sense that it would create and maintain an orderly, moral, and dutiful society. Though he might have sat down to plan carefully a well-ordered rational system if he had had the time, he was so caught up with his military problems that the reorganization of the state had to take second place, which may explain why the government reforms happened so late in his reign and in so haphazard a manner.

Peter discovered that he needed to have an institution that could run the government while he was away at war or visiting one of his many construction projects, and to that end he created the Senate, but not until 1711. Peter confided to the Senate the right to rule in his absence and, indeed, tried to force it to do so. Senators had to take an oath of loyalty to the tsar and realm, to dispense justice fairly, to collect revenues and recruits, and to serve the tsar and state interest "to the last drop of their strength" and to renounce all personal interest in the pursuance of their duties.[19] Peter was never happy with the performance of the Senate, apparently feeling that the Senators did not accomplish as much business as he thought they should, and he tried various means to improve their work, finally creating the post of procurator-general of the Senate, whose job was to watch the Senate and make sure that it performed its duties. The procurator-general did not have a vote in the Senate, but he reported directly to the tsar any infraction of duty on the part of the Senators.

MERITOCRACY AND THE TABLE OF RANKS

Peter tried to force the government to abandon cronyism and bribery and to embrace service to the state as an ideal in his General Regulation, published in 1720. He replaced the ancient *prikazy* with Colleges of War, Foreign Affairs, Justice, Commerce, Admiralty, State Revenues, State Expenses, State Accounting, and Mines and Manufacture. The presidents of the colleges sometimes sat on the Senate, to which they reported. In 1724 Peter created under-procurators to watch the colleges and report to the procurator-general in another attempt to weed out corruption and to force the men in the government to work. Peter was clearly very frustrated by what he saw as laziness on the part of most of his servitors, who apparently found it difficult to transition from the old more leisurely way of doing business through their networks to a steady job without regard to their personal aggrandizement or enrichment. In 1722 Peter created the Table of Ranks, which was supposed to alleviate this problem. The Table consisted of 14 ranks that encompassed the military, civil, and court service. In order to attain a higher rank, and with it a responsible and more powerful post, every man had to prove himself through service to the state. No one was supposed to be able to rise through the Table on birth or favoritism, only through merit. Entrance into the Table for those of non-noble birth conferred nobility at the lowest grade, 14, for military ranks and at grade 8 for the non-military servitors. Although commoners sometimes entered the Table through merit and service, the main point of the Table was to encourage the nobility, whom Peter considered the natural leaders of the country, to work harder at their jobs in order to advance to a higher rank. Thus, Peter attempted to tie noble privilege to promotion through merit and ability in order to force his servitors to reorient themselves to the idea of serving the state rather than their own interests. In another effort to streamline government, he began revision of the law code, but it was never finished and never implemented. It is important to note that the creation of new institutions and regulations did nothing to limit the power of the tsar. Peter remained an absolute ruler with no institutional or legal limitations on his powers, and in 1721 he took the title of emperor to reflect Russia's new position in Europe and his own expansion of power. That Peter still saw himself as above all laws is demonstrated by his Law on Succession of 1722, which stated that the emperor would name his successor; this law completely abrogated the ancient Muscovite (and European) tradition of hereditary succession and meant that women could now assume the throne because it specifically stated that the throne did not have to go to male kin, but to whomever the tsar chose. Peter wrote this law in part because his only surviving son, Alexei, had been a disappointment to his father; Peter found his son to be weak and lazy. Alexei was eventually implicated in a treasonous plot and died under mysterious circumstances, probably from torture. The new law showed Peter's belief that as tsar, he could impose his will even after his death, regardless of institutions or traditions. Unfortunately, however, Peter died without naming a successor, so it is not clear whom he had in mind to succeed him.

CHURCH REFORM

Peter also subordinated the Church to the state in no uncertain terms. Although he had no desire to undermine faith in Orthodoxy, which was, after all, one of the bases for his claim to the throne, he refocused the state's purpose away from its previous religious orientation. The political ideology of the Third Rome had implied that the true purpose of the tsar in the past had been to keep the Orthodox faithful and prepare for God's kingdom on earth by maintaining the true faith in Russia. Peter and his successors believed that the Russian ruler's job was to expand the political and international interests of Russia and that the Church should restrict itself to purely spiritual matters. Peter asserted that the Church absorbed far more of Russia's resources, both in terms of land and revenue and in terms of labor, than was justified by its purposes. To limit the power of the Church, Peter replaced the office of Patriarch with the Most Holy Synod, modeled on the colleges; with 11 churchmen overseen by an over-procurator who reported to the tsar himself, it no longer had any pretensions to an independent leadership. The Church was now simply another administrative branch of the government, institutionally subordinate to the tsar and the state. Peter also disliked monasteries, seeing in them only a way for the lazy to avoid their duties, and he strictly limited monastic activity and recruitment.

LOCAL GOVERNMENT

Peter attempted to reform provincial and town government, but with very limited success. His main concern was ensuring that the provincial and town governments send him taxes and recruits as required. Ivan III's system of military governors had grown increasingly corrupt and ineffective. Peter divided his kingdom into eight permanent provinces and replaced the old military governors with new permanent provincial governors who were in charge of all aspects of governing the district, in addition to overseeing conscription and taxes. Each province was responsible for supporting designated military units. In the towns, Peter created town councils, elected from the wealthiest inhabitants, and placed them in charge of seeing that revenues and recruits made it to the central government, overseeing and managing the city economy, and overseeing justice by policing the towns and creating courts. In general, the new system did not work much better than the old, given that most of the provincial and town staffs remained the same and engaged in the same kind of corruption that they had under the old system. Peter also had trouble staffing his new provincial and town governments because nobles were not interested in doing the paperwork involved; they preferred simply to govern their own serfs—over whom they had complete legal authority—and ignore the rest of the local government. Peter's new system did manage to send him enough recruits and revenues to keep his military machine going, but the local people suffered just as much from corrupt officials as they had before. Peter himself admitted that the provincial reform probably made a bad situation worse.

THE RESULTS OF GOVERNMENT REFORM

Peter's reformed state was a conglomeration of old and new; it was not a modern, professional, bureaucratized state but also was not the Muscovite Christian patrimony he had inherited. Peter ruled as absolute sovereign—in modern fashion because he believed his highest duty was to the state, but not constrained by any force but his own conscience to do so and leaving plenty of opportunity for future rulers to ignore or redefine state interest in any way they chose. Birth, networks, cronyism, and corruption were still rife in the new government, but there were also policies and procedures to be followed, and much more emphasis was placed on performance than had been true in the past. As one historian has pointed out, Peter's government was not so different from the absolute monarchies in Europe of the same period. All were an amalgamation of old and new, with modern armies and bureaucracies still dominated by hereditary nobility employed in the service of a Christian monarch who was theoretically answerable only to God and claimed to serve the state's interest: Frederick II of Prussia called himself the "first servant of the state," and Louis XIV of France declared, "l'état c'est moi."[20] Certainly Peter succeeded in inserting Russia into the world of European power politics. By the time of his death, Russia had embassies in all the major European capitals instead of the single embassy that existed in Warsaw when Peter assumed the throne. The Russian ambassadors were dressed in the latest European fashions and were clean-shaven, with wigs and fashionable wives, and could conduct their negotiations in French, German, or Italian. One of his most prominent ambassadors, Andrei Matveev, was instrumental in creating the first European law on diplomatic immunity while in London, following his own arrest for debt in that country.[21] But in terms of domestic life, Russia was still under-governed, and the government relied on the tsar's oversight and intervention to work well. The further away Peter was, the less stable the society was. Even in Moscow itself, foreign observers complained of the brigandage in the streets, saying that one could not venture out after dark without danger of robbery or murder. Government officials at all levels continued to use their positions to exploit the weak and to build up their own fortunes and power without regard to their duties. It is important to remember, however, that this state of affairs was not confined to Russia. Europe in the eighteenth century was similar—the further away one was in status or location from the ruler, the less access one had to justice of any kind. Peter's government retained remnants of the old Muscovite ways, but by the end of his reign, he had created a state that was on a par with the other monarchies of Europe and that had the foundations of a modern bureaucracy.

Muscovite ambassador in the time of Ivan IV. North Wind Picture Archives.

NOTES

1. George Vernadsky, *Kievan Russia* (New Haven: Yale University Press, 1973), 136–209.

2. The term *khan* is a title derived from the Turkish *kagan,* which means emperor. Chingis adopted the title, and it has become part of his name. For more on this see Charles Halperin, *Russia and the Golden Horde: The Mongol Impact on Russian History* (Bloomington: Indiana University Press, 1987), 23.

3. Halperin, 21–32.

4. Halperin, 77.

5. Donald Ostrowski, *Muscovy and the Mongols: Cross-Cultural Influences on the Steppe Frontier, 1304–1589* (Cambridge: Cambridge University Pres, 1998), 118.

6. For a detailed yet highly readable account of the rise of Moscow, see Robert O. Crummey, *The Formation of Muscovy, 1304–1613* (London: Longman, 1987).

7. Crummey, 41–42.

8. Crummey, 85.

9. Michael Cherniavsky, "Ívan the Terrible as Renaissance Prince," *Slavic Review* 27 (1968): 195–211.

10. Andrei Pavlov and Maureen Perrie, *Ivan the Terrible* (London: Pearson Education Ltd., 2003), 142.

11. David G. Rowley, *Exploring Russia's Past: Narrative, Sources, Images,* vol. 1 (Upper Saddle River, NJ: Pearson Prentice Hall, 2006), 157.

12. Catherine Evtuhov, David Goldfrank, Lindsey Hughes, and Richard Stites, *A History of Russia: Peoples, Legends, Events, Forces* (Boston: Houghton Mifflin Company, 2004), 173.

13. Lindsey Hughes, *Sophia: Regent of Russia 1675–1704* (New Haven: Yale University Press, 1990), 91–95.

14. Lindsey Hughes, *Russia in the Age of Peter the Great* (New Haven: Yale University Press, 2000), 17–18.

15. Hughes, *Russia in the Age of Peter the Great,* 64–65.

16. Hughes, *Russia in the Age of Peter the Great,* 66.

17. Hughes, *Russia in the Age of Peter the Great.*

18. James Cracraft, *The Revolution of Peter the Great* (Cambridge: Harvard University Press, 2003), 60.

19. Hughes, *Russia in the Age of Peter the Great,* 101–102.

20. Cracraft, 65–66.

21. Cracraft, 73.

2

Modernizing Russia

Over the course of the eighteenth and nineteenth centuries, Russia struggled with modernization. Peter the Great had placed Russia on a westernizing path designed to bring her into the European political arena as one of the great powers. His successors did not challenge this goal but continued to see Russia's destiny in terms of her place among the great powers of Europe. The eighteenth-century rulers consolidated Peter's reforms, but none emerged as a great leader until Catherine II took the throne from her husband in 1762 and forced Russia further into European politics and brought the Enlightenment to Russia, pushing the modernizing tendencies beyond the physical and social and laying the foundations for the intellectual upheaval that would challenge the nineteenth-century rulers. The first half of the nineteenth century was a period of great change and reaction in Russia. The Napoleonic Wars, the emergence of a civil society, increased discontent with serfdom and with the autocracy, problems with nationalities, and revolt among the elite all created a highly volatile situation that the first two emperors of the century chose to repress. The Crimean War at mid-century demonstrated Russia's economic and military weakness and finally forced the government to look for an alternative to serfdom. The problems created by the emancipation and eventually by industrialization fueled the fires of discontent, leaving both upper and lower classes ready to revolt. The Russian government never figured out how to deal effectively with the forces for change that were sweeping over the country during the nineteenth century: the tides of industrialization, mechanization, urbanization, and education all contributed to the pressure cooker that eventually erupted in revolution in the early twentieth century.

BETWEEN THE GREATS

The first four emperors after Peter, Catherine I (1725–1727), Peter II (1727–1730), Anna (1730–1740), and Ivan VI (1740–1741), did not stay on the throne long enough to institute any important changes. The quick succession of rulers gave the highest-ranking noble families a chance to reestablish themselves at court, but they did not manage to undermine the institution of the autocracy. Elizabeth (1741–1761) enjoyed the longest and most illustrious reign between the two Greats, although her extravagance left the treasury broke— upon her death, they discovered 15,000 dresses in her possession— and the plight of the Russian serfs declined still more. Elizabeth granted nobles the right to buy and sell individual serfs without land and away from their families and the right to exile problem serfs to Siberia or into the army. She, like Anna before her, gave thousands of acres of populated estates to her favorites, thereby sending tens of thousands of state peasants into private serfdom. She raised taxes to try to pay for her luxuries and wars, which engulfed hundreds of thousands of peasant recruits. Elizabeth has been described by historians and contemporaries as thoughtless and frivolous, but others have made the argument that her lavish lifestyle and her ostentatious construction projects were part of her job—for Russia to compete with the other crowned heads of Europe, Elizabeth needed to play the part. She was also very successful in foreign policy, consolidating Russia's position in Europe. At the end of her reign, she entered the Seven Years' War, where Austrian and Russian forces fought Prussia in Europe while the English fought French forces in British North America and at sea. The Seven Years' War was an expensive and difficult war for Russia, who had her usual difficulties in provisioning and paying her troops. Still, Russian forces took much territory from Frederick II, and Russian troops briefly occupied Berlin in 1760. Elizabeth died in 1761, leaving her nephew, Peter III, to take the throne. Peter was a great fan of Frederick and immediately called for an end to the war, withdrawing his troops from all of the territory that the Russian troops had captured. This was a great piece of luck for Frederick and resulted in a peace that was much more favorable than Prussia could have expected. This also contributed to Peter III's unpopularity and his subsequent loss of power.

Peter III (1761–1762) was perhaps Russia's most unpopular ruler, partly because of his handling of the Seven Years' War, but also because he showed great disdain for his country and his people. Peter had expected to take the throne of Sweden and was raised in his father's province of Holstein as a Lutheran. He was brought to Russia at the age of 14 to be groomed as Elizabeth's heir. Peter showed no interest in learning about the country he was to rule. He was baptized into the Orthodox faith but showed no signs of adhering to its tenets. He did not learn to speak Russian. He preferred to dress in the Prussian military style and greatly enjoyed watching his soldiers drill—an activity that did not endear him to his guards. Elizabeth had married him off to Sophia of Anhalt-Zerbst, rechristened Catherine in the Orthodox Church. Catherine, unlike her husband, took a great interest in her new country. Because her marriage was very disappointing to her—she wrote of Peter's childish pastimes, his passion for drill, his inept attempts at flirtation—she focused instead on learning as much about Russia and the Russian court as she could. She gave birth to a son, who may or may not have been Peter's child but was acknowledged as such and then taken from her and raised by Elizabeth. Catherine studied Russian and read voraciously, taking particular interest in the works of the Enlightenment that were being published in Europe at this time. She watched the court, learning about court intrigue and the various factions that controlled Russian politics. Upon Elizabeth's death, Peter was crowned emperor, and Catherine saw how unpopular he was with the rest of the court. His withdrawal from the war and his disastrous mistake of returning all of Russia's gains to Prussia deepened the court's dislike of Peter. The only act during his brief reign that did not anger his nobles was his decree on the Emancipation of the Nobility in 1762, which freed the nobles from all compulsory state service. Even this, however, did not engender loyalty to him. He was contemplating legislation that deeply offended all Russians; he planned to remove all icons from Russian churches and to force Orthodox priests to adopt Lutheran dress. He also threatened to disband the Guards Regiments. Rumors spread that he was going to divorce Catherine and marry his mistress. Finally, Catherine and the Guards united to overthrow Peter, who was killed during the insurrection. Catherine II was crowned in 1762 as the Empress of Russia.

CATHERINE THE GREAT (1762–1796)

Catherine II, also known as Catherine the Great, completed many of Peter the Great's reforms. Whereas Peter had used brute force to wrench Russia out of her traditional ways and place her on the path of westernization and modernization, Catherine worked with the nobility to introduce the more sophisticated aspects of Western culture and learning into Russia and to further expand Russia's influence in Europe. However, like Peter before her, Catherine did nothing to improve the lives of the vast majority of Russian

Catherine II (1762–1796) of Russia in Coronation Robe, 1770. Bildarchiv Preussicher Kulturbesitz/Art Resource, NY.

subjects; serfdom continued unabated and even spread during her reign. Catherine's accomplishments were not as stunning as Peter's largely because she built on his framework—there were no massive military or social reforms during her reign, but Russia's military might and standing in Europe increased substantially under Catherine. Her long reign brought a time of stability to Russia, and her court, more refined and comfortable than Peter's, became one of the most stunning in Europe. Catherine often spoke of Peter as her spiritual father, and she too saw herself as a servant of the Russian state, dedicated to expanding Russia's power and prestige as well as leading her noble subjects to what she believed was a higher intellectual and cultural level.

THE LEGITIMACY PROBLEM

Catherine began her reign in the same way that most of her eighteenth-century predecessors had—by seizing power. Unlike her predecessors, however, she had no heritable right to the throne. This fact would color her attitudes and actions for the duration of her reign. Like Peter, Catherine worked very hard; unlike Peter, she did not force everyone around her to do the same. Peter had the advantage of being a clearly legitimate heir to the Russian throne, and his absolute assurance that he was the true emperor allowed him to ignore the wishes of his nobles and even to repress them brutally whenever he found it necessary. Catherine did not have this luxury. She was, in fact, not a legitimate heir to the throne. When Peter III died without naming an heir, the next logical person to take the throne was their son Paul, acknowledged as Peter's son whether he was or not. But Paul was a child, and Catherine and her fellow conspirators did not wish to work through a regency, so Catherine was crowned empress in her own right. Nor did she bring Paul into her court to train him as her successor as he got older, apparently always seeing him as a threat to her own power; indeed, several plots against her during her reign centered on replacing her with Paul, although there is no evidence that Paul himself had anything to do with any of the plots. Therefore, Catherine understood that she ruled at the pleasure of the nobility given that at any time, a powerful faction could back Paul and remove her from power. Because of her rather precarious position, Catherine had to balance the interests of the nobility against all other considerations. For this reason, her reign is sometimes called the Golden Age of the Nobility.

LOVERS AND REPUTATION

Of course, Catherine is most famous for her love affairs. The obsession with Catherine's sex life often overshadows all of her other accomplishments and failures, spawning not only contempt for her, but also jokes and myths about the empress's life. The most outrageous and well known of the myths asserts that Catherine's voracious sexual appetite resulted in her death from attempting to have sex with a horse. She actually died of a stroke in her private chambers. The fact that such a ridiculous story could be so widely accepted necessitates saying a few words about Catherine's sex life. Catherine had 12 lovers during her reign, most of whom had nothing to do with governing Russia. Her lovers usually lasted a few years and then were pensioned off handsomely. They were often young men who shared her taste in literature and art. Only three of her lovers had state positions, and they were all very capable men who continued in their government service even after the love affairs were over. Certainly Catherine was not a model of Victorian virtue, but neither did she allow her love life to dictate her goals or activities as the ruler of Russia, nor is there any evidence of any unusual sexual activity. Like Peter I (and most rulers before and after her), she took lovers as a part of her home and social life. Because she chose not to marry officially, which would have complicated not only her own reign but also the succession, her lovers formed an important part of her domestic life. Unlike Elizabeth, Anna, or even Peter, Catherine was not given to large raucous parties or drunken debaucheries. She often entertained at small private dinners and card parties, giving the occasional large state function when required. She rarely drank even wine unless her physician prescribed it for her. It is ironic that although Catherine's court was far more reserved and domestic than any of her eighteenth-century predecessors, she is the one with the reputation for sexual depravity. Historians have usually attributed this reputation to male spite at her success as a ruler. Although both Anna and Elizabeth presented problems as rulers, it is more difficult to fault the logic and sense of Catherine's decisions; her sex life, however, presented an excellent target.

ENLIGHTENED ABSOLUTISM

Catherine began her reign determined to continue Peter's reforms and to bring Russia more fully into the European sphere. Peter concerned himself exclusively with power and prestige, closely imitating the institutions, technology, and lifestyle of the powerful European monarchies he so admired. By the late eighteenth century, the ideals of the Enlightenment had caused educated Europeans to start looking more critically at political and social institutions and had spawned a new set of values by which Europeans judged their leaders. Catherine was a part of this new trend in European thought and sought not only to increase the efficiency of her government but also to justify her reign through some other means than divine right or military power. It was not that she spurned these ancient and highly effective means of legitimizing her throne, but Catherine was deeply committed to giving Russia a rational, humanistic government that would be responsive to the needs of her people, particularly in the areas of education and physical and moral health, as well as to military requirements. This is not to say that Catherine's reign was without problems. Like all of her predecessors, Catherine failed to do anything to improve the lives of the peasants, and in fact, their lives deteriorated still further under her reign. She continued to engage in warfare, which fell heavily on the peasantry in terms of taxes and recruits. She gave populated estates away to favorites, to her former lovers, and as a reward for outstanding service to the state. She did nothing to limit the landlord's power over his serfs. Her efforts at rule of law and spreading education did not extend to serfs. Despite her enlightened ideals, she chose to ignore the greatest evil in her realm. Catherine would no doubt argue that she ignored serfdom because she could do nothing about it without undermining her own position as empress; she relied on the nobility not only for her throne but also to oversee and direct all of the necessary functions of the state and military apparatus. There were other problems with ending serfdom that are discussed in more detail later.

THE LEGISLATIVE COMMISSION

Catherine's most ambitious attempt at change was the Legislative Commission, called to gather information and get advice on her empire in preparation for a recodification of the laws. The Legislative Commission was made up of nobles, townsmen, Cossacks, homesteaders, industrialists, non-Russian tribesmen, and state peasants—no serfs or clergy were involved. She wrote detailed instructions to the Commission, charging them to review Russia's needs and to propose measures that she could take to improve Russia. The instructions were, in a sense, her manifesto: 526 articles that outlined her principles of an enlightened government and rule of law. Catherine wanted her subjects to debate national policy so that she could learn from the debates and create policy. She did not intend to share power. The Commission sat for two years but proved a huge disappointment to the young ruler. She had hoped that the various groups could work together to come up with goals for Russia, but instead, each group went off on its own to prepare its own list of grievances and requests—most of which were at odds with one another: The peasants wanted an end to serfdom and the right to farm the land without interference from the nobility. The merchants wanted the right to buy populated estates and a monopoly on trade. The nobles wanted to possess the right to engage in trade, to retain their privilege of being the only people allowed to own populated land, and to maintain their power over the serfs. Catherine did get reams of information on conditions in Russia that were invaluable to her in formulating her policies, but no hint that any of her subjects were able to look past their own narrow interests to formulate policy for the country as a whole. Catherine determined that she had to rely on her own judgment as the only person in Russia who was above all other estates and able to weigh all concerns equally. Of course, as has been shown, she did no such thing, given that she needed noble support to retain her throne, but the Commission provided a good excuse for not creating any kind of permanent legislative body to help rule Russia.

Catherine used the information gained from the Legislative Commission as a guide for reforming Russia. She learned that she could not touch serfdom—it had proved a highly volatile issue at the Commission, and the reactions of the noble delegates to any indication that serfs might be viewed as human subjects of the crown had set off impassioned speeches concerning the necessity of maintaining absolute noble control over the serfs to ensure peace and prosperity. Catherine turned to other issues and set up commissions to investigate the problems that she hoped to address. One commission reorganized the army to improve mobility and placed more emphasis on discipline and training, arguing that these factors were just as important to an army's strength as numbers. Border garrisons were standardized and expanded, and by 1765 Russia had 303,000 men in her army, with the number growing to 413,000 by 1796. The royal navy was also expanded and its officers sent abroad for training.[1]

PROVINCIAL GOVERNMENT REFORM

One of the most ambitious of Catherine's reforms was the Statute on Provincial Administration in 1775. This reform was a reaction to the Pugachev revolt (discussed later), which highlighted Russia's lack of control over her provinces and borders. This was largely due to the lack of administration and administrators—in 1763 Russia had just 16,500 paid officials, whereas Prussia, only 1 percent of Russia's size, had 14,000.[2] Of course, serf owners took care of administering their serfs, and villages took care of most of their internal affairs, but the central government had no way to deal with provincial trouble quickly when necessary. The provincial reform divided Russia into 38 provinces and then subdivided further into districts. Each province had a capital with a governor who was appointed by the center and answerable to the empress, as well as a commander in chief, a deputy governor, and a chief of police. The law also established a system of courts and appeals courts separated by estate—one for nobles, one for townsmen, and so on—that was supposed to simplify procedures and limit opportunities for appeal.[3] Serfs were not covered by this system and continued to be administered solely by their owners. Boards of Public Welfare were supposed to run schools, hospitals, orphanages, almshouses, mental asylums, workhouses, and such. In 1782 the Police Statute regulated law and order and the maintenance of streets and buildings, waste disposal, lighting, firefighting, beggars, religious dissidents, and public behavior. Although it is not clear how well these reforms worked, they were the first attempt since Peter I to improve Russia's provincial government.

SENATE AND CHURCH REFORMS

Catherine also worked on further streamlining the central government. She reworked the Senate, changing it from an institution that met as a single body into six specialized departments, each tasked with overseeing one aspect of the government. She secularized all Church property as well, transferring all of its populated land to the state and eliminating the category of church peasant. This meant that the Church had to function on an annual subsidy of one-third of its former income. Catherine, as a product of the Enlightenment, believed that the Church should have no power in government or in the economy but should instead concentrate on the moral health and welfare of her subjects. By relieving the

Church of its economic independence, Catherine ensured that it could not hinder her political agenda.

FOREIGN POLICY

Catherine's greatest successes were in foreign policy. During her reign, Russia added several million square miles of territory, almost of all it at the expense of Poland, which had ceased to exist by the end of her reign, and the Ottoman Empire. She was also at war during much of her reign, with Turkey in 1768–1774, resulting in the first partition of Poland, and again in 1787–1792, in a conflict that involved much of Europe and pitted Russia and Austria against the Turks, the Prussians, Sweden, and Britain. She sent troops into Poland in 1792 and had to continue to occupy much of eastern Poland until its final dissolution in 1794. Like the earlier rulers of the eighteenth century, Catherine believed deeply in the necessity of expanding her empire and maintaining her position vis-à-vis the other European powers, particularly those closest to her, Prussia, Austria, and the Ottomans. She was perfectly willing to send hundreds of thousands of her people to die in what she believed to be the service of the state—necessary to maintain great power status and preserve Russia's prestige. Her wars proved too costly to be paid for by a raise in taxes, however, so she was the first ruler to borrow on the international money markets. This new empire also presented more headaches for the administration, given that most of the new subjects were not Russian and not Orthodox. By 1780, fewer than 50 percent of the empire's subjects were Russian. For the first time, Russia had a sizable population of Jews, Catholics, and Protestants as well as Muslims, Buddhists, and pagans to govern.[4] Catherine believed that it was best to allow the new subjects to continue to use their own languages and follow their own traditions and to slowly Russify them. All of this meant an expansion of government and new departments to deal with the new peoples, further increasing the tax burden on the peasants.

CATHERINE AND THE NOBILITY

Like Peter I, Catherine believed that the gentry were the natural leaders of her population, and she worked on educational reform in hopes of widening the noble's outlook. Catherine also promulgated her Charter to the Nobility in 1785. In this document, Catherine acknowledged the right of nobles to own populated estates and to enter or leave state service at will as well as their freedom from taxes and corporal punishment. The Charter affirmed nobles' right to their property, stating that they could not be deprived of titles or estates without a trial by their fellow nobles, and even when convicted of serious crimes, nobles had the right to pass on their property to their heirs. She hoped that the nobility would take advantage of their release from serving the central government to take over the governance of the provinces as provided for in her Statute on Provincial Administration, but few nobles were interested in getting involved in the headaches of provincial government. Nobles who did not serve the state at some point in their lives were prohibited from holding provincial office or voting in local noble assemblies. Although the Charter certainly reaffirmed the nobles' privileged position in society, it granted no new rights or privileges. The nobles still had no institutional place in the central government or any way to limit the emperor's power. Still, after a century of changing emperors and a chaotic court, the Charter extended a certain level of stability to the noble estate.

PAUL (1796–1801)

Paul comes as a close second to Peter III as Russia's most unpopular emperor. Paul had been taken from his mother, Catherine II, when he was an infant and was raised by Empress Elizabeth. When Elizabeth died, Paul was given over to his tutors. Paul apparently deeply admired his father and shared his love of all things military. He was very embittered by his father's overthrow and shocked and saddened by his father's murder. He was even more enraged by his mother's refusal to admit him to the circles of power. Catherine had hoped to name Paul's oldest son Alexander as her heir, but both her advisors and Alexander refused to accept this decision. When she died, Paul's revenge began. His first act upon assuming the throne was to promulgate a new Act of Succession that excluded women from the throne by instituting primogeniture; the emperor's eldest son would succeed to the throne. Paul next attacked the court and noble privilege, replacing Catherine's sparkling court of highly educated and cultured statesmen with military officers and turning the palace into a barren military barracks. He was uninterested in philosophy, literature, or art; hated all things French; and insisted that all members of the court behave as if they were in a military hierarchy. He believed fervently in his right to complete power and control over his subjects, and he responded to any attempts to undermine the military discipline and hierarchy of the court with arrests. He greatly admired Peter I's control over the nobles and wanted to get back to the notion of universal service to the state. He was also notorious for being highly touchy and expecting his orders to be carried out immediately and without question, so that men who were summoned to the emperor's presence went complete with money and traveling clothes in case they were shipped off to Siberia for some imagined slight or sent on an ambassadorial mission on the spot. Paul also launched an attack on noble privilege by interfering with the nobles' control over their serfs. He decreed that nobles could not force the serfs to work more than three days a week on noble land, so that the serfs could work three days on their own land and rest on Sunday. Although this may seem like a benevolent gesture intended to mitigate some of the worst evils of serfdom—and indeed, Paul believed that he needed to address the problem—Paul's main intent was to undermine noble privilege. The decree was not enforceable for most of his empire, but it did upset the nobles, who saw it as an attack on their position. Although the edict did little to help the serfs, it did much to convince the nobility that Paul had to go. Life at court was chaotic and unstable once again.

Paul's hatred of his mother also affected his foreign policy. He immediately dropped out of the First Coalition against Napoleon, which his mother had joined, and thus avoided the First Coalition wars, although his hatred of France and particularly the Revolution forced him into the Second Coalition in 1798–1799, during which time the Russian general Suvarov showed himself to be a brilliant general. The Second Coalition ultimately failed, and Paul blamed his partners, particularly the Austrians, for their failure to support Suvarov. He then turned his attention to the south, planning to invade India, which would have begun a war with Great Britain, Russia's most valuable trading partner and ally; it was this harebrained scheme that finally convinced his son, Alexander, to listen to the pleas of the nobility and agree to overthrow his father. Alexander, who apparently loved his father, stipulated that Paul would not be hurt in the overthrow, but his coconspirators had other plans. Paul was killed during the turmoil, and Alexander assumed the throne in an atmosphere of hope but with a deep personal sense of guilt and sorrow.

ALEXANDER I (1801–1825)

Alexander I is one of the most mysterious emperors in Russian history. Raised by his grandmother, Catherine the Great, Alexander received an enlightened education. The young emperor ascended the throne at the age of 24, apparently full of ideas for reform. His reign was interrupted by the Napoleonic Wars and the devastation that they caused. In the last years of his reign, Alexander appeared to become reactionary, embracing mystical religion, heavy censorship, and the secret police, and abandoned his earlier plans to change Russia. Yet he was not wholly repressive, given that he refused to suppress the secret societies that sprang up in response to his failure to follow through on his reforms, societies that would erupt in open revolt upon his death.

THE ENLIGHTENED RULER

Alexander ascended the throne over the body of his father, Paul. Although the young Emperor knew that Paul had been a disastrous ruler, he deeply regretted his part in the overthrow and death of his father. If the men who had advised his actions had hoped that they could control Alexander, they were quickly disappointed. Alexander reinstated the nobility at court and returned to his grandmother's European style, but he did not avail himself of the advice of the older and more powerful families. Instead, Alexander created his own advisory council of four young, like-minded men, his "Unofficial Committee," jokingly called Committee of Public Safety, after the revolutionary body in France that led the terror during the French Revolution. These young men met for coffee every morning and helped Alexander formulate some of his early reforms. Alexander understood that monarchy could no longer be defended as the only viable form of government given that the French and American revolutions had proved that other options existed; monarchy could be justified only if it proved to be a better form of government than a republic. Alexander's enlightened education led him to consider giving Russia a constitution, but he never went that far. Instead, he took less drastic but still important measures such as opening Russia's borders, reinstating the old-style military uniforms, and abolishing Paul's secret police. He reaffirmed the Charters to the Nobility and the Towns, indicating that he was going to continue in the direction laid down by Catherine II and Peter I.

GOVERNMENT REFORMS

Alexander immediately set about continuing the process of modernizing Russia. He set up a commission to recodify the laws and replace the ancient and now highly confusing law code of 1649. The process took nearly three decades, and the new code did not come into action until after Alexander's death. He strengthened the Senate, and the colleges were reorganized and replaced with eight ministries. Alexander also created a Council of Ministers, but it did not have an existence independent of the emperor and met only when the emperor called it; the emperor had the sole right to decide disputes between ministries. He also created a Council of State to oversee the work of the ministries. The Senate's job was to see that the ministries kept in line with the emperor's policies and to act as the supreme court of Russia. Alexander also tried to extend his central administrative reforms to provincial governments by linking the provincial councils, which acted as advisory councils to the provincial governors, to the ministries. Although the reorganization of the administration certainly streamlined the bureaucracy, it still did nothing to minimize the personal power of the emperor. The heads of the ministries often acted independently of the sovereign, but they were answerable only to the emperor, who could dismiss them at will. The autocracy remained in place.[5]

Alexander's reforms, modest as they were, met with much opposition from the Senate and the established noble families. The Senate had survived the eighteenth century as the only institution with any pretense to power and was staffed, moreover, by old nobility who did not like to see their authority, limited as it was, overridden by bureaucratic institutions. They feared and resented the service gentry and the bureaucratic machinery, which they believed would institute despotism by carrying out the emperor's orders without any consideration for their consequences. Other factions at court also opposed the reforms, particularly those who had hoped for a more liberal form of government. Whereas the Senate wished to limit the emperor through its own oligarchic control, others hoped for something more along the lines of the English system of government. Still others simply hoped to manipulate the existing system to benefit themselves through proximity to the emperor. All in all, opposition to reform was widespread but completely fragmented among the various interest groups at court.[6]

THE NAPOLEONIC WARS

Alexander's plans to reform Russia were cut short by the Napoleonic Wars. Russia joined the Third Coalition with Britain and Austria against France in 1805, and there followed a disastrous series of wars, culminating in Russo-Prussian loss to Napoleon at Friedland in 1807. The Treaty of Tilsit, signed between Alexander and Napoleon on a raft in the Niemen River in 1807, was packaged as an agreement between two great empires, but in truth, Russia had little choice, and the advantages were largely on the French side. Alexander had to recognize Napoleon as an emperor and acknowledge the kings Napoleon had installed in Holland and Sicily. Russia lost her Adriatic port of Cattaro and the Ionian Islands but gained part of Prussian Poland. Alexander also had to agree to join the Continental System, Napoleon's attempt to destroy the British economy by breaking off all trade between Britain and the continent. The treaty remained in effect until 1812 and should have provided Russia a breathing space to regroup, but the nation was involved in wars almost the entire time. In addition, the treaty proved disastrous economically. The Continental System did little to hurt Britain but severely hurt Russia, whose greatest trading partner had been Britain. The nobility in particular found the restrictions on trade irksome because it cut them off from their main source of luxury items. By 1810, Russia had abandoned her boycott of British goods and instead levied heavy tariffs on French imports, and by 1812, Napoleon was ready to engage Russia.

The Napoleonic invasion of Russia has been recounted in many histories as well as in novels, poetry, and movies. Napoleon sent his army, 600,000 strong, into Russia at the end of June and began a long, slow march to Moscow. Russian armies retreated before him, destroying crops and stores as they went to prevent the French from supplying themselves. After the battle at Borodino, where both armies suffered staggering losses amounting to 100,000 men, the French entered Moscow only to find that city deserted and empty of supplies. Alexander had evacuated the city, and the mayor, after releasing the inmates from prisons and lunatic asylums, had set fire to Moscow. Napoleon's troops could go no further. The Russian forces north of the city managed to keep the French from moving on, and the French supply lines were impossible to maintain. Alexander refused to negotiate with Napoleon while any French soldier remained on Russian soil. In October the French realized that they must retreat. The Russian army then harassed the French all the way back to the Russian border, forcing the French army to retreat over the scorched ground they had covered on their way to Moscow. The combination of the Russian winter and the lack of supplies destroyed what was left of Napoleon's huge army; fewer than 20,000 of the 600,000 soldiers who had entered Russia survived to leave it. Alexander then ordered his armies to pursue the French back through Europe, eventually ending up at the Battle of Nations in Leipzig in October of 1813, where Napoleon's forces were defeated; the Russian army entered Paris in the spring of 1814. Napoleon was exiled to Elbe; he escaped in 1815 and made it to Paris, where he took command of the army once again. His "Hundred Days" campaign finally ended at Waterloo, where he was utterly defeated and exiled to the island of St. Helena.[7]

IMPACT OF THE NAPOLEONIC WARS

Russia emerged from the Napoleonic Wars as the greatest land power in Europe, finally realizing Peter the Great's dream. Although Russia's vast distances and inclement weather were crucial to Napoleon's defeat, the Russian leadership used these advantages effectively, and the Russian march to Paris showed the rest of Europe that Russia was a dangerous enemy to waken. When she emerged from her borders and unleashed her apparently limitless resources and manpower, the results were terrifying. This was not lost on the participants at the Congress of Vienna, where the statesmen of Europe attempted to recreate the European order that Napoleon had destroyed. Alexander himself represented Russia at the Congress, the only monarch to attend. Of most concern to Russia, a new Polish state was created out of the Prussian parts of Poland and given a constitution, with the Russian emperor as the constitutional monarch of Poland, an arrangement that satisfied neither Poland nor Russia. The Concert of Europe, Prussia, Russia, Austria, and Great Britain was created to act as a watchdog group for any signs of revolution or aggression to avoid future conflicts. Alexander also pushed through a renewed Holy Alliance with Austria and Prussia as the three Christian emperors of Europe dedicated to preserve "Christian precepts of justice, charity, and peace" in international relationships and to unite them "by the bonds of true and unbreakable fraternity."[8]

MYSTICISM AND REACTION

The last 10 years of Alexander's reign are often described as reactionary. The victory over Napoleon seems to have renewed Alexander's faith in his divinely ordained mission as ruler of the last great Orthodox nation. Alexander's religious mysticism differed little from that of his contemporaries, many of whom also moved away from secular enlightened thought to embrace a romantic religious philosophy. Alexander began building the Church of Christ the Savior to commemorate the Russian victory over Napoleon. As before, Alexander fit right in with the intellectual trends of his day; it was his translation of these beliefs into government policy by attacking secular education (discussed later) that placed him into conflict with much of educated society.

THE DECEMBRIST REVOLT

Partially in response to Alexander's abandonment of enlightened reform, secret societies began to spring up in the years following the wars. Some of them were tied to the Masonic lodge, which had become popular in Catherine's day and attracted many men simply because it was fashionable. However, in 1821 Alexander was informed of a group of secret societies that were plotting the overthrow of the autocracy. Despite the fact that his informants provided lists of members who were all officers in the army and solid evidence of their plans, Alexander refused to have them arrested. Called the Union of Welfare and the Union of Salvation, the organizations had begun as humanitarian societies based on models their founders saw in Paris at the end of the war. The goals of both organizations were very vague, but their members openly discussed an end to serfdom and their hopes for a constitution. Neither society was well organized, and both were fragmented among a variety of groups who had radically different ideas for the future of Russia, from the Northern Society's plan for a constitutional monarchy to the much more radical Southern Society's hopes for the dissolution of the monarchy entirely and freedom for the serfs.

In December 1825, Alexander died suddenly while in Taganrog, several hundred miles from the capital. Despite the clear Law of Succession, a crisis arose. Alexander had died without any surviving sons, which left his oldest brother Grand Duke Constantine heir to the throne. Two years earlier, however, Constantine, who was also commander in chief in Poland, had married a Polish lady and renounced his claim to the Russian throne in favor of their younger brother Nicholas. The arrangement had been kept a secret, and Nicholas, unsure of the situation, had the court and the army take the oath of loyalty to Constantine. Meanwhile, Constantine had the army in Poland swear loyalty to Nicholas. For more than two weeks, no one sat on the Russian throne, as the youngest royal bother, Mikhail, was dispatched back and forth between

Nicholas and Constantine, both of whom insisted that the other take the throne. Nicholas finally acknowledged that he would have to accept the job, and word leaked out to the army that Nicholas would be the next emperor. The Northern Society of the Union of Welfare took the opportunity to stage a revolt, telling their troops that Nicholas was trying to usurp the throne from Constantine and instructing them to refuse to take a new oath to Nicholas. Constantine was erroneously viewed as being more liberal than Nicholas because he governed Poland, which had a constitution. On December 14, about 3,000 troops gathered on Senate Square and refused to take the oath to Nicholas, shouting "Constantine and Constitution." Over the course of the day, Nicholas repeatedly asked the rebels to capitulate but finally, reluctantly, had loyal troops fire on the rebels and arrest them. Meanwhile, the leaders of the "revolution" were nowhere to be found; the man who was supposed to declare himself dictator, Prince Sergei Trubetskoi, lost his nerve and spent the day wandering around the city.

The Decembrist Revolt, as this incident came to be known, was an unmitigated failure for a number of reasons. The leaders had no clear notion of what they wanted to do and, beyond inciting the palace troops to refuse Nicholas, had no plan of action. The one thing that they certainly did not want to do was begin a French Revolution, and for that reason, they made no attempt to spread their rebellion throughout the city or the countryside. Their fear of "the mob" was greater than their desire for change. Although it seems that they had a vague notion of a constitutional monarchy, they had not agreed on a blueprint for its implementation and had no plan for consolidating their hold over the rest of the country if they had succeeded in taking the palace at St. Petersburg. Despite the fact that it failed, the Decembrist Revolt had profound consequences for Russia. Nicholas I began his reign with a horror of revolution, and it was not lost on him that the conspirators were all young officers in his army. He had the five leaders executed and sent the rest of the participants to Siberia, which meant that the most promising young nobles of that generation were either killed or exiled. Many historians have attributed the oppression that characterized Nicholas's 30 years on the throne to his fear of another uprising.

NICHOLAS I (1825–1855)

Nicholas I began his reign by destroying the Decembrist Revolt, but he had more to deal with in his reign than the disaffection of his young officers. One historian has succinctly described Russia's condition at the time of Nicholas's ascension:

The plight of the enserfed peasantry, the misery of the common soldier, the precarious condition of the state's finances and the Empire's entire economic system all demanded attention. So did the economically impoverished nobility, the Empire's underdeveloped industry and Russia's unfavorable balance of trade with the West. And the bureaucracy needed to be reformed so that it would administer the Empire in the interests of the state as a whole and serve as an instrument for expressing the Emperor's will. Beyond that, the Empire needed a courts system which worked smoothly, fairly, and efficiently; it required a system of taxation which did not fall mainly upon the poorest elements; and it needed an army which did not consume the lion's share of the state budget.[9]

Nicholas's response was to create what this historian has called the "Nicholas system," in which the autocrat himself dealt with all the problems facing Russia; rather than relying on other groups to help him govern, Nicholas relied on his own judgment and expected his ministers to carry out his directives without question. This was far from an innovation but instead the culmination of the autocratic system that had been in place since the time of Peter I; Nicholas simply took it to its logical extreme based on his sense of his God-given responsibility to rule Russia.[10]

OFFICIAL NATIONALITY

Nicholas's sense of his mission was embodied in the concept of Official Nationality that developed over the course of his reign and was articulated by his advisors in the 1830s: "Orthodoxy, Autocracy, and Nationality." Orthodoxy came first on the list as a corrective to the secular ideals that came out of the Enlightenment—Nicholas firmly believed that government and earthly hierarchy emanated only from God and the divinely ordered universe of the Orthodox faith. Therefore, his duty to rule came directly from God, and his responsibility was to God alone. His belief in autocracy clearly followed from his faith—he did not believe that people could rule themselves, and therefore, only an autocrat ordained by God, who loved his subjects and was above all of them equally, could rule well. The third pillar, nationality, cannot be understood simply as the kind of nationalism that emerged in nineteenth-century Europe. Although Russian intellectuals did begin to develop a Russian nationalism similar to European nationalism—glorification of the

Russian past, people, language, and culture—the nationality part of Official Nationality embraced quite a different concept. Nationality for Nicholas and his advisors meant the organic and indissoluble link between the Russian emperor and his people, not necessarily just the ethnic Russians, but all of his subjects who understood the God-ordained relationship between emperor and people; all Russians must—and indeed desire—to obey their God-appointed emperor who alone was responsible and able to guide Orthodox Russia along her path.

Nicholas was deeply concerned about the future of Russia. He is often portrayed as reactionary, and indeed, his military bearing and devotion to what he believed were Russia's traditional forms of government and society posed a striking contrast to the cosmopolitan courts of Catherine II or Alexander I. But Nicholas was not an unthinking reactionary, nor was he unaware of the evils in Russian society. He kept the reports of the Decembrist investigation on his desk throughout his career as a reminder that Russia had significant problems that he needed to address. He abhorred serfdom and created a commission to investigate its abolition but, like his predecessors, could find no satisfactory alternative to it. He endeavored to ferret out and address the evils of the huge and corrupt bureaucracy and hoped to ease the problems that plagued his people, but at the same time, he feared any sort of social upheaval and believed fervently in the importance of hierarchy and chain of command, which certainly hindered his efforts to uncover corruption among his officials. Finally, he ruled Russia during a very difficult period. Revolution erupted all over Europe during his reign, unrest was rampant, and the old empires were beginning to crumble. Nicholas sought to stave off these evils from Russia and to help his fellow monarchs retain power and stability in Europe. As the rest of the continent exploded with the changes of the industrial revolution, Russia remained agrarian, limited by serfdom and the attendant agricultural conservatism that serfdom perpetuated. The absence of the agricultural revolution that had hit Europe left Russian agriculture inefficient and labor-intensive, with very little surplus to generate the kind of capital needed to build factories. The institution itself prohibited the development of the mobile labor force needed to work in the factories. Russian limitations on travel and education and her continued use of protectionist trade policies prohibited the development of the technologies required for large-scale industry. Finally, Russia's lack of paved roads and slow development of railroads made transportation particularly difficult, which also impeded trade and industrial development. As Europe moved forward at a historically unprecedented rate of technological progress that spurred on massive social, economic, and political transformation, Russia continued to develop at a much slower rate, which would prove disastrous to her position in Europe by mid-century.

TOOLS OF OPPRESSION

Nicholas preferred not to work through the cumbersome bureaucracy and relied instead on His Majesty's Own Imperial Chancellery, an institution that had originally been created to manage the emperor's personal household. Nicholas reorganized it into six sections, each with a different function, and frequently directed his government activities through one of the Chancellery sections rather than through the government itself. The most famous department was the Third Section of His Majesty's Own Imperial Chancellery, which turned into a secret police force. Nicholas envisioned the Third Section as his eyes and ears in the bureaucracy and among the elite, watching and listening for any signs of corruption or treason, but it quickly turned into a network of spies and informants that searched for any sign of disloyalty. Agents of the Third Section reported not only on government activity but also on conversations at private parties, read private mail, and generally spied on all members of the elite. Although everyone knew that the Third Section existed, its members operated in secrecy, so that no one knew who might be spying. The organization was highly inefficient and notable for not uncovering a single conspiracy against the government in its entire existence, although it investigated, harassed, and interrogated thousands of victims. Despite the inefficiency of the Third Section, censorship became increasingly onerous, all independent societies were closed down, and university courses were censored, with "unnecessary" subjects such as philosophy being discontinued. Most intellectuals found themselves under arrest at some point during their lives.

GOVERNMENT REFORMS

Despite, or perhaps because of, his distrust of the bureaucracy, Nicholas continued his predecessors' work of trying to make the administration of Russia more efficient and rational. A new law code, based on the work begun under Alexander I, was finally finished and put into place in 1833, and special codes for Siberia, the Baltic states, and Finland were eventually published. The civil service grew enormously, from 38,000 officials in 1800 to 113,900 by mid-century.[11] The nature of civil service also changed from just another government posting filled by whoever was available to a professional occupation with specialized training and examinations that required university training for the highest posts, making birth less important than ability. Lower levels of the bureaucracy also expanded enormously and were filled by the non-noble *raznochintsy* (see chapter 5). Many of the new bureaucrats staffed the local government, which was expanded in order to increase the efficiency of tax collection and application of tax revenue at the local level. The tax collectors, inspectors, and postal officials were overseen by local officials who answered to a provincial governor. At the center, the ministries were reorganized, and ministers were given much more power and had many more officials at their disposal.

WAR

Nicholas's reign was plagued by war and international crises. At the beginning of his reign, he had to defend his lands against Persian aggression and almost immediately thereafter went to war with the Ottomans. In both cases, Russia was victorious, but at great cost to herself. She obtained favorable treaties from the Ottoman Empire, which roused the suspicions of England, France, Prussia, and Austria. In 1830 revolution broke out again in France, followed by an uprising in Belgium and then a revolt against Russian rule in Poland, which resulted in loss of all Polish autonomy from Russia. After nearly 20 years of peace, Russia was once again pulled into European affairs with the Revolutions of 1848. Nicholas was thoroughly dismayed by the seemingly endless rebellions that took place in Paris, Berlin, Vienna, and nearly 50 other cities across the continent. He was prepared to send troops to help any legitimate government, but all refused his help except the Habsburgs who had to request the help of Russian troops to put down the Hungarian nationalist uprising. Russia defeated the Hungarians, but her outdated weaponry and tactics made that victory much more costly than it should have been.

PROBLEMS IN THE NICHOLAS SYSTEM

The Revolutions of 1848 heralded the beginning of the most oppressive years of Nicholas's reign. His government proved unable to deal with the disastrous cholera epidemic and famine that hit Russia in

1848. His old advisors from the beginning of his reign, men whom he had known most of his life and who had helped him establish the Nicholas system, had died or retired over the course of the 1840s. In order for the "Nicholas system" to work, it was necessary for the emperor to have as clear a picture of Russia as he could get; after all, only the emperor could create policy. The men who surrounded Nicholas after 1848 preferred to keep Nicholas happy. The events of 1848 had inspired much stricter censorship and a reinforcement of hierarchical relationships to the extent that government officials were allowed to fire their employees for no reason at all. All this meant that Nicholas had no source of information other than his advisors—newspapers reported only what the censors permitted, and government officials and bureaucrats had to obey superiors without question or complaint or lose their jobs. Nicholas became a prisoner of his own security and censorship systems and was completely unable to ascertain the true state of his empire. His lack of information and his misunderstanding of the dramatic changes that had occurred in the rest of Europe led him into the disastrous Crimean War.

THE CRIMEAN WAR

The Crimean War was a watershed event in Russian history. After a century and a half of forward momentum in her quest for European greatness, Russia suffered a shattering defeat that highlighted all of the problems in her empire. The sovereign's ignorance of the social and economic problems in his empire; Russia's economic, technological, and military backwardness; and the nation's isolation from and misunderstanding of the political, economic, and social changes that were growing in the West were all revealed in the crucible of the Crimean War. Russia's loss highlighted her backwardness, but equally telling are the reasons that she entered the war. The issues that led to the Crimean War were not new and had been the subject of debate since the beginning of the century, but in the post-Napoleonic period, the rest of Europe had undergone important political and economic changes that had altered the diplomatic landscape. Despite the evidence of the revolutions of 1848, which he had watched with such alarm, and Russia's military problems in the Hungarian campaign of 1849, Nicholas did not realize the profound consequences of the political changes or that the Russian army, despite its size, was hopelessly behind the armies of the rest of Europe. England was deeply concerned with

Russia's activities in the regions of the Black Sea and Persia and was suspicious of Russia's plans for Istanbul and the Straits. Nicholas had long sought a contingency plan with Britain concerning the disposition of Ottoman holdings when that crippled empire finally fell, and he believed that through his personal relationship with the English crown and the British envoys to Russia, he had successfully communicated his sincere wish to come to an equitable arrangement with the other great powers of Europe. The precipitating cause of the war was a conflict with France over the issue of Christian shrines in the holy land. Nicholas, who understood neither the political system of England nor the political system of France, had no concept of international negotiations as a part of internal political power struggles and misunderstood his relationship with both powers; he believed that his personal assurances to the British crown had defused any confusion over his intentions in regard to the Ottomans, and he not only completely miscalculated the French king's need for some kind of concession on the shrines, he also discounted the importance of French and British economic ties in the Ottoman Empire, India, and Afghanistan. The idea that the crown of England could not conduct foreign policy as the sovereign ruler but had to satisfy an ever-changing parliament did not occur to him, nor did the idea that the French crown might go to war over shrines that the French had all but ignored for a century in order to gain political capital at home. The Ottomans, on the other hand, understood all of these political niceties very well and manipulated all of the misunderstandings to their own advantage, hoping to get the great powers to fight it out and regain some of their lost territory and prestige in the process. The Ottomans succeeded, and war broke out in 1853.

Over the course of the war, Russia's failure to keep up with Western military technology and her lack of infrastructure became painfully apparent. Russia had 1.5 million men in her army, but only 4 percent of them were supplied with percussion rifles; the rest were inadequately supplied with the much less accurate smoothbore muskets, which also had a much shorter range than the percussion rifles that most French and English soldiers carried. Even these old-fashioned weapons were in short supply; overall, the Russian arsenal contained only 52.5 percent of the weapons authorized for their infantry. Many of these weapons were in poor condition because Russian soldiers often modified their muskets to sound more impressive on the parade ground, modifications that made them less accurate or even completely useless in a battle. Even

new weapons were often so badly made that they failed to function in battle; out of 1,500 rifles produced in Warsaw in 1854, 1,490
were defective by the time they reached the soldiers at Sevastopol
in 1854.[12] Still, the first year of the war did not go badly for Russia. Although she suffered some losses, she also enjoyed success
on several fronts, and it was not until the end of 1854 that the siege
of Sevastopol began to spiral into a disastrous defeat for Russia. In
addition to the military problems, supply doomed the garrison at
Sevastopol. The absence of railroads meant that supplies had to be
sent by oxcart, often over roads that had become bogs. Nicholas
died a broken man in the winter of 1855. By his death he finally
understood that he had left his son and heir an empire in turmoil
even if he did not understand why or how Russia had lost so much
of her former glory. It would be up to Alexander II to try to cope
with the problems of modernization that had finally overtaken
Russia.

ALEXANDER II (1855–1881)

Alexander II had not been raised to be a reformer, but the misery
of Russia's ignominious defeat in the Crimean War taught Alexander that he would have to make changes in the Russian economy
and society if he expected to regain Russia's position as a great
power. The war highlighted all of the problems that had been building in Russia since the Napoleonic era: The lack of good roads and
railroads had made the supply of Sevastopol impossible to maintain. The slow growth of industry, limitations on scientific exchange
with the West, and tight controls over education had forced Russia
to rely on outdated weapons supplied by foreign industry. None
of these problems was directly caused by serfdom, but Alexander
understood that they could not be solved without finally emancipating the serfs: Great industrial growth required free labor and
a certain amount of educated labor; serfs could supply neither. A
strong industrial economy required reliable roads and railroads,
which would present problems for serf owners, who would find it
increasingly difficult to control their serfs' movement, and which
would also allow for the faster spread of rebellion when it arose.
Developing effective technology, particularly military technology,
required an educated public and scientific research, and in order to
keep up with military changes in western Europe, Russia needed
to open her borders for the scientific and technical community to
keep an eye on further developments. The oppressive regime of

Nicholas I had discouraged all such interaction and inquiry, and it was difficult to see how that oppression could be relaxed without emancipating the serfs. Finally, one of the biggest problems highlighted by the Crimean War was that Russia's huge army was ineffective. In order to fight in the south and maintain her hold over Poland and her long borders, she needed to recruit ever more men. It proved impossible to recruit and train enough men quickly and effectively; the enormous Russian military machine found itself short of trained soldiers despite the huge amounts of money it had spent trying to meet the demands of the war. The other side of the manpower problem was demobilization; after the war, Alexander could hardly demobilize soldiers and send battle-hardened men back into serfdom without serious civil unrest. Russia was the only major power without a trained reserve army, but a reserve army was not possible in the conditions of serfdom. Ending serfdom would not immediately solve Russia's problems, but it would allow for other changes that would directly address some of her most pressing concerns. Although the matter is disputed among historians, most would agree that the main force behind the decision to end serfdom was the necessity for military reforms, particularly the need for a large reserve army. Serfdom began in the seventeenth century as a way to support the Romanov army; it ended two centuries later for the same reason.

THE PROBLEM OF EMANCIPATION

Alexander began his push for reform by building on the secret investigations into emancipation that had begun under his father. These investigations highlighted the myriad of problems that emancipating the serfs presented. From a governmental standpoint, serfdom had long been the basis for local administration in the countryside. Although provincial government had developed much since the time of Peter I, the vast majority of Russia's population was under the authority not of the government, but of a gentry landlord. Landlords were responsible for ensuring that their serfs paid their taxes and produced conscripts for the army; landlords were the police force and the judicial system for their serfs; landlords provided whatever social services existed in the countryside and were responsible for building and maintaining local infrastructure. From the administrative standpoint alone, emancipating the serfs was a huge undertaking because it would also require the immediate introduction of local government throughout the vast territories of Russia. The immediate bureaucratic needs that would arise were a logistical nightmare. Then there were the economic problems—how to free the serfs without destroying the Russian economy or impoverishing either the serfs or the gentry. The Russian government needed the gentry, who formed the core of the bureaucracy and the military. To deprive the gentry of their land was unthinkable; the government would have to increase all salaries substantially to make up for the loss of income, but the government did not have enough money to pay their gentry servitors a wage that would compensate adequately for the loss of estate income. On the other hand, land without labor would mean that these servitors would have to find a way to work their estates themselves, which would take them away from their government service. On the other end of the spectrum, freeing the serfs without land would immediately produce tens of millions of homeless and impoverished vagrants—also an unthinkable option. The serfs could not afford to buy land from their noble landlords, nor could the landlords afford to give the land away for nothing. Finally, the social problems were equally daunting. Serfdom had provided the social structure of the Russian countryside for centuries; how would its abolition change the social structure? How would the peasants regulate their lives without the controlling influence of a landlord? The emperor and the upper classes were well aware of the problems that industrialization had caused in western Europe—the horror of industrial slums, the disease, the millions of impoverished workers who had lost their traditional social and cultural constraints in the process of economic change—and no one in Russia was interested in following the path that had led to the Revolutions of 1848 or to the cholera and typhoid epidemics that plagued industrialized cities in the West. The huge social upheavals that led to political turmoil were to be avoided at all cost. Alexander was faced with the difficult question of how to free the serfs and address all of the attendant problems as well.

Alexander's response was to ask the educated population of Russia for advice. For the first time, the emperor asked the public to debate this question of policy and to make suggestions for the emancipation. Newspapers and journals abounded with editorial pieces and essays discussing the "serf question." The four years spent in debate did not influence the final legislation a great deal, but it did force the upper classes to come to terms with the fact that serfdom was ending and allowed them to feel that they were involved in the process. By the time the Emancipation Manifesto was published in 1861, almost all of the upper classes were resigned to the idea, and most believed that it was right and necessary to free their serfs. Meanwhile, Alexander worked with his advisors to come up with a solution to the problem as well.

THE EMANCIPATION

Right from the beginning, the emancipation pleased no one. At its best, the Manifesto granted the peasants personal freedom from their former landlords—peasants could marry without permission, they no longer owed the landlord dues or labor, and they were no longer under the power of their landlord for justice or mediation. But the emancipation process was complicated and difficult, as evidenced by the more than three hundred pages of legislation that governed the process. In order to address the economic problems, the legislation required that serfs buy land from their former landlords. The problem of land was made more difficult by the fact that the land itself varied so much around the empire. In the southern, black-earth regions, land was extremely productive and therefore very valuable. The gentry from these regions wanted to keep as much land under their own control as possible and insisted that the price the peasants pay for the land be commensurate with its value, whereas the peasants of these regions, of course, wanted to keep as much land as possible but not pay very much for it, given that they had very little money. In the north, however, the land was not very productive, and in fact many northern serf owners employed their serfs in occupations other than farming—some had factories on their land, and others engaged in logging or fishing or any number of other industries that were more lucrative than farming. In these regions, the gentry wanted to unload as much land as possible, but they wanted compensation for the loss of serf *labor,* not the land. The serfs, on the other hand, did not want to take the land because it was of minimal value; they simply wanted to be free to pursue their work without the oversight or the economic drain of their landlords. All over Russia, land on estates varied as well, so that in all regions, the most productive land was coveted by both sides. And all over Russia, the serfs deeply believed that they should not have to pay for land that they had worked. The peasant ethos was that the land belonged to the person who worked it; the notion of legal ownership to them was simply a lie created by the gentry to fleece the peasants of the fruits of their labor. The idea that they should pay for land that they had always worked seemed ridiculous and deeply wrong.

To answer the widely divergent interests across the empire, the emancipation legislation allowed for great flexibility in distribution of and payment for land. Each landlord was responsible for negotiating with his peasants to create a contract that divided up the land and set the price that the peasants would pay for it. The legislation set minimums on the amount of land peasants could or must purchase and maximums and minimums on the purchase price. Within these broad parameters, the landlords and peasants could work out the details of the agreement. By setting these parameters, the government ensured that northern peasants could not refuse to buy a certain amount of land for an established minimum price (which was far more than the land itself was worth), and in this way, the legislation ensured that northern serf owners would get compensation for the loss of their serf labor under the guise of payment for the land. On the other hand, by setting a maximum purchase price, the state also ensured that southern peasants would be able to afford to purchase some land from their landlords. There were also provisions for special cases: house serfs were to be freed without land, given that they had not worked land, and peasants had the option of taking the "beggar's allotment," a piece one-quarter the minimum for the region, without having to pay for it.

This process generated a great deal of confusion and frustration. Those gentry who owned several estates had to come up with separate agreements for each of them. Because most of the peasants were illiterate, they could not read the legislation, and it was easy for unscrupulous landlords to take advantage of their ignorance, although all of the agreements had to be approved by state-appointed commissions before they could go into effect. The legislation said nothing about land that was not under crops, so much of the land that the peasants had always viewed as common land—pasturage, woodlands, roadways, and waterways—did not appear in the agreements and remained by default in the hands of the landlord, who could then charge the peasants for its use. In order to make the process move more quickly, the legislation also viewed peasants as a corporation within their village, so that landlords did not work out individual agreements with each peasant family but with each village; this also paved the way for corruption as landlords bribed the village elders or plied them with vodka in order to get a favorable agreement. At the end of the process, the peasants universally felt that they had been robbed, and during the nine years of negotiations, peasant unrest was common. Rumors about the emancipation ran wild, most famously the assertion that the "real" emancipation decree had simply granted freedom and land to the peasants but had been suppressed by the evil gentry who had substituted this fake proclamation.

Not only was the legislation regarding land disposal confusing in the extreme, but in addition, the payment scheme was equally complex and ultimately benefited neither group. Because peasants had no cash with which to pay for the land, the state had to hold the mortgages. Every village had a 49-year mortgage that it paid to the central government; these payments were known as redemption payments. Every village now paid redemption as well as taxes to the state, and most villages ended up paying far more for their land than it was worth. The discrepancy between the land's actual worth and the amount they paid for it grew wider over the years as the population exploded, and it became increasingly difficult for the peasants to make enough money from their crops to support themselves and make their tax and redemption payments. The effect on the peasants varied, of course: many found their lives relatively unchanged from the pre-emancipation period, others found themselves slipping to or below subsistence level as they struggled to make ends meet with insufficient and expensive land, and a few prospered, using their new ability to purchase land and hire labor to expand production or finding ways to leave the village and move into the new industries that had begun to develop in the last half of the century.

The gentry also had a mixed response to the emancipation. The state could not immediately afford to pay the gentry for the land that they lost in their agreements, nor could the gentry wait 49 years for payment. In order to compensate the gentry more quickly, the state paid them in government bonds that had a 25-year maturity period. Gentry who kept their bonds for 25 years could then cash them in for the full price of their land (less inflation). Gentry who cashed them in sooner took a loss. The vast majority of gentry had already mortgaged their serfs to the state, however, and before they received their bonds, the state paid off their mortgages. As with the peasants, the impact of this system varied widely from person to person. Many gentry received nothing in exchange for the land that they sold to their peasants because their entire redemption went to pay their mortgage, others received a small amount after their debt was paid off, and on up the spectrum to those who received the full amount in bonds. Once a landowner had his bonds, he could hold them for all or part of their maturity period, cash them in immediately at a significant loss, or sell them, for something in between their present value and their mature value, to one of the many speculators who sprang up to deal in government bonds in the aftermath of the emancipation. In real terms, this meant that some gentry families were financially wiped out in the emancipation because of their preexisting debt and their desperate need for ready cash to make up for the loss of serf income, many more entered into a period of slow but steady economic decline as they struggled to maintain their previous lifestyles at a much reduced income, some broke even, and a very few became fabulously wealthy either by exploiting the bond market or by investing their money in new industries or agricultural improvements. Overall, the effect on the gentry was negative as most sank deeper and deeper into debt.[13]

ZEMSTVO REFORM

As indicated previously, the emancipation was only the first step in a series of reforms designed to bring Russia into military parity with the rest of Europe and reforms to create systems to replace those that serfdom had provided. The most pressing problem was that of local government. With the loss of the landlord, a new method of administering the countryside had to be implemented immediately. The villages were placed under the control of their communes, which now took on all local administration. The communes were responsible for the collection of local taxes and redemption payments and the distribution of land. The commune also mediated disputes among its members, acting as a judicial authority. These powers gave the commune absolute authority over its members—no one could leave the village without the permission of the commune, nor could members marry, set up new households, or make agricultural changes without the permission of the commune, which was, as before, often controlled by the more powerful members of the village and highly corrupt. The commune, however, could control only local issues, and the state needed a way to connect rural villages to the regional, the provincial, and finally the central government. The first step was the Zemstvo Reform in 1864, designed to create government administration at the district and provincial levels. The *zemstvo* was an elective body in charge of local infrastructure: it held responsibility for overseeing distribution of resources during times of hardship; maintaining roads and bridges; providing for health care and education, social welfare, police, and insurance; overseeing church, school, and hospital construction; disseminating up-to-date information on agriculture and animal husbandry; regulating the postal service and conscription; levying local taxes and managing funds from the central government; and serving as the communication link between local and central government. Voting was managed by curia (the population was divided into curia based on wealth and each curia voted separately for their delegates), which gave the nobility and wealthy townsmen a distinct advantage, although the peasantry generally made up close to half of the delegates to the district zemstvo. The highest level of zemstvo was the provincial one; the legislation did not provide for a national zemstvo, nor were any of the subsequent emperors willing to create such a body. Still, the zemstvo provided the first opportunity for local self-government and the first chance for Russians to experience the electoral process. The zemstvo provided a new focus for political activity away from the capital and in the provinces, spawning a new class of professional people who staffed the zemstvo activities and took their education and ideas with them to the countryside.

JUDICIAL AND EDUCATIONAL REFORMS

The most progressive reforms to come out of Alexander II's reign were the judicial and educational reforms. The Judicial Reform of 1864 placed the Russian judicial system on a par with the rest of Europe. Whereas the judicial system previously had been merely another branch of the administration, the reform separated the judicial system from the rest of the administration and established trial by a jury of peers for all criminal cases. The new system allowed for the public to observe court cases and created a network of courts in all districts, with appeals courts up to the provincial and national levels and with the Senate acting as the Supreme Court. These courts were not available to peasants, who were confined to their own peasant court system, but the reform created a modern, largely uncorrupted system for the rest of the population. The reform also created a Justice of the Peace, an elected official who could mediate in minor and noncriminal offenses, including those between peasants. In the area of education, universities were given the right to self-regulation in 1863, and in 1864 the Ministry of National Enlightenment opened elementary schools to all, including peasants. Later legislation created high schools for both classical and practical education, and in 1870 women were given the right to attend them. In the same vein, censorship was relaxed, and short publications became exempt from censorial review.

MILITARY REFORMS

The Great Reforms culminated in the military reforms. Again, one of the lessons of the Crimean War had been that Russia needed a more flexible and better-trained army, and the military reforms were the first step to that process. The main problem was the lack of a reserve component, which meant that Russia had to maintain a huge standing army at all times and that she had to scramble to train new recruits during times of war. In 1874 the Military Statute changed the terms of military service to universal service for six years followed by nine years on leave and reserve service until age 40. Not only did this supply Russia with a large trained reserve component, but it was also one of the first reforms to bridge the gap between the peasants and everyone else. Even after emancipation, peasants lived under their own laws—for tax and redemption purposes, they were part of the corporate legal identity of their communes rather than individuals; for legal purposes, they had their own set of courts; for zemstvo elections, they voted as a curia. The 1874 statute made military conscription a universal duty for all male citizens regardless of status. Although in practice the wealthy could buy their way out of service or, through education or nepotism, place their children in higher-ranking positions, the legal military obligation of the young male peasant was exactly the same as that of a young nobleman: both were required to serve in the same army and for the same length of time.

THE LAST YEARS

Alexander II holds a controversial place in Russian history. Both contemporaries and historians hail him as the great liberator emperor, the man who finally set Russia back on the path to progress that Peter I had embarked on a century and a half earlier. Alexander's reforms paved the way for the beginnings of industrialization, for the necessary infrastructure to modernize, and for the foundations of widespread education and health care. On the other hand, his reforms generated a huge amount of dissatisfaction and even despair with the autocratic system and spawned a large and ultimately successful revolutionary movement. His contemporaries and historians both point out that because he restricted the reforms so much, little changed for the average peasant, that the emancipation settlement impoverished much of the gentry, and that he was unwilling to relinquish any of his autocratic power to the inevitable forces of liberal progress. He ranks with Peter I and Catherine II as one of the most loved and hated emperors to sit on the Russian throne, but he has the unique distinction of being the only Russian autocrat to be assassinated by a revolutionary group determined to radically alter Russia's destiny. We discuss the evolution of the revolutionary movement and the assassination later, but ironically enough, Alexander was killed by a bomb thrown at his carriage while on his way to a meeting with some of his advisors where they were to discuss further political reforms to include a national commission made up of representatives from the zemstvo and town governments. The proposed commission was to discuss changes in the central government, changes that might have led to a sharing of power and a weakening of the autocracy. The death of Alexander II ended all hope of a constitutional government for Russia because his heirs reacted to his assassination with increased oppression and a reassertion of central authority.

ALEXANDER III (1881–1894)

The Great Reformer was succeeded by his son, Alexander III, who quickly made it clear that the revolutionaries' hopes that the government would collapse upon the death of the emperor were naïve. Alexander, like Nicholas I, began his reign under the cloud of attempted revolt, and Alexander was determined to crush all opposition to the autocracy while at the same time attempting to fix the problems in Russian society. Alexander III revived Nicholas I's mantra of Orthodoxy, Autocracy, and Nationality, but with a much stricter interpretation; whereas Nicholas I had allowed other religions and nationalities to continue to honor their traditional teachings, Alexander III extended the concepts of Orthodoxy and Nationality to all of the peoples of the empire in the hope that the empire would be easier to control with a more uniform bureaucracy that replaced local elites and practices with a standardized Russian system that operated in the Russian language. A strict campaign of Russification began and led to a backlash of nationalist sentiment in regions that had been relatively peaceful under the old system. The Russification campaign was joined with a brutal pacification program designed to reinstate central control in the Russian provinces as well.

REACTION

Alexander III's first act upon assuming the throne was to enact the "Temporary Regulation," giving the government the power to bypass the new judicial system in all cases involving treason. This effectively meant that Alexander could use his army and his bureaucracy to try, convict, and sentence anyone who did anything that could be construed as revolutionary, which Alexander broadly interpreted as anything that undermined or questioned the Russian government, Church, or culture. As it turned out, the "Temporary Regulation" lasted until 1905, giving the state broad powers of coercion and oppression against anyone who questioned it. Alexander further undermined the reforms by placing more control over the zemstvos. He believed that most of the problems in the countryside stemmed from the radicals who inhabited the zemstvo system; he further believed that it was necessary to keep the peasantry more firmly under the control of the upper classes and the state. To this end he created the much-hated position of *zemskii nachal'nik,* or land captain. The land captain's duties were to oversee the work of the zemstvo; he had to approve all the delegates elected to the zemstvo and approve all of the decisions that it made. He also had broad powers of intervention and the ability to identify and detain anyone suspected of revolutionary activity in his district under the Temporary Regulation. The land captain was appointed by the central government and was by definition a nobleman. This meant that in most cases, the land captain came from the family from whom the peasants had received their emancipation only 20 years before. Finally, the fact that all of the assassins had come from the ranks of university students was not lost on Alexander III, who passed a new University Statute that severely restricted access to higher education and limited the curriculum taught. Thus, Alexander III effectively undermined the judicial, zemstvo, and university Reforms that his father had developed.

NICHOLAS II (1894–1917)

Nicholas II has the dubious distinction of being the last emperor of Russia. He is by turns vilified and pitied for his ineptitude as a ruler during a very difficult period of Russian history. Perhaps a stronger and more resourceful ruler could have stayed the tide of revolution, but it is important to remember that Russia had been developing revolutionary tendencies for nearly a century before revolution finally broke. Although Nicholas would have been a mediocre ruler under the best of circumstances, he was completely unable to grasp the enormity of the problems that Russia faced and therefore was unable to cope with them.

George V, king of the United Kingdom (left), and Nicholas II, ca. 1913. Eon Images.

INDUSTRIALIZATION

One of the main reasons for the emancipation had been to allow Russia to modernize her military, both the organization itself and its weaponry. New industries were vital to the revival of Russian military power. But weapons production requires support industries and infrastructure to succeed—Russia needed better roads, railroads, and mining and refining facilities if she was to produce all of her own weapons. Under Alexander III's finance ministers, Russia pushed railroad construction and looked for investors in Russian industry. Nicholas II continued Russia's industrial expansion, led by the very able minister of finance, Sergei Witte. Witte's plan was for Russia to use foreign investments and loans to seed Russian industry and liberate her from imports and to expand Russia's railroad as much as possible. To this end, Witte placed Russia on the gold standard to encourage foreign investment and counseled alliance with France, who, after the unification of Germany, found herself isolated in Europe. The agreement with France secured both loans and investment capital for Russia's developing industry. Witte's program for creating industry in Russia included many unpopular measures, such as high tariffs on imported goods and a state liquor monopoly, which created a great deal of animosity toward him. He also tried to persuade Nicholas that the peasant commune should be disbanded in order to encourage peasants to develop family farms and to allow more workers to enter into industry. Nicholas resisted these efforts, believing that the commune was the only mechanism that could keep the peasants in line. Despite these limitations, industry grew enormously in the 1890s and early 1900s and brought with it all of the problems that the Russian government had hoped to avoid—rapid urbanization with slums, sanitation problems, worker unrest, underground union activity, strikes, and a general disruption of traditional societal constraints as increasing numbers of peasants left the countryside and moved to the new industrial centers.

TURN-OF-THE-CENTURY CRISES

Meanwhile, Russia's continued expansion into the east finally resulted in the disastrous Russo-Japanese War from 1904 to 1905. Russia's defeat at the hands of tiny Japan sent shock waves not only throughout Russia, but throughout Europe as well. Many Russians viewed the loss as proof that the Great Reforms had been a failure. After all, Alexander II had begun the reforms as a result of the loss of the Crimean War to the powerhouses of France and Great Britain; now, 50 years later, Russia had suffered a much more humiliating defeat against a non-European newcomer to power politics. As Russia entered 1905, it was clear that she was losing the war. This simply added to the already volatile atmosphere that had been building in Russia, particularly since the late 1890s. Famine in 1897, 1898, and 1901 contributed to panic in the countryside and to the sense that the government could not cope with the problems of the new era. Nicholas responded to the agrarian crisis cautiously, by relaxing some of the control that the commune had on its members but reaffirming communal agricultural practices. An industrial crisis from 1900 to 1903 further exacerbated the economic situation and resulted in widespread illegal strikes and in Witte's dismissal.

BLOODY SUNDAY

As tensions rose, the government used increasingly oppressive measures to contain popular discontent. The authorities in St. Petersburg tried to stem the tide of worker discontent with police unions; undercover agents of the police set up worker organizations that allowed workers to blow off steam while keeping them under government surveillance. One of these unions was begun by Father Gapon, who decided to engage in a peaceful demonstration, asking Nicholas to consider the workers' plight. Despite warnings from the police not to undertake the demonstration, several hundred workers and their families marched to the Winter Palace on January 9, 1905, carrying icons and their petition to the emperor, which included some radical demands such as amnesty for political prisoners and calls for a constituent assembly. Nicholas was not in residence, but his guards fired into the crowd, killing several hundred unarmed demonstrators and launching Russia into one of the most chaotic years she had yet experienced.

THE REVOLUTION OF 1905

The response to Bloody Sunday, as it was called, was immediate and widespread. In the first five months of 1905, 800,000 workers went on strike, and peasant rebellions broke out all around the empire; finally a mutiny aboard the battleship *Potemkin* in June signaled that even the military was becoming unreliable.[14] Meanwhile, the official press chided the government for its handling of Bloody Sunday, and the underground press called for revolution. Not all of the unrest came from liberal or leftist groups, however; the turmoil of 1905 also unleashed violent anti-Semitic, inter-ethnic, and Russian nationalist uprisings around the empire, resulting in murderous pogroms and conservative ultra-nationalist gangs roaming the streets of the major cities. The Black Hundreds, as these groups were called, beat up and sometimes killed anyone they perceived to be a threat to Russian tradition. The government failed to respond to these challenges, hampered by the fact that much of the army was still in the Far East, and in October over a hundred million people took part in a general strike, which succeeded in closing down not only factories but also railroads, telegraphs, printing presses, and government offices. On October 17, Nicholas finally conceded defeat and issued the October Manifesto, which granted freedoms of speech, press, assembly, and religion and promised a national legislative assembly. The Manifesto satisfied the liberals, and they withdrew their support from the strikers, many of whom wanted to hold out for economic concessions as well. Without the support of the upper classes, however, the more revolutionary elements could not sustain the strike, nor could they launch a successful resistance to government forces, which were finally beginning to return to European Russia, and by 1907, all vestiges of the revolution had ended.

IMPACT OF 1905

The results of 1905 were mixed. By the end of the year, the peasants had gained some important concessions—an end to the redemption payments and a reduction in taxes. Workers had the right to form unions and to strike, and the election of the Duma, as the new legislative assembly was called, necessitated the creation of political parties and heated debates over government policy in the now free press. Unfortunately, Nicholas almost immediately regretted his concessions, and as soon as his army was back in European Russia, he began to undermine his new institution. In 1906 he issued the Fundamental Laws, which reaffirmed that the emperor was the unquestioned autocrat of all Russia, answerable to no one but God. The election laws were also very conservative: the population voted indirectly and by curia or categories so that, for example, 1 landowner's vote equaled those of 3 bourgeois, 15 peasants, and 45 workers, although because peasants constituted such a large portion of the population, they controlled about 40 percent of the Duma seats.[15] The Duma was further hampered by the fact that it had no real legislative power—it could not propose legislation, it could deliberate only on issues presented to it by the government, and it had very limited budgetary power. The government also created a State Council as a senior house to the Duma. Nearly half of the members of the Council were appointed by the emperor, and the other half were elected by conservative groups in the population. Still, the first Duma was eager to begin work and spent much time debating the land question, the uppermost issue in the peasants' agenda. After watching the Duma argue for a few weeks, Nicholas disbanded it and called for new elections. The second Duma became polarized over the land issue and was also disbanded. At this point, Nicholas rewrote the election law to limit the franchise further. The third and fourth Dumas served out their terms but were completely under the thumb of the State Council and the government.

STOLYPIN'S GOVERNMENT

The main focus of the period from 1907 to 1914 was an attempt to further modernize Russia while limiting the freedoms of the political opposition. Peter Stolypin, prime minister from 1906 to 1911, finally convinced Nicholas that the peasant commune had to be allowed to break up. Stolypin believed that the commune was corrupt and allowed the lazy and the drunk to drain resources away from the strong and sober—in fact, he called his plan for the countryside the "wager on the strong and sober." Stolypin's plan forced the communes to allow their members to withdraw and to take their land with them and encouraged communes to consolidate their members' landholdings and eliminate strip farming. Stolypin believed that those who left the commune and consolidated their lands would become small family farmers who would be more likely to embrace new crops and technologies, ultimately solving Russia's agricultural problem. Because industry was continuing to grow, Stolypin believed that many of those who would be dispossessed by a breakup of the peasant commune would be able to find work in the city. Ultimately, very few peasants took advantage of their new ability to leave the commune.

Stolypin was also known for his brutal repression of any and all dissent. In order to bring the countryside back to order after the disruption of 1905, he set up military tribunals to try all peasant rebels, who were charged with treason and denied their judicial rights. So many peasants were hung in the first two years of Stolypin's tenure that the noose became known as "Stolypin's necktie." The government also cracked down on newspapers, closing them down and arresting their editors and publishers. He was also responsible for the new election law after the second Duma was dissolved, which changed the franchise to allow the nobility, about 1 percent of the population, to elect 50 percent of the Duma and which privileged Russian voters over non-Russian voters.[16] Stolypin was finally assassinated in 1911; no significant government figures emerged again until after the revolution of 1917.

ON THE EVE OF WAR

Of course, the final years of Imperial Russia were overshadowed by the increasing tensions in Europe. The political position of the Balkans became increasingly polarized between Austrian desire to maintain her empire and the demands of the other nationalities, particularly the Serbs, for national independence. Russia had been heavily involved in this area of the world since the late 1870s, hoping to further develop ties to her Slavic "younger brothers" and to gain more influence in the area. Many educated Russians felt a great deal of sympathy and responsibility toward the south Slavs and believed that it was part of Russia's mission to foster independence for all of the Slavic Orthodox in the region. This involvement led to serious confrontations between Russia and Austria in 1908 and to the Balkan War of 1912–1913, in which Russia openly supported the Serbs and the Bulgarians. As Austria became more aggressive in her claims on the area, nationalist tensions rose. Finally, on June 28, 1914, a Bosnian student assassinated the heir to the Austrian throne, giving Austria, with German support, cause to declare war on Serbia. Russia began to mobilize her army, followed by France. Germany responded by declaring war on Russia on August 1 and on France on August 3. Great Britain declared war on Germany on August 4, and Japan declared war on Germany on August 23. World War I had begun.

CONCLUSION

Russia faced enormous challenges during the eighteenth and nineteenth centuries—consolidation of the Petrine Reforms; the Napoleonic Wars; emancipation; industrialization; political, economic, and social upheaval; and the beginnings of organized revolutionary movements. The changes in the rest of Europe were perhaps the biggest challenge of all; Russia could not maintain her position in European power politics without undergoing the same technological and economic changes that her contemporaries experienced, nor could she make these changes without the concomitant social and political upheavals. In the nineteenth century, the Russian elites struggled with these transitions and tried desperately to limit the impact of progress on their political and social positions. The Russian emperors were not the only forces that limited change. The Russian gentry may have believed that it should have more political power, but any movement toward a more liberal or democratic government would have meant relinquishing their privileged economic and social positions—a sacrifice most members of the gentry were not willing to make. Although the Russian elite were by no means unified in their hopes and expectations for political change in Russia, they were all convinced that the peasants were not truly capable of ruling themselves. Educated Russia persisted in viewing the peasantry as children who required guidance if they were to survive and prosper. This paternalistic attitude took a number of forms, from those who believed the peasants were evil and ignorant to those who saw the peasants as innocent children simply requiring a little guidance and education to realize their full potential. The reforms after humiliation in the Crimean War unleashed a backlash from all of these forces, as all levels of society struggled to deal with the unique problems created by the state's attempts to limit change to the specific areas that would allow Russia to reemerge as an important player in European power politics while maintaining a political and social system that could not support the new economic and technological requirements of progress. The last emperor of Russia proved singularly unable to deal with any of these problems. The concessions that he made in the Revolution of 1905 were quickly undermined by his attempts to regain total control in subsequent years. The economic and social problems of industrialization remained largely unaddressed, leading to unrest and an upsurge of strike activity in the years before World War I. Ultimately, the limited reform efforts of the last three emperors proved inadequate to launch Russia into the age of modernization quickly enough for her to compete with the other European powers in the war. The emperor's apparent lack of concern for the desperate economic situation faced by most of his subjects finally destroyed the last vestiges of respect and awe that the autocrat had enjoyed since the Romanov dynasty assumed the throne. The huge losses Russia sustained over the course of the war combined with the desperate economic situation on the home front contributed to the fall of the Romanov Dynasty in February 1917.

NOTES

1. John T. Alexander, *Catherine the Great: Life and Legend* (New York: Oxford University Press, 1989), 86–87.

2. Catherine Evtuhov, David Goldfrank, Lindsey Hughes, and Richard Stites, *A History of Russia: Peoples, Legends, Events, Forces* (Boston: Houghton Mifflin Company, 2004), 288.

3. Alexander, 186–188.

4. Evtuhov et al., 282.

5. Marc Raeff, *Understanding Imperial Russia* (New York: Columbia University Press, 1984), 118–119.

6. Raeff, *Understanding Imperial Russia,* 125–127.

7. The statistics for exactly how many soldiers were involved are still somewhat disputed; these are taken from Evtuhov et al., 326–328.

8. Quoted in Evtuhov et al., 332.

9. W. Bruce Lincoln, *Nicholas I: Emperor and Autocrat of All the Russias* (Bloomington: Indiana University Press, 1978), 77.

10. Lincoln, 77–78.

11. Evtuhov et al., 356.

12. Lincoln, 344–345.

13. We explore the impact of the Great Reforms on all levels of society in greater detail in subsequent chapters.

14. Alexander Polunov, *Russia in the Nineteenth Century: Autocracy, Reform, and Social Change, 1814–1914,* trans. Marshall S. Shatz, ed. Thomas C. Owen and Larissa Zakharova (Armonk: ME Sharpe, 2005), 219.

15. Polunov, 224.

16. David G. Rowley, *Exploring Russia's Past: Narrative, Sources, Images,* vol. 2 (Upper Saddle River, NJ: Pearson Prentice Hall, 2006), 84.

3

The Elites: Princes, Boyars, and Gentry

The further back we go in history, the more difficult it is to find descriptions of life, and those that we can find usually deal with the elite. In order to create a picture of life, historians use a wide variety of sources: chronicles kept by churchmen and by court scribes (who were often churchmen themselves), law codes, travelers' accounts, biographies of saints, memoirs, literary texts, archeological and ethnographic studies, descriptions of festivals and rituals, songs, poetry, fragments of letters, household lists, accounting books, icons, portraits, woodcuts, and efforts by the Church to regulate life through literature, manuals, prayer books, penitential questions, standardized penances, and directions to priests on how to handle common problems. All of this taken together still gives us only a sketchy view of life because very little of the evidence was generated by ordinary people. Our view is necessarily dominated by the Church and the state, the two institutions that generated most of the extant documentation of life in early Russia. One of the most valuable sources for our understanding of daily life is the *Domostroi*, a book published by the church during the time of the Metropolitan Makery, detailing how a well-run Russian Orthodox family should be managed. The book included not only advice on raising children and the relationship between spouses, but also detailed guidance on basic housekeeping, managing servants, storing food, and so on.[1] In this chapter, we examine the lives of the Russian elite from the Kievan period through the early twentieth century.

KIEVAN SOCIAL AND ECONOMIC STRUCTURE

The social structure in Kievan Rus was divided into several categories: The prince and his family, along with a large retinue of retainers and the local aristocracy, were at the top of the hierarchy. These last two groups eventually melted into one another to create the nobility that would dominate Russian political, economic, and social life in the early imperial period—the boyars. Below this group was the middle class. Kievan Rus differed from its west European counterparts in that trade and urban centers formed an important component of its economy and therefore its political and social structure throughout the medieval period; approximately 13 percent of the population lived in towns, including the princes and their retainers. A middle class, therefore, could be found in the towns, largely composed of those who engaged in trade.[2] Beneath them were the lower classes, mostly composed of peasants. Most of the peasants in this area were free or at least partially free. Over time, and largely as a result of the frequent wars on their land, many peasants became bonded to the nobility because they were forced to seek loans to stave off starvation when their crops were destroyed. In most cases, however, the peasants were free to leave once the loans were paid; the category of serf had not yet developed in Kievan Rus. Peasants were the only people who paid taxes, and they made up the majority of the population. Below the peasants were slaves. These were sometimes free peasants who had sold themselves into slavery and were sometimes captives from the wars. Slaves in Kievan Rus had no rights and no property but could sometimes purchase their freedom. Although the presence of a landed warrior aristocracy and peasants may sound like feudalism, Kievan Rus was far from a feudal system. Land was held freely, not in connection with military service; it was given by the princes in gratitude for services already rendered, without a contract to guarantee future military service as in the feudalism of western Europe. Trade and money were important parts of the Kievan economy and contributed to the growth of large urban centers, unlike the almost wholly agricultural and rural economy of the feudal West. Finally, the authority of the local elites was far more limited than in the system of feudalism.

THE KIEVAN ELITE

In Kievan Rus, life for the upper classes differed markedly from their west European counterparts and from the later post-Mongol period. Most of the aristocracy owned estates, but they spent much of their time in the cities where the princes resided. Important boyars imitated the princely court at their manors, and, because they usually lived in the cities, appointed stewards to manage the affairs of the manor. For boyar men, life revolved around the princely court as they counseled the prince, participated in his wars, and jockeyed for position. The estates usually concentrated on raising horses—valuable military equipment—rather than on growing crops. The boyar and his family lived in town and enjoyed more social interaction and a higher level of education than any in western Europe; the importance of trade and complex diplomatic relationships meant that literacy was much more highly prized in Kiev than in the largely agrarian Western lands. Aristocratic women were usually educated alongside their brothers in such topics as grammar, mathematics, philosophy, healing, astronomy, rhetoric, Greek, and Latin. It is not surprising that the women of the Kievan princely family who married foreign princes and kings (such as the Holy Roman Emperor Henry IV) astounded their new courts with their abilities and education. At a time when few men in the West could even sign their names, Kievan princesses and noblewomen could often read Plato in the original Greek. Kievan law permitted women to own and administer their own property, so elite women sometimes had estates of their own to manage. Widows had a particularly powerful position for the time because they could inherit property from their husbands and were often given full power of guardianship over their husbands' property and their children. Wives of princes and more powerful boyars also sometimes advised their husbands, received embassies, and issued declarations under their own names. Widows of princes sometimes acted as regents for their underage sons and ruled absolutely until the boy reached the age of majority. These women had to know how to manage property, conduct diplomacy, and hear judicial cases and issue judgments and even how to conduct a war. Of course, relatively few women held such positions, but most upper-class women played a large role in managing the household property, running an extensive establishment, and participating in internecine quarrels and power struggles.[3]

IMPACT OF THE MONGOLS AND MUSCOVITE POLITICS

Life for the elite changed radically after the Mongol invasion. As the power of Kiev waned and the Rurikid princes struggled for ascendancy, the importance of military retainers became more and more pronounced. As Moscow emerged as the dominant city, more of the elite families removed to Moscow to be nearer to court. For most of the elite in the Mongol era, wealth came not from trade, as it had in Kiev, but from agriculture. The rise of Moscow and the spread of her power placed more populated land in the hands of those who loyally served the grand prince. The pomeshchik system that emerged under Ivan III reinforced the general shift away from trade and toward agriculture as the most important economic foundation for the aristocracy. As warfare became more important and trade less important, the court and its retainers became less interested in education. Although there are no literacy statistics available to us, it seems clear that it became less common for the elite men and women in Moscow to be as highly trained in the variety of languages and disciplines as they had been in the Kievan court. To be useful to the rulers of Moscow, elite men needed to be warriors first and foremost. Elite life continued to center on the city rather than the estate, but the cosmopolitanism and sophistication of Kiev was lost. Instead the elite focused on warfare and on improving their family's standing in the mestnichestvo system. As discussed earlier, the only way to power in Muscovite Russia was through connection to the tsar, who could not only grant lucrative appointments and lands but could also confer power simply by favoring certain men or families at court. Aside from the tsar, the only other source of privilege was the mestnichestvo system, which depended on family connections. The only way to affect one's standing in mestnichestvo was through marriage. Therefore, the life of the elite at court focused on jockeying for position through alliances with other families, political intrigue and schemes, and attempts to attain the tsar's confidence.

LIFE AT THE MUSCOVITE COURT

Life at court changed gradually but dramatically as the tsars gathered the lands into their kingdom. As new territories and new elites were added, the court necessarily expanded, but the center of the court remained the tsar and his few trusted boyars. The term *boyar* had come to mean those who sat on the Boyar Duma, the council that advised the tsar, and at any given time, no more than 15 men could claim the title, which was sometimes passed from father to son or from brother to brother, but not always; the tsar could appoint the men he chose to the council, but boyars almost always came from the old Moscow elite whose families had helped the Muscovite princes grow from their relatively obscure position in the Rurikid line to the exalted position of tsar. The boyars were the closest to the tsar, and although they might also hold offices of high prestige, their power came directly from the favor of the tsar. Beneath them was a much larger group of courtiers, composed of both old Muscovite families of lesser rank and elites from the new territories. These men were not boyars; they were a motley group of non-titled aristocrats from old Muscovite families, pomeshchiki, lesser-ranking nobles or high-ranking nobles from newly integrated territories who were permitted to keep their titles and lands. From these courtiers, the tsar would choose his military and civilian officers, governors, and administrators, and they would also form his bodyguard during battles. For these men as well, real power could only come from proximity to the tsar, not from any particular office they might hold. This large and ever-increasing mob of courtiers vied for lucrative military or provincial commands, for important positions at court, and for the attention of the tsar, the only man who could grant the highest and most valuable posts. The Russian nobility, therefore, grew from a variety of sources and backgrounds, but all were essentially military men, and all understood that the only avenue to increased power, prestige, and wealth came directly from the tsar. The Russian nobility spent as much time as they could at court engaging in court intrigue: angling for advantageous marriage alliances, plotting against rival individuals or factions, and above all, watching one another closely for signs that anyone was getting too close to the tsar and, therefore, getting more power than the rest of the court. If any one family gained too much power or influence, they could expect the other clans to work to bring them down—often with spectacular success and deadly consequences for the heads of the unlucky families.

The Time of Troubles shows better than any other time period the degree to which the Moscow elite was fragmented. By 1610 the English Parliament had been established and was accumulating more power for the elite against the king. In France the Estates General, though not as powerful as the English Parliament, had become a necessary part of governance, and the French kings would spend the next century trying to limit the growing power of their various elite groups. The Russian nobility, by contrast, had a golden opportunity in 1610 to create for itself some corporate institutional power. With no tsar, the nobility could have established any kind of government that it chose. It chose to find a tsar. Noble factions, fragmented by years of shifting allegiances, had created an elite that had no corporate identity. The Russian nobility still operated on a clan basis, with power emanating only from a central figure, the tsar. Without that figure, noble factions could not be controlled, and the government could not function. No revolutionary or reform voices were heard from either the nobility or any other powerful group—only demands for a new tsar.

THE ELITE UNDER THE EARLY ROMANOVS

The elite came out of the Time of Troubles much shaken but still firmly at the top of the political and economic hierarchy of Russia. The installation of Mikhail Romanov in 1613 ensured that the social and political structure that had developed under the Rurikid princes would continue. Both Mikhail and Alexei continued to rule in much the same way that the earlier tsars had done—they reigned as supreme autocrats, theoretically answerable only to God. They were staunchly supported by the Church but were superior to it; the Church never posed the kind of threat to royal power in Russia that it did in western Europe because the tsar was clearly the head of the Church. The early Romanov tsars relied on the Boyar Duma to advise them but were not legally or morally bound by its decisions, although for practical reasons, they might have a difficult time openly defying the entire Duma. Alexei strengthened his own position by expanding the Boyar Duma, promoting men of lesser rank to boyar status and effectively undercutting the power of the boyars. Boyar power was also challenged by the growing number of pomeshchiki entering the elite. The pomeshchiki watched anxiously as the new cavalry units—who were paid a salary rather than granted land—presented the possibility that they would lose their land and noble status. The Law Code of 1649 allayed their fears by establishing the pomestie as fully hereditary—a law that for the most part simply acknowledged the fact that pomeshchiki had long been treating their grants of land as heritable property. Although a distinction still remained between the land of the old nobility and that of the pomeshchiki, this law blurred the distinction between the two groups as the pomeshchiki now formed an established lower stratum of nobility. To further support the pomeshchiki, the new law code established serfdom by prohibiting peasants from leaving the estate on which they were born, removing the statute of limitations on recovering runaway serfs, and imposing stiff penalties on anyone who harbored runaway serfs. The new law code made all of the social estates hereditary and placed the landed aristocracy, whether old boyar or pomeshchik, at the top of the hierarchy in alliance with the tsar. As a result of this code, the noble estate became much larger but also more closed, and it became increasingly difficult for anyone who was not born to a landed family to obtain land. Those with land, the nobility, helped the tsar govern those without land, serfs and lower townsmen, in exchange for their elite status.

THE TEREM AND WOMEN'S POLITICAL POWER

The importance of family connections had a profound impact on the lives of elite women. Even in Kievan times, the women at the princely court had their own living quarters known as the terem. Despite their separation, women of the princely families often played important roles in the political and cultural life of Kievan Rus, and elite women had always enjoyed the right to own property. Elite women in the Kievan period ran large households and oversaw complicated marriage negotiations. We have already noted their unusually high level of education. The Muscovite court was not as highly educated as the Kievan princely houses had been, nor was it as well connected to the other great European houses. The separation of elite women intensified over the course of the fifteenth through the seventeenth centuries so that by the seventeenth century, elite women were secluded from contact with men outside their immediate families in the terem. The origins of and reasons for this increased control over women are subjects of much debate among historians, but it seems likely that the change had to do with the increasingly complicated kinship and marriage alliances that dominated political networks—a family could alter its position in the system of mestnichestvo only through marriage. By keeping women sequestered, heads of families could more effectively control marriages. Secluding women did not just mean that they lived in a separate part of the house; elite Muscovite women did not appear in public unless they were veiled or hidden from view in some other way. Men and women did not socialize together; the elite did not attend any balls, concerts, or theaters in mixed company. This is not to say that the elite did not socialize—they did—but men and women socialized separately. Women visited one another in their separate quarters and in the terem of the Kremlin.

There is also ample evidence that seclusion did not mean powerlessness. Elite women were instrumental in the political functioning of the Muscovite system through their own female networks; they lobbied for their husbands' interests, gathered information from one another and passed it on to their husbands or fathers, and perhaps most importantly, played a significant role in arranging marriages. One author has argued that the seclusion of women enhanced their value as brides and mothers, while allowing them to continue to play an important role in the political networks of the elite.[4] Another historian has argued that the royal terem in particular held a great deal of public power under the Muscovite rulers, emphasizing the extent to which the early Romanov tsars relied on mothers and wives for guidance, especially in matters regarding religion, and as the de facto (although never official) ruler when the tsar himself was away at war.[5] Although elite women were secluded during the sixteenth and seventeenth centuries, women of the lower classes were not. Peasant women and townswomen could not be secluded because their labor was just as important to the family's survival as the labor of men. Peasant women worked in the fields along with their husbands and sold produce at markets, and widows sometimes took the place of a dead husband in village meetings. Townswomen managed stores and sold goods at markets or in shops, and widows sometimes ran the family business when the husband died. Only elite women could afford seclusion, and therefore, seclusion became one of the marks of status, highly prized by the elite.

WOMEN AND PROPERTY

The use of land to pay servitors in the form of pomestie also affected women's legal status. Historically, women had been able to inherit and own land. But although women were still able to own property, they could not inherit pomestie, nor could it be used as part of their dowries because it was tied to service to the state. Pomestie became more common, leaving more women without the opportunity to inherit land or receive it as dowry. In theory, of course, pomestie was not heritable at all, but over time, it tended to go to the holder's son or male kin who then was responsible for fulfilling the service obligation. Women could not fulfill the obligation and therefore could not inherit. In the absence of a son, a son-in-law might petition to take on the pomestie when a pomeshchik died, but he did not have to do so. Nor could wives inherit any part of the pomestie upon the death of pomeshchik husbands, although a widow's portion was set aside from which she could collect the rents while she lived. As more people combined pomestie lands with *votchina*, or family land, it became more difficult and complicated for women to own property, although they certainly continued to do so. The law regarding women and property changed several times over the course of the seventeenth century, eventually stating that widows and unmarried daughters had to be compensated with land or income from land when the head of the household died and that they retained the right to control the land until marriage or remarriage.[6] The law became sufficiently complicated, however, that fewer men chose to leave any kind of land to the females of his family, preferring to take the safer legal route of leaving it to sons or brothers, with smaller provisions for their female family members.

THE PRE-PETRINE SOCIAL STRUCTURE

Life for the nobility continued much as before except that it was now a larger and closed estate. The Law Code of 1649 meant that no one could acquire noble status except through birth or through special appointment by the tsar himself. Noblemen continued to cluster around the tsar, vying for his attentions and favors, and to fulfill the top posts in his army and government. The nobles in the Boyar Duma and those given high commands in the army were often those from the old families, but mestnichestvo was becoming less important as a tool for assigning military posts. Tsars since Ivan IV had refused to honor the mandates of the mestnichestvo system during times of war, and the system was officially abolished in 1682 during the brief reign of Fedor III (1676–1684). Although the Law Code of 1649 appeared to turn Russia into a system of closed estates, the actual lifestyles of people within each estate could vary widely from the norm. People who were classified as peasants might live in a town and run businesses. A provincial serviceman might work his own land if he did not have serfs or did not have enough serfs to support him. Impoverished individuals might enter into slavery in order to avoid taxes. People of any estate—except serfs—could take monastic vows and remove themselves from their family's sphere. Overall, however, the early Romanovs created a more stable and orderly society than Russia had enjoyed since the invasion of the Mongols.

THE PETRINE REFORMS

The life of the elite changed drastically with the Petrine reforms. The rapid changes of the eighteenth century made noble life chaotic until the time of Catherine the Great, who brought 30 years of stability and intelligent leadership to Russia after such a long period of chaos. Peter I changed Russia forever, but his reign was tumultuous precisely because of his sweeping reforms. No one could rest easy during Peter's reign, from the lowliest serf to the tsar's closest friend, because no one knew when he would be called upon to undertake some monumental task for the tsar—whether it was the serf conscripted to labor in the construction of St. Petersburg or a nobleman sent to study abroad, no one knew when his life would be disrupted by the tsar's activities. The tsar's insistence that his nobility adopt a Western lifestyle was particularly unsettling, not because Western culture was entirely alien, but because the Russian elite was well aware of the differences and believed Russian culture to be superior. Moscow had a German Quarter and many foreigners in residence who wore their Western fashions. Elite Russians were aware that Westerners shaved their beards and cut their hair; wore wigs; smoked tobacco; socialized in mixed company at balls, concerts, and plays; and generally dressed and behaved quite differently from Russians. The differences were attributed to the deficiencies of Western versions of Christianity, which had rejected Orthodox truth and allowed people to dress and socialize in a most shocking and sinful manner. The Orthodox Church taught that men were made in God's image and should therefore not alter their natural appearance by shaving or cutting their hair. The Church condemned tobacco as sinful. Russian clothing was loose and covered the entire body, probably as a result of the cold climate that made bare arms, legs, and bosoms uncomfortable and encouraged loose layers to maintain warmth, but the Church also approved of covering the body—and for women, the hair—when in public. The Russian elite did not engage in balls, concerts, or public theater; men and women did not socialize together because the isolation of women was closely linked to family honor for the nobility, and Russian homes, even elite homes, were not constructed for such large gatherings. The Petrine changes required that the elite change not only their clothing but also their entire outlook on life, including the way they conducted themselves in public, the education of their children, their religious beliefs, the construction of their houses, and their relationship to their estates and serfs.

NOBLE CULTURE

Peter is perhaps best known for his attack on Russian traditional culture. Russians dressed very differently from people in western Europe, but many other aspects of Russian culture also differed markedly from the West: The seclusion of women in the terem, for example, had no counterpart in western Europe. Russian art focused almost exclusively on religious subjects and tended to the iconographic style; the Italian Renaissance bypassed Russia completely. Russian architecture also tended to the Byzantine style and had not undergone the changes that had occurred in the West. Music and literature were limited to religious use. Peter changed all of that and forced the Russian nobility to adopt Western clothing, artwork, architecture, and amusements, but even these cultural changes were linked to his efforts not only to westernize and modernize Russia, but also to turn her into a service state. His insistence on the Western-style appearance of both his subjects, by dressing them in Western fashions and forcing them to adopt Western cultural amusements, and their property, by insisting on Western architecture, art, education, and business practices, was a part of his insistence that everyone serve the state in all things—building a Western-style mansion in St. Petersburg was as much a service to the state as serving in battle. These reforms, the details and development of which are explored further in subsequent chapters, were deeply resented during Peter's lifetime. These cultural changes directly affected only the urban and upper classes. For the vast majority of the Russian population, the peasants, the cultural reforms had no effect on daily life except to increase the duties that they owed to their masters and the state. The trickle-down effect of Peter's reforms did not manifest itself in terms of better education, new clothes, or exotic foods for the lower class, but the lower class did have to pay for all of these new luxuries that members of the upper class were forced to enjoy.

ENTERTAINMENT AT COURT

In 1718 Peter issued his Decree on Assemblies, which mandated that men and women socialize together. Peter had set the example for mixed-sex parties much earlier, in 1702, at the three-day celebration of the wedding of a court jester; during the first two days, the guests dressed in traditional Russian fashion with separate celebrations for men and women, but on the third day, everyone had to put on Western dress and come together at a feast with dancing and merrymaking. These changes were particularly difficult given the fact that family honor had long been tied to the seclusion of women, and women had long been admonished to eschew all contact with men outside their families. In one fell swoop, Peter insisted on low-cut dresses, mixed dining, and even more horrific, mixed dancing at balls. This was a traumatic shift for men as well as women as parents watched their traditional notions of family honor evaporate and their control over their children's marriage choices erode.

In addition to his insistence on Western-style dress and social events, Peter had a taste for the bizarre and the ridiculous. His Western banquets and balls were often supplemented by decidedly un-Western entertainment. He was notoriously fond of dwarves and frequently included some amusement featuring dwarves in his parties; the most famous of these was a party thrown a few days after his niece's wedding at which a mock dwarf wedding was staged. The noble guests had tables at the side of the dining hall and watched as a wedding between two dwarves and their wedding feast, attended by dwarves, took place in the middle of the hall. Peter was also fond of costume parties and insisted on heavy drinking at all of his affairs, to the point that men and women would drink themselves into a stupor. Attendance was mandatory at all of the tsar's functions, which could last for several days—guards were posted at all exits to ensure that no one left early. Anyone who failed to attend or who failed to take part in the festivities with enthusiasm would be punished, usually by being forced to drink an enormous amount of vodka. Stories of Peter's parties evoke bizarre images of elite men and women from 15 to 90, dressed at the height of European fashion, attending events that were in part a sophisticated banquet and in part a circus in which they themselves had to perform. Foreigners were shocked at the odd amusements and the enormous amounts of vodka that Peter insisted all imbibe regardless of health or age—one pregnant courtier fell ill and gave birth to a stillborn infant after Peter insisted that she drink as heavily as everyone else, but events such as this did nothing to change his insistence on wild partying. His niece, the Empress Anna, had similar tastes. Her most notorious party was the "ice wedding," in which one of her courtiers was married off to a Kalmyk woman; the couple

Marriage of dwarfs at the court of Peter the Great. North Wind Picture Archives.

was then forced to spend their wedding night in a palace on the frozen Neva River, lying naked on a bed of ice wearing ice nightcaps and slippers. Such behavior made life at court uncomfortable. Peter's daughter, the Empress Elizabeth, however, conducted her court with much less emphasis on the bizarre and satisfied her taste for the unusual by hosting costume balls that were much more in keeping with the west European culture of her day. Catherine II's court was a model of European sophistication.

Some stability at court was achieved under Elizabeth, who did not have a taste for the bizarre, but it was not until Catherine II assumed power that things at court settled down. Although she was ever watchful for conspiracies seeking to replace her with her son Paul, she usually used less drastic measures than her predecessors to bring the nobles into line—the Empress Anna, for example, had a courtier's tongue cut out after he wrote a letter describing her in unflattering terms. Catherine's intelligence and her 17 years spent observing the court before her ascension gave her a more subtle approach to court intrigue, and she proved very adept at manipulating her court without often resorting to arrests or torture. Her clear preference for supporting the nobility allowed them to relax a bit after so many years of chaos and upheaval. This, along with their emancipation from service, allowed the nobility to begin to cultivate a more sophisticated lifestyle, to spend time reading and discussing philosophy, art, music, and even politics. The Russian nobility actually began to resemble the Western aristocratic society that Peter had admired so much but that had not had time to mature until Catherine's reign. The time between Peter's reign and Catherine's reign had seen the evolution of the elite from their forced outward acceptance of Peter's somewhat twisted view of upper-class life. Under the intervening tsars, particularly Elizabeth, social refinement had become the norm.

A SERVICE ELITE

Nobility had long been associated with state service, and the Petrine reforms explicitly tied the two together for the first time—those who did not serve the state lost their noble rank and with it their right to own populated estates. Peter's concept of society was a pyramid of service: at the bottom, the serfs served the nobles by providing their economic support; the nobles served the emperor through military and state service; the emperor served the state and God. Peter I's concept of state service became deeply embedded in the lives of the nobility—so much so that Peter III's emancipation of them less than 50 years later did little to alter their lives; they continued to serve the state as the best way to prosperity and because service had become a part of the noble heritage. Before Peter I, only the nobility in Moscow expected to dance attendance on the tsar at all times. These nobles left their estates to be managed by foremen or by family members while they served the tsar in war and peace. All of the other nobles—those from the provinces, younger brothers, lesser branches of great families—lived on their estates and served only when called to war. Peter's new rules meant that all noblemen had to serve all of the time, leaving their estates largely devoid of noble males over the age of 15. It meant that noble families with ambitions either to gain high rank or to keep it had to train and educate their sons to prepare them for life as professional officers or as civil servants. It meant that fewer noble families actually lived on their estates at all, given that wives and children frequently followed the head of the house to his posting either in Moscow or in the provinces.

The biggest change for the nobleman was the unending requirement to serve, one grueling or boring or uncomfortable assignment inevitably followed by another, sometimes from the military to the civil service and back, with little or no rest in between and often no consideration of the nobleman's personal interests or talents. This constant movement, combined with the fact that any given noble's estates would be scattered around the empire, contributed to the fragmentation of the nobility and helps to explain why the noble estate in Russia did not develop a corporate identity and challenge the emperor's autocratic power; no close ties or friendships could easily survive the rootless and mobile life of the noble servitor. As one historian has described it,

the nobleman felt strongly that he had been put into the service of a machine—huge, callous, and impersonal. Yet he could not give up the hope that a personal approach and an appeal to the human feelings of the ruler (and his ministers) might alleviate his condition; hence the pathetic form of the appeals and petitions [to be relieved of duty]. They are graphic illustration of the nobility's desperate attempt at counteracting—nay, at denying the new relationship between serviceman and monarch. But they met with the working of bureaucratic routine and mountains of papers. Little wonder that the nobleman's resentment fastened not so much on the permanence and regularity of service as on its depersonalization.[7]

Although most nobles continued in state service even after their emancipation, many, particularly those without large holdings, served for only a few years and then retired to manage their estates. Catherine II's Charter to the Nobility and her provincial reforms gave nobles increasing control over local affairs, which made estate life more attractive for those who did not wish to leave service entirely. But many nobles remained strangers to their estates and their serfs, and their lifetime of service did not create any avenues to power outside of those controlled by the central government. Even in their provincial assemblies, the nobles who were elected to serve had no authority independent of the central government—they were always and only representatives of the emperor, the only source of sovereignty in Russia.

The nobility's relationship to the sovereign and their attitude toward service changed in the first half of the nineteenth century The relationship between emperor and nobles was at its most comfortable under Alexander I. All in all, Alexander was exactly the type of emperor that the Russian nobility understood. They were all, by this time, well acquainted with Enlightenment principles. Although the nobility held a wide variety of opinions on how Russian politics, economics, and culture should develop, they were all convinced that the well-born, educated segments of society could most effectively lead the country. The relationship between Alexander and his nobility was a cross between that of Peter I and Catherine II. Like Peter, Alexander's right to the throne was unassailable, and he could directly rule over his court. Unlike Peter, however, Alexander and his nobles thought very much alike. Whereas Peter ran over his nobles, forcing them to his will, Alexander worked easily with his court. In this sense, his court was much more like Catherine's—Alexander and his nobles worked together and exhibited a mutual respect. Unlike Catherine, however, Alexander had nothing to fear from his nobles and was therefore much less dependent on their goodwill. In Alexander, then, we see the culmination of Peter's legacy—an absolute ruler working cooperatively with his nobility for the greater good of Russia. He and the gentry shared a set of beliefs fostered by their enlightened education and held one another in mutual respect. At the same time, their positions were crystal clear: Alexander was the unquestioned sovereign, and the gentry were his loyal servants. Such a symbiotic relationship between monarch and gentry had not existed since before Peter I made such drastic changes to gentry life, and this newfound comfort led to a flowering of gentry culture. Increased opportunities for education and travel expanded the educated elite's understanding of the philosophical trends that they had adopted from the West and prompted Russian intellectuals to begin their own explorations of philosophical, scientific, and literary subjects. There was also excitement and a great deal of concern at the beginning of Alexander's reign because it seemed that the young tsar might make some fundamental changes to the Russian political and economic system. Reaction to this possibility varied widely as the younger generation tended to look forward to what they believed would be enlightened change, whereas the older generation feared such drastic measures as a threat to their way of life. Ultimately, the changes did not take place; instead Russia found herself involved in the Napoleonic Wars.

In the final years of Alexander's reign and throughout Nicholas I's reign, the relationship between nobility and emperor became increasingly strained. Many nobles resented Alexander's apparent rejection of enlightened ideals and even more hated the oppressive atmosphere of Nicholas's government. The primary effect of the Decembrist Revolt on elite culture was to create a sense of distrust between Nicholas I and his nobles. As Nicholas struggled, unsuccessfully, to heal Russia through the Nicholas system, the elite had only two choices: to work for the government without question or comment or to leave government service. Of course, many of the educated gentry could not afford to leave government service and continued to serve in the increasingly stifling atmosphere created by Nicholas's oppressive measures. Others chose to stay in service out of a sense of duty or ambition, but all who remained in government service found themselves under strict but haphazard supervision and subject to a variety of humiliating requirements designed to ensure their absolute loyalty to the emperor. Many noblemen who could afford to quit state service did so and isolated themselves on their estates, feeling that it was immoral to serve under the reactionary Nicholas. The Third Section was always watching for subversive ideas in the capitals, and many nobles who admired Western political systems felt safer on their estates, far removed from the capitals. Their flight from service came at a great cost, given that many of them felt strongly that it was their duty to serve their country, and they comforted themselves with educating their children and sometimes by experimenting with modern agricultural techniques in hopes of improving the economic lives of their serfs.

DEFINING THE GENTRY

The gentry in eighteenth- and nineteenth-century Russia was an amorphous group who shared certain privileges, primarily exemption from personal taxation and the right to own populated estates. Although this was a very small proportion of the overall population, it was of the first importance to the state because the nobility formed the backbone of the army, navy, and civilian government. The gentry estate grew over the course of the century, ending up at about two percent of the population by the end, and was far from homogeneous. The new emphasis on service rather than birth undermined the traditional definition in both Russia and western Europe that nobility was a matter of birth. The old noble families would argue that nobility was an inherited "quality of character and mind," but the fact that one could now achieve nobility through service indicated that "education and cultural leadership" could also be the defining characteristics of nobility.[8] Over the course of the eighteenth century, the noble estate became even harder to define, leading Catherine II to divide the gentry into six categories: actual nobility who had received grants from the sovereign, military nobility who had attained a commissioned rank, nobility who had reached the eighth rank in the civil service, nobility from foreign sources, titled Russian nobility, and old noble families who could not produce documentary proof of their status.[9] Beyond identifying the various types of nobles, these distinctions bore no legal meaning—all nobles were exempt from the poll tax, had the right to purchase or receive populated estates, and were accorded all of the other privileges as laid out in the Charter to the Nobility.

NOBLE STRATIFICATION

Despite the fact that all nobles were legally equal, real distinctions lay in variations of wealth and proximity to power and influence. At the top were the nobles, usually of ancient lineage, who served the tsar—or after 1721 the emperor—at court and in the highest ranks of the military and government. These few families would own several estates scattered around the empire and counted their serfs in the thousands. These men lived their lives in the capitals or wherever their duties took them; they hired foremen to run their estates and rarely visited their holdings. Beneath them were nobles of high rank who also served in the military or government but who were not close to the emperor and who owned lesser estates, numbering their serfs in the hundreds. These men had to pay more attention to their lands and might divide their time between their service posting and their estate or leave their lands in the hands of their wives to run. Beneath them were the two largest segments of the nobility, the first of which were the gentry who owned small estates that they managed themselves; this level of noble probably could not afford to hire a foreman and had to rely on his wife or his serfs to run the estate while the nobleman was in service. At the very bottom were gentry with no lands, men who had to live entirely on their meager state salary. Of course, there were also those who moved up or down in wealth and power: Peter I's right-hand man, Alexander Menshikov, started out life as the son of a pie seller. He spent several years at the side of the emperor before attaining noble status and receiving grants of land. All of the emperors of the eighteenth and nineteenth centuries discovered men of lesser rank who were then elevated and given rich estates, so that at any time, one might find a lesser nobleman or, more rarely, a commoner at the side of the emperor, wielding much influence, but without wealth or high rank. These men usually attained both wealth and rank as favors from the emperor and were thoroughly despised by the older families at court who felt that the newcomers had no place in their sphere.

The economic and geographic differences among the elite continued and even intensified in the nineteenth century, and the elite became increasingly fragmented by other fissures as well, particularly by the changes in service to the state. As the bureaucracy became more complex, government service became more professionalized and stratified. The number of lower-level bureaucrats increased enormously, and these positions were held more often by men from the impoverished gentry, the middle-level merchant classes, or the clergy. These jobs carried no rank but formed the backbone of the government administration. It was possible for the son of an impoverished nobleman to move up through connections and ability, but most of these clerks would remain in the lower echelons of the government throughout their lives. As government jobs became more highly specialized at the lower and middle levels, more and more of them were filled by non-noble professionals who mixed with the lower-level nobility in the workplace and even in their social circles. Another group of government servants that grew enormously was the provincial servitors. It became more and more common for men who began their careers in the provinces to stay in the provinces as central and provincial government became more highly specialized. This led to more gentry society in the provinces and the growth of gentry culture in provincial capitals. Middle-level bureaucrats who might achieve a rank could be found in both places but as their positions became more specialized, were not interchangeable and could not be easily moved around the government administration in the way that they had been in the past. Even at the highest ranks of provincial and central bureaucracy, professionals were needed. Men who hoped to hold high office could no longer rely solely on the good will of the sovereign to give them a post; they needed to possess a university education and be able to demonstrate their competency through a series of exams. The days of government servitors moving from the military to the bureaucracy and back on a regular basis were over. The more professional the bureaucracy became, the more it served to fragment the elite.

Still other gentry chose not to work in government service at all. Although they might be called to serve in times of crisis, such as the Napoleonic Wars, these men spent most of their lives on their estates, engaging in a particularly provincial society. Especially after the Napoleonic Wars, these men often developed vast libraries of foreign literature and periodicals, which they would read and sometimes discuss with their neighbors. Over the course of the reign of Nicholas I, this segment of the gentry grew as men found service to the crown distasteful and unsatisfying in the increasingly stultifying atmosphere of Nicholas's government. These men occupied a unique position, living a restricted life in the provinces with a very limited social and cultural sphere yet immersed in the latest literature from the West; they were hardly provincial bumpkins, yet they were far removed from the noble life of the capitals or the provincial centers.

All of these changes meant that the nobility were even less of a corporate body than they had been in the past. Even at the highest levels, noblemen who could claim a long noble heritage found themselves rubbing shoulders with men who had achieved noble status through their education and administrative skills. The older nobility might despise the newcomers as upstarts, but they could not escape their influence either at work or in the social arena. As one went down the noble scale through the middle ranks to the impoverished gentry, more and more of the newly ennobled or non-noble administrators could be found. Although those who could claim generations of inherited nobility at all levels thought of themselves as a special category, they were not legally different from those who attained hereditary nobility through their own efforts, by achieving the eighth rank in civil service or the first officer rank in the military; those who were in the Table below these ranks were personal nobles who could not own serfs. For a nobleman who hoped to move up in government service, making pointed distinctions based on birth could be disastrous to his career because he might very well have to rely on one of the new men to promote him. The power that the new nobility wielded meant that they could not be ignored by high society, and they appeared at salons, balls, and concerts alongside the old-line families. At the lower levels, nonnobles mixed with old families who had fallen on hard times. So although the old nobility might resent the new arrivals, they in fact often had much more in common with and spent much more time with the new men than they did with older noble families who had fallen below or risen above them in government service or those who were occupied in the provinces either with government service or with their estates. The new nobles did not form any kind of coherent body either; many of them wanted to be accepted into the highest ranks of society along with the older families, whereas others were more interested in their work than in high society. The old nobility could not form a coherent block against the new, but the new nobles did not try to unite against the old.

The nobility who remained in government service differed from those who did not in other ways as well. The two groups each tended to think of the other as sellouts. Those in government service felt that they embodied the Petrine ideal of selfless service to the general good (the state) and viewed those who remained on their estates as throwbacks who lived off the labor of their serfs and contributed nothing to the overall good of Russia. Those on the estates, particularly during the reign of Nicholas I, believed those in government service to be mindless drones, carrying out the wishes of an archaic and despotic sovereign far removed from Russian reality. Although they often deplored their own reliance on what they increasingly came to see as the evil system of serfdom, they believed that by involving themselves in their estates and improving agriculture and by creating a more humane environment for their serfs, they were doing what they could to improve Russia. They chafed under the forced inaction that the Nicholas system imposed on them by restricting all active roles in politics or social change to those in government service, but they felt that working for such a corrupt system was merely to perpetuate it and add to its evils. Thus, these two groups each saw themselves as taking the only conscientious path to improve Russia, and both saw the other as selling out either to the government or to a life of lazy acceptance. These two groups of nobles rarely came together because they moved in very different social circles, but they both endeavored to send their sons to university. Sons from both categories were imbued with a deep sense of duty and desire to serve Russia; at university they met, studied together, formed reading circles, and argued over the future of Russia. As the century wore on, and the Great Reforms failed to improve the lot of the serfs, their numbers grew, and many of these university students eventually came to the conclusion that the previous generations on both sides had been wrong; Russia could not be changed through either state service or humanitarian efforts. The only answer lay in overturning the system entirely.

ELITE EDUCATION

Peter's desire for a service elite had profound consequences for noble education. Peter needed servants who understood the complexities of modern government, economics, and warfare, so he founded schools for young nobles and for children of the other free categories. Ambitious families soon learned that their children needed to speak French—and preferably German and Italian as well—to ensure their ability to rise at Peter's court. He sent hundreds of men abroad to study at Western universities and to acquire technical expertise, although his plans to send young noblewomen abroad to study were stopped by the overwhelming objections of noble parents. Peter founded printing presses that concentrated on state publications and technical manuals but that also printed books that he thought would be useful to his people. He himself loved to learn new skills and respected educated men; he hoped that the elites of Russia would embrace education not only to bring technical expertise to Russia but also to create Russian scholarship outside of purely religious studies. In a similar vein, Peter wanted Russia to develop arts after the manner of the West, and to that end, Peter's sister Natalia opened the first court theater.

Over the course of the eighteenth century, the education of children became vital to the survival of the noble family, particularly the male children. Peter I made education of noble boys mandatory and enforced this measure using passports. When noble boys were about seven, they were registered and issued a passport. By the age of 15, the boy was supposed to return and take an examination. Boys who passed the examination were admitted to service and declared adults. Boys who failed the examination could not renew their passports and had to enter service at a lower rank. They were not considered legal adults and could not marry until they passed the examination. The consequences of having a son fail the examination were dire enough that families went to great lengths to ensure that their sons had an adequate education, usually sending their sons to boarding school after they received their first passport. When Anna permitted graduates of the Cadet School to enter directly into the Table of Ranks, the value of education went up even more. Elizabeth opened Russia's first university in Moscow and an art academy in St. Petersburg. By the end of the eighteenth century, it was unthinkable for a noble family to raise a son who had not received a solid formal education, covering at least the basics. By the end of Catherine II's reign, being a cultured gentleman had become a prerequisite for success in the sovereign's court, and many noble parents aspired to educate their children far beyond the basics required to enter service.[10]

Catherine II continued educational reform in hopes of creating a more sophisticated elite. Through the Statute on National Schools in 1786, she opened gentry, town, and provincial schools and even mandated coeducational high school and primary schools in provincial and district towns for all children of the free (non-peasant) classes. These schools were not very successful, and relatively few parents sent their children to them. Most nobles continued to educate their children privately or through the cadet schools. Catherine also expanded printing presses in Russia and started publishing journals, even writing articles herself for many of her favorite publications. She encouraged her subjects to write as well, sponsoring essay contests and inviting discussion on a variety of topics. These reforms may not have succeeded in producing the "new people" that Catherine wanted to create in Russia, but they laid the foundation for future expansion of the educated public, which emerged with a vengeance in the nineteenth century.

CHANGES FOR NOBLEWOMEN

Catherine also founded the Smol'nyi Institute, the first boarding school for gentry girls, reflecting the new emphasis on women's education among the elite. Chastity and religious observance were still of the utmost importance, but it became increasingly important for noble girls to acquire the kind of education that would help further their husbands' careers and enable them to raise properly educated children. The noble concept of family life shifted from the Church's view of the family as the producer of the Orthodox faithful to embrace Peter's concept that the main purpose of the family was to raise children to be successful servitors of the state. Before the Petrine revolution, little thought was given to raising children beyond their religious and moral upbringing and teaching them the skills they needed to survive. Along with the rest of eighteenth-century Europe, the post-Petrine Russian elite began to view mothers as the first educators of their children; children had to be molded into good service-oriented adults. For women to set their children on the proper paths, they needed new skills; the accomplished noblewoman was still supposed to be chaste, virtuous, and obedient, but now she also needed to speak several languages, play an instrument, sing, draw, and be able to converse on a variety of subjects. These accomplishments would make a woman a valuable helpmate to an ambitious husband but would also help her to raise children who could do all of these things as well.

Girls' education was also affected by the new notion of romantic love that had finally penetrated into Russia. Although some noblemen still preferred a meek wife who effaced herself and simply carried out his orders, more and more noblemen chose to marry women who were their intellectual equals. In order to raise a marriageable daughter, therefore, parents taught girls to guard their chastity and their moral virtue and remain meek but also to carry on intelligent conversation and to read good books; girls were taught to dance, sing, play, and draw. In addition to these ornamental skills, girls had to learn how to run the household, which was a woman's primary job—no minor task for the wife of a great noble who might have several estates and townhouses to manage. Even the most elite woman would need to know how to oversee the household to ensure that her servants were doing all of the work properly—preserving fruits, vegetables, and meats; sewing; darning; weaving; cleaning; and providing for any guests in the house.

AN ENLIGHTENED COURT

By Catherine's time, the nobility had acquired a much more sophisticated outlook on life; they had become indistinguishable from their European counterparts in dress, behavior, housing, entertainments, and even language. Perhaps the most striking difference between the Western and Russian nobility of the late eighteenth century was the Russian nobleman's commitment to state service. The gentry in Russia still had a weak corporate identity, further fragmented by the stratification of their estate as discussed earlier. Although it was not in Catherine's best interest to have a noble estate that had a strong corporate identity, which might encourage the nobles to try to limit her power, she believed that the only way Russia could move forward was to increase the education level and widen the noble outlook on the world. The Legislative Commission had revealed to her the extremely narrow and self-interested view that persisted among the gentry. She was also painfully aware of the rampant corruption that still existed in her government, which she also attributed to narrowness of outlook. Enlightened education was the answer.

Catherine taught the nobility to think like educated Europeans as well look like them. Her educational reforms, though not as successful as she had hoped, reinforced the idea that both men and women who wished to be viewed as cultured and sophisticated had to be educated, thoughtful, and well versed in the important topics of the day. In addition to philosophy and natural sciences, the printing presses were busy with religious books and novels—probably the favorite pastime of young noble women. By the end of the century, both men and women of the elite read widely (or at least pretended to) and added the salon to their social schedule. Catherine even made a woman, the Princess Dashkova, the founding head of her Academy of Sciences in 1783, the first woman ever to hold such a position in Russia or in Europe. Dashkova also founded the Russian Academy and edited a journal. Catherine wanted a reading public and opened many new publishing houses in Russia. She began several literary journals, encouraging her noble subjects to write on all sorts of controversial topics, and contributed essays herself. She had works of the Enlightenment published and hosted salons at court to discuss them. She favored the works of Montesquieu and Voltaire that seemed to justify absolute rule in a country like Russia and was deeply shocked and frightened by the events of the French Revolution, which led her eventually to increase censorship and slow the publication of possibly revolutionary literature. She was greatly disturbed by Alexander Radishchev's 1790 publication of *A Journey from St. Petersburg to Moscow,* in which he described and deplored the inequities in the Russian countryside, particularly the evils of serfdom. Radishchev was a wealthy noble of the "new type," having been educated in the Imperial Corps of Pages and at government expense at the University of Leipzig—the kind of noble that Catherine had consciously attempted to create. Catherine condemned the book as inflammatory and accused the author of being full of "the French madness," but she commuted the sentence of death imposed by the Petersburg Criminal Court to 10 years exile and hard labor.[11]

NINETEENTH-CENTURY EDUCATIONAL REFORMS

After the Napoleonic Wars, the government began to limit access to education. Alexander I created a new Ministry of Spiritual Affairs and Education, placing all of the schools and universities he had created under the direction of the over-procurator of the Holy Synod and founder of the Russian Bible Society, which sponsored the first translation of the Bible into vernacular Russian. The new ministry emphasized religious instruction in schools, but not just Orthodox instruction. Schools in Muslim, Jewish, and Old Believer areas were allowed to incorporate their beliefs into instruction. Toward the end of his reign, Alexander became much more suspicious of the independent religious societies, and in 1822 he allowed his advisors to close the Masonic Lodges, the Ministry of Spiritual Affairs and Education, and the Bible Society and to burn all copies of the translated Bible; he then gutted the University of Kazan when the district governor claimed that it was a hotbed of anti-Christian activity and instituted much tighter censorship of the press. Nicholas I continued in this vein, endeavoring to limit access to education based on social status, believing that it was safer for people to have just as much education as they needed to carry on their duties. Therefore, it became almost impossible for any but the nobility to obtain secondary education or attend a university. The Ministry of Education was controlled by the man who had articulated the doctrine of Official Nationality, and he worked tirelessly to ensure that all schools adhered to the spirit of the policy. Nicholas attempted to standardize all schools, even private ones, and sent out teams of inspectors to ensure that schools and universities taught the right subjects to the right students. Alexander II granted more freedom to the universities and allowed women to attend special courses to train as midwives, nurses, and teachers. Attendance at universities expanded steadily over the course of the late nineteenth and early twentieth centuries, although the presence of the radical movement among students resulted in periods of severe censorship of curriculum and suspicion of both students and professors. Alexander also opened primary education to all of his subjects and expanded the network of elementary and secondary schools throughout his empire.

AN ENLIGHTENED NOBILITY

The fear that the French Revolution generated and the state's heavy censorship did not, however, turn the reading public away from discussion of important topics. The salon actually became even more prevalent during the reign of Paul, who hated the intellectual and cultural emphasis of his mother's court. His replacement of the sophisticated court of Catherine with the barrack-style life he preferred combined with his callous treatment of the nobility resulted in the gentry fleeing to their estates or to Moscow, where they continued their social activities far removed from Paul's influence. During Catherine's reign, the most prominent salon was at court, but during Paul's reign, the salon moved to private drawing rooms, allowing the nobility more freedom in their discussions now that no sovereign sat listening to their views. In an ironic twist, Paul's attempt to wipe out the Enlightenment influence gave it new life and encouraged the nobility to air more independent views and to develop their intellectual tastes without the oversight of the emperor. This completed the transformation of the elite from their entirely submissive outlook of the pre-Petrine era, through their tutelage at court under Catherine, into the beginnings of an intellectually independent civil society. By the end of the century, it would have been difficult to see much difference between the Russian elite and their European counterparts.

THE BIRTH OF CIVIL SOCIETY

The Napoleonic Wars affected the gentry in a variety of ways, but the most notable change was in the gentry attitude toward Russia and their role in her development, a change that historian Marc Raeff has identified as the birth of Russian civil society. The eighteenth century had created an educated elite who read Western philosophy and literature but who rarely questioned the political or social order in Russia. The nobles who marched to Paris and back in 1812–1815 saw that Russia was very different from other European countries where the elites played an active role in government. For the first time, they understood that their education in Enlightenment principles could be applied to government and to social relationships. Their experience of their own people changed as well. Young officers were impressed by what they perceived to be the patriotic behavior of the Russian peasants; for the first time, the elite youth saw the lower orders as their fellow countrymen rather than as a dark mass that had to be controlled. Although they still believed that the peasantry needed elite leadership, the new feeling among the educated was that the peasantry could and should be led to something better than serfdom. The combination of these two discoveries led to the development of a social consciousness and the desire to play an active role in Russian political culture.[12] This new attitude took many forms: some joined the Decembrists, others struggled to find a way to effect change within the system, and still others did little themselves but educated their children to work for change.

This changed with Alexander II's reign. As many nobles faced economic catastrophe precipitated by the emancipation, more of them were forced back into state service. Some attempted to manage their estates according to the latest European models, hiring their former serfs to work their remaining lands, buying new equipment, and experimenting with cash crops such as sugar beets or tobacco, new seeds, and fertilizers. Some of these families became quite wealthy, but many of these nobles found their attempts to modernize agriculture frustrating. They were still forced to rely on peasant labor, and the peasants proved no more willing to try new methods after the emancipation than they were before. Other nobles chose to rent or sell their lands to peasants. The nobles who tried to go back into state service did not do much better because the government did not have enough positions for all of the nobles who now needed to obtain employment. The ranks of impoverished nobles grew, as did the numbers of middle-level nobles struggling to survive on their government salaries or the produce from their estates. Some families became fabulously wealthy by turning to new industries, but these were few and far between. Overall, the economic position of the nobility declined considerably following emancipation.

The Great Reforms did have the effect of stimulating gentry involvement in society. Many were galvanized by the Reforms and believed that Russia was finally on her way to a freer society with more opportunities for political involvement. The educational opportunities and the new professions that emerged from the university and zemstvo reforms opened up new possibilities for gentry youth. Some studied seriously, earned a degree, and embarked on careers in medicine, education, law, or engineering with the idea that they could help Russia in her development in these new areas. Others went to universities and became radicalized, joining revolutionary movements that would lead many of them to arrest, exile, execution, or underground activity. We look more closely at the new professionals and revolutionaries later, but the generations after the 1860s believed for the first time that they could effect change in Russia and that it was their responsibility to do so. This meant that the increasingly oppressive reigns of Alexander III and Nicholas II fell heavily on the young gentry, eager to be of service to the people but increasingly limited to service to the cumbersome state. The events of 1905 galvanized them once again, and most of the nobility and gentry eagerly assisted in the General Strike of 1905 by creating strike funds for the lower classes and becoming active in political groups. The October Manifesto satisfied many of this class because it seemed the beginning of liberal government in Russia, and many joined the Kadet party (Constitutional Democrats), believing that the Duma would be able to push Russia further along the path of reform. Although the emperor's obvious reluctance to work with the Duma and the subsequent change in election laws disappointed many gentry liberals, they mostly continued to participate in legitimate political activity throughout the prewar period. Of course, not all of the nobility and gentry approved of the political changes, and those who clung to the old ways joined parties to the right of the

Kadets, hoping to help Nicholas II curb the changes that seemed to be coming thick and fast between 1905 and 1914.

IMPACT OF THE REFORMS ON GENTRY WOMEN

The lives of young gentry women were perhaps even more profoundly affected by the Great Reforms and subsequent counterreforms than were the lives of their male counterparts. The issue of what the proper role for women was in Russia became a heated subject for debate in the late nineteenth century. The "woman question" gained momentum after the emancipation and became a necessary part of any discussion of the future of Russia. Revolutionary and radical movements embraced the idea of women's emancipation and equality, but liberal and reform groups also debated this question. Articles on the evils of women's lack of education, the terrible plight of women in industrial work, the heavy burdens of the peasant women, and of course, the evils of prostitution all inspired much speculation on where women belonged in a modernizing country. From the Populist and Marxist insistence on complete equality between the sexes to the Orthodox and conservative insistence that women stay in the home and submit meekly to their husbands and fathers, the pages of the periodical press teemed with arguments over the proper place for women, but real changes occurred even as the discussion raged. For the first time in the 1870s, women could attain higher education either through special courses made available to them at the universities or by traveling abroad, usually to Zurich, to obtain university degrees. The special courses in the Russian universities did not grant degrees but did grant certificates that allowed a young woman to gain employment as a teacher or a midwife. The government decided to allow women to go abroad to get degrees that were not available to them in Russia because they were in desperate need of doctors and midwives. Both of these opportunities were highly controversial, and the government continually tried to curb the interaction of male and female students at the universities and spied on the women who were in school abroad. Both groups were accused of wanton sexual behavior, and a common accusation was that they used their medical knowledge to perform abortions on one another. In fact, most of the young women who were brave enough to take advantage of either opportunity were very serious about their educations and extremely ascetic in their lifestyles. Many of them were terribly poor and could barely afford to feed themselves as they studied.

Women received no political advances from the Revolution of 1905; they were excluded from voting and could not hold public office, but this did not prevent them from becoming involved in the political discourse of the time. A small feminist movement had begun in Russia, and after 1905, it lobbied for the franchise for women. Upper-class women also became involved in philanthropic societies. Marriage and children continued to be the primary activity and duty of Russian women, but the politically charged atmosphere of the early twentieth century drew many women out of their homes and into the public arena, agitating for suffrage, laws to protect working women and children, stricter controls on prostitution, and a wide range of other activities. Upper-class women had never engaged in such public activity before in Russia.

GENTRY ON THE EVE OF WAR

By the time World War I broke out, the Russian elite remained a highly fragmented and disparate estate, but a good portion of it had undergone a radical transformation from the cowering service gentry of the eighteenth century to a highly educated and articulate group of men and women who deeply believed in their duty to serve Russia. Although they did not agree on the manner of that service or on their goals for Russia, the sense of commitment to their nation was strong. Their lack of cohesion or strong corporate identity meant that any challenge they posed to the existing political system could not be consistent or powerful enough to force any real change without the support of significant portions of the other estates. But they were isolated from these other groups as well, not only by their wealth and status but also by their conviction that they were the natural leaders of Russia and that the lower orders needed gentry leadership in order to survive. This paternalistic attitude, developed over centuries of isolation from the vast majority of Russians and cultivated by their particular educational and cultural backgrounds, made it difficult for the gentry to exercise their leadership over the resentful lower classes.

NOTES

1. Carolyn Pouncy, trans., ed., *The Domostroi: Rules for Russian Households in the Time of Ivan the Terrible* (Ithaca, NY: Cornell University Press, 1994).

2. George Vernadsky, *Kievan Russia* (New Haven: Yale University Press, 1973), 105.

3. Natalia Pushkareva, *Women in Russian History from the Tenth to the Twentieth Century,* trans. Eve Levin (Armonk: M.E. Sharpe, 1997), 12–28.

4. Nancy Shields Kollmann, "The Seclusion of Elite Muscovite Women," *Russian History* 10, no. 2 (1983): 186.

5. Isolde Thyret, *Between God and Tsar: Religious Symbolism and the Royal Women of Muscovite Russia* (Dekalb: Northern Illinois University Press, 2001).

6. Pushkareva, 171–177.

7. Marc Raeff, *The Origins of the Russian Intelligentsia: The Eighteenth-Century Nobility* (New York: Harcourt, Brace & World, 1966), 44.

8. Raeff, *The Origins of the Russian Intelligentsia,* 54.

9. John T. Alexander, *Catherine the Great: Life and Legend* (New York: Oxford University Press, 1989), 194.

10. Raeff, *The Origins of the Russian Intelligentsia,* 132.

11. Alexander, 283–284.

12. Marc Raeff, *Understanding Imperial Russia* (New York: Columbia University Press, 1984), 137–145.

4

The Peasantry

Throughout Russian history, the difference between urban and rural life was great. Cities housed the great lords, cathedrals, palaces, and all cultural events. The countryside housed the peasantry and a scattering of noble families. Until the late nineteenth century, peasants were almost all illiterate, and most lived right around the subsistence level. These differences grew over the course of the imperial period so that by the time of the emancipation, the peasantry felt little connection to the other estates in Russia. Despite the wide gap between elite and peasant, "Russia" has always been evocative of the peasant rather than the elite. Particularly after the changes of the eighteenth century, the elite seemed removed from "Russia" in their imitation of Western fashion, entertainments, language, and philosophy. All Russians were united in Orthodoxy, but this increasingly became the only cultural connection between the peasantry and everyone else. Over the course of the nineteenth century, the focus of elite thought became increasingly centered on the peasantry, first with the problem of emancipation and later with the problem of modernizing and educating the countryside. The peasantry mostly resented this attention, feeling that the elite were simply self-serving parasites who wanted only to squeeze the peasantry dry and interfere with peasant life. Even in the early twentieth century, the Russian peasantry seemed disconnected from the other orders in Russia, serving only to bear the burdens of increased taxation, conscription, and rising prices without having any ability to fight back except through isolated revolts.

Of course, this picture of the peasantry as a dark and isolated if enormous segment of the population is largely the result of our lack of sources from the peasants themselves. Our knowledge of peasant life is based almost entirely on the reports of those segments of the educated population who observed, oversaw, or worked with the peasantry. The sources are often colored by the reporter's personal views of the peasantry, which gives us a highly skewed view of peasant life. Some observers idealized the peasantry, some felt guilty, some hated the peasants, and some saw them simply as a means to an end. As government became more pervasive in the countryside in the nineteenth century, it generated a certain amount of raw data on the peasantry that provides further clues to peasant existence. The Church provides another source of insight, given that it was the only institution that had a presence in virtually every village in the empire. But even these sources are biased because they report only on aspects of the peasant existence that were of interest to state or Church authorities. In the late nineteenth century, intellectuals and revolutionaries developed a keen interest in the peasantry, resulting in ethnographic studies and reports from the field on peasant life. The emergence of the zemstvo officials also provided new insights into peasant existence. All in all, our understanding of peasant life becomes richer and more detailed the closer we get to World War I. But even with the massive amounts of data generated in the last 50 years of imperial bureaucracy, we are confronted with the problem that the Russian peasantry formed an enormous and very diverse group of people spread out over millions of acres of land, who developed a wide variety of living arrangements, traditions, rituals, and customs that varied not only from region to region but even within individual villages. The picture we paint here of peasant life can reflect only a small slice of that rich and diverse culture.

PEASANTS AND SERFS

In the early twentieth century, peasants made up about 87 percent of the population.[1] After 1649, peasants were divided into four categories: state peasants, Church peasants (until 1764 when the Church was divested of its estates), crown peasants, and serfs. About 50 percent of all peasants were serfs, and this percentage increased over the course of the eighteenth century as the crown gave populated estates to their courtiers and forced the Church to relinquish its populated lands to private or state ownership. Most peasants engaged in agriculture, although in the north, where the soil was not very good for farming, many peasant villages turned to fishing or craft production as their main source of income. The structure and daily life of the peasant village changed very little from Muscovite days until the twentieth century.

KIEVAN PEASANTS

Peasants formed the majority of the Kievan population. They lived in communities called *mirs*, villages that had emerged from the clan ties of the pre-Kievan days. The members held pasture, meadows, and forests in common as well as sharing fishing and hunting rights. They were also collectively responsible for paying taxes. The Kievan peasant village had no clear legal or government institutions.[2] Peasants were not literate and, in the Kievan period, usually not very Christian, given that the adoption of Orthodox Christianity did not immediately affect daily life for any but the most elite families of Kievan Rus. Because almost all of the land in Kievan Rus was covered with forest, peasants used a slash-and-burn technique to clear land. Trees were stripped of their bark and allowed to die. Because the trees no longer grew leaves that provided shade, the ground around the trees could be planted for a year or two while the trees died. After the trees were dry, they were felled and burned and the ash plowed into the soil to increase its fertility once more. After the soil lost its fertility again, the farmers moved on to a new section of the forest. The peasants had to keep the cycle moving and prepare sections of forest in advance. After lying fallow for many years, fields could sometimes be cleared and used again. The plow used was called a *sokha*, a wooden structure with iron shoes that was pulled by a person or a draft animal. The cleared land was usually planted with grain—rye in the north and millet in the south and sometimes buckwheat, oats, wheat, barley, peas, lentils, flax, and hemp. They planted winter rye late in the year to supplement their spring and summer crops. Harvested grain was stored in pits lined with birch and pine bark or in barns. Peasants also kept livestock such as horses, cattle, oxen, sheep, goats, poultry, and pigs, which grazed in the summer. Berries, mushrooms, fruit, and nuts from the forest supplemented the peasants' diet along with fish and game. Beekeeping also provided wax and honey for commercial and domestic use. Despite frequent small wars between the princes of the various cities, life in Kievan Rus was relatively stable in comparison with life in medieval western Europe, although still short and harsh by more modern standards.

PEASANTS UNDER THE MONGOLS

The focus of the revived economy after the Mongol invasion shifted from trade to agriculture and led to a restructuring of peasant life. As the scattered survivors picked up the pieces, most villages of Kievan Rus gave way to independent family farms or small groups of farms that governed themselves in local matters and farmed whatever land they cleared. Free peasant farmers who paid taxes in kind continued to dominate agriculture, although more land passed into the hands of the elite as the Muscovite princes extended their power. Farming was no longer geared toward the market, however; instead the elite rented out their lands to tenant farmers and charged rent, fees, and service payments. Labor was in high demand, so this system did not victimize the peasants as much as it may seem—landlords would offer low rents or temporary tax exemptions to attract farmers to their lands. Peasants were free to move as long as their debts were paid, and this allowed them to take advantage of the attractive offers made by competing landlords. There is also archeological evidence that peasants were able to purchase some of the luxury goods that arrived on the trade routes from the East, indicating that they benefited at least a little from the expanded trade made possible under the Mongols. On the other hand, the peasants certainly bore the greatest burden of the Mongol tribute.

PEASANTS UNDER MUSCOVY

The rise of Moscow and the installation of the pomeshchiki under Ivan III had a profound impact on peasant life. The whole point of the pomeshchiki was that they served the tsar, which meant that they could not farm their own lands; in order to fulfill their service obligations, pomeshchiki had to have peasants to work their estates. The lands that the tsars distributed were already inhabited in any case, and when the tsar gave them to one of his servants, that new landlord took over all of the rights that the previous owner (if any) had to collect rents and other payments. From the peasant's point of view, the change in ownership might be almost invisible—the peasants continued to make the same payments, just to a different family. For other peasants, the change could be dramatic. Lands were often divided up without regard for the settlements already on them, and it was possible for land to be divided right in the middle of a village, resulting in villages having to break up in order to serve their new lords. In addition, the wealth of the lord made a huge difference to the peasants on his land. A boyar with a very large estate or with many estates could afford to make fewer demands of his peasants than a pomeshchik with only one small holding. The unlucky peasants who found themselves on land granted to a minor servitor could expect the demands on them to rise significantly as the pomeshchik squeezed as much as possible out of his small holding to support himself and his family. The large landholders could sometimes assist their villages in bad years; the small landholders often starved along with their peasants. Overall, the new system of landholding resulted in enormous changes for some peasants and no change at all for others; the number of free peasants (peasants without a direct landlord) steadily dwindled as the tsars gave more and more land to servitors, resulting in an ever-increasing layer of gentry between the crown and the peasant—a layer that the peasants had to support in addition to paying taxes to the crown. To make matters worse, taxes had increased substantially over the course of these years. Ivan IV had tried to spread the tax burden more evenly by taxing peasants based on what they could afford to pay. He created a system in which surveyors evaluated the quality as well as the quantity of the land and assessed it accordingly. But despite this attempt to even out the tax burden, taxes in 1620 were more than 12 times what they had been in 1560.

WARFARE, TAXES, AND PEASANT FLIGHT

War was a frequent and often devastating occurrence for the peasants throughout this period and ultimately resulted in their full enserfment in 1649. In the Kievan period, civil wars between princes and wars with the steppe nomads or with Byzantium popped up frequently but were usually short-lived and isolated. The Mongol invasion completely disrupted life for most people, but as Moscow began to emerge, the old pattern of short limited wars also reemerged. The period between the liberation from the Mongols and the installation of Mikhail Romanov on the throne of Russia was a time of transition and intermittent turmoil that culminated in the Time of Troubles. The consolidation of power in the hands of the Muscovite grand princes involved frequent small wars and much jockeying for position among the elite and the emerging elites. Even during times of relative peace within the borders of the new kingdom, during the early years of Ivan the Terrible's reign for example, Russia was involved in border disputes and wars with other powers that required high taxes and kept many of the pomeshchiki away from home as they fought the wars. The end of Ivan's reign and the Time of Troubles that followed were chaotic for the entire kingdom. From 1480 to 1613, no one could feel assured that life would not erupt into some kind of disaster—war being the chief concern during most of that period as the Muscovite princes struggled to gather the other regions under their power and as Russia defended herself from her neighbors.

It was in the Muscovite princes' best interest to interfere as little as possible with the economies of the newly subdued territories—after all, the more prosperous a region, the more the grand prince or tsar could get out of it in taxes and in other revenues. The leaders understood this and endeavored to uphold the trading or agricultural interests of their new lands. The process of acquiring new territories, however, often resulted in disruption of trade as cities were cut off from their sources of supply to encourage them to acquiesce to Moscow's power. Farmland could be ravaged by the battles that took place between Moscow and the local elites trying to maintain their independence. For these reasons, the period of expansion was one of economic disruption and turmoil. As mentioned previously, the peasants might find themselves in difficult circumstances after the struggle as their lands were parceled out to various nobles, sometimes resulting in the movement of entire villages to new lands. In addition, the larger borders meant that the Muscovite grand princes and later tsars had to maintain an ever-increasing army to preserve their gains, and the cost of these new armies fell most heavily on the peasantry and lower townsmen, the only part of the population subject to constant and direct taxation in addition to all of the indirect taxes the government could impose. Peasants responded to these new hardships in very traditional ways. Some fled their new lords, either to look for refuge in a larger, more established estate or to flee the new kingdom altogether, moving to the borderlands to settle in territory that had less oversight. These borderlands were dangerous because they lacked the protection that the cities and the tsars could offer, but they had the advantage of being rent-free and, if far enough away, tax-free. The pomeshchiki were particularly vulnerable to peasant flight; their smaller estates squeezed peasants harder, encouraging the peasants to consider even the desperate choice of flight to unknown, and their estates could ill-afford the loss of labor. For the larger landholders, peasant flight could be an asset because peasants were more likely to flee to their estates from the smaller estates. Pomeshchiki, therefore, lobbied the tsar to pass laws that would require peasants to stay on the land and oblige other landowners to return any refugee peasants to their original landlord. The struggle over peasant movement grew more intense as time went on, and the tsars were forced to decide whom to support—the wealthy nobles who benefited from peasant mobility or their new service gentry who desperately needed their peasants to stay put. Over time, the pomeshchiki, backbone of the army and the growing administration, won this struggle.

The use of the pomeshchiki in the army and government administration emphasized the central importance of agriculture to the emerging nation, with the pomeshchiki relying on the produce of their estates to support them and arm them for war; this was acknowledged in the law code of 1497, which stipulated that peasants could not leave their landlord's service except during the two weeks surrounding St. George's Day on November 26. Of course, the peasants also had to clear all of their debts to the landlords before leaving. Although this law certainly inhibited peasant movement, it was not as restrictive as it may first seem. By mandating that peasants stay until the end of November, the law ensured that crops would be fully harvested and stored before peasants began to move. November was also a good time to travel because the dirt roads in Russia, muddy bogs during the summer months, would be frozen and more easily traversed. On the other hand, this legal limitation on peasant mobility was the beginning of a series of measures to restrict peasant movement in order to protect the pomeshchiki's economic position, measures that would eventually lead to the full enserfment of the peasantry in 1649.

THE ROMANOV DYNASTY AND THE CONSOLIDATION OF SERFDOM

Tsar Mikhail had a difficult task in helping Russia recover from the upheavals of the Time of Troubles. He needed a reliable army to protect his fragile kingdom, he needed to get the economy going, and he needed a consistent income for the government treasury. The key to all of these things was a productive peasantry. Settled productive peasants could fund his army by supporting the pomeshchiki, pay predictable taxes into his treasury, and hopefully produce enough to feed the entire population. To further this goal, Mikhail extended the time limits that pomeshchiki had for recovering fugitive peasants. The problem of peasant flight from less prosperous estates to more prosperous estates or to the borderlands continued, however, prompting Tsar Alexei to fully enserf the peasants in his law code of 1649. Peasants no longer had any right to mobility without the explicit consent of their landlord; they were legally tied to their land. Peasants were not the only group to lose their freedom of movement—landless artisans and workers in towns were also forbidden to leave without permission. This did not mean that peasants no longer fled—the lure of the Cossacks, of the borderlands, and of wealthy boyar estates continued to draw peasants away from the small pomeshchiki, but after 1649, no statute of limitations existed on their recovery, and severe penalties fell on those who harbored fugitive serfs.

IMPACT OF SERFDOM

Despite the hardships peasants endured, the fact of enserfment did not change their lives as much as one might suppose. The new law gave the nobility absolute control over their estates and their serfs, but Russian law had been tending in that direction since the time of Ivan III; the law simply institutionalized the process of enserfment that had been going on for many generations. In some ways, serfdom created stability and confirmed the peasants' right to work the land to which they were tied. The fact that most landlords spent their lives away from the estate—at court, in administration, or at war—meant that most serfs had little or no contact with the nobility. Serfs managed their own village affairs, sometimes under the oversight of the landlord's foreman, but often villages were simply left to run themselves as long as they delivered their taxes, payments, and labor obligations when required. Landlords could, of course, involve themselves as much as they liked in the lives of their serfs— the most common way was in the practice of taking their household servants from their serf population. House serfs suffered the same indignities and lack of privacy and control over their own lives that house servants across Europe suffered, and female house serfs were sexually very vulnerable to the whims of their owners. Although the plight of the house serf was certainly very bleak, house serfs formed only a tiny portion of the overall serf population. Landlord involvement in village life was rare simply because landlords were rarely around. It is also important to note that only about half of the 906,101 peasant households (90 percent of the population of Russia) reported in the 1678 land survey belonged to the nobility. The other half lived on Church or crown lands or were state peasants.[3] State peasants did not belong to anyone but were organized into villages that largely governed their own affairs but still owed heavy taxes and labor obligations to the state. Finally, despite the new law, serfs who were determined to flee still did so, and sometimes, the state turned a blind eye to peasant flight when it served state purposes; peasants who fled to the south and enlisted in the garrisons that protected the southern border were generally ignored, as were peasants who successfully integrated themselves into town life and paid taxes there. The quality of life for the serfs depended very much on circumstances outside their control—the quality of their land, the weather, the lottery of conscription, and the type of landlord they served.

THE STEPAN RAZIN REVOLT

That the peasants resented the new restrictions regardless of their actual impact is illustrated by the fact that one of the worst peasant revolts since the Time of Troubles occurred in 1670–1671, led by the Cossack Stepan Razin. Razin began the revolt by gathering support from the disaffected population of Russian peasants who had fled the increasing control of the nobility and settled in the Cossack territory. They first attacked cities in their vicinity, killing the representatives of the tsar, and then turned toward Moscow, gathering support along the way from religious dissidents, peasants, and the urban poor. Razin was not leading a rebellion against Alexei but claimed to be purging officials and boyars who were preventing the common man from enjoying his freedom. That this rebellion was exceedingly diverse with muddled goals is reflected in Razin's battle cry, "For God and the Prophet, for the Sovereign and the Cossack Host!"[4] Razin's rebellion was essentially a revolt of the downtrodden against the prosperous rather than any kind of coherent attempt to restructure the system. Just as the rebels during the Time of Troubles claimed that they sought only to put the "rightful" tsar on the throne, Razin and his followers claimed to be fighting to restore the proper relationship between the tsar and his people, a relationship that had been sundered by the evil bureaucrats and landowners who oppressed the common man. The tsarist army defeated the rebels, but Razin got away, and the army pursued him, suppressing further revolt by brutally executing hundreds in their search for the rebel. He was finally captured and taken to Moscow where he was tortured and then executed by quartering. Peasant rebellion was a common occurrence in Russia, but the Razin rebellion was notable for its size, its duration, and the difficulty the government had in putting it down. Without the leadership of the Cossacks and the deep dissatisfaction with the spread of serfdom and increasing control of the central government and the nobility, the rebellion could not have succeeded for as long as it did.

THE VILLAGE

In order to understand how the peasants lived, it is important to examine the structure of the peasant village. Peasants were not individual smallholders, nor were they plantation workers; instead, they lived in villages surrounded by their fields. The village was run by the commune or *mir*, usually composed of the village elders, who interfaced with the landowner and the state and controlled internal politics. The commune was responsible for managing the land, assigning responsibility for and collecting taxes and dues, planning the agricultural year, mediating local disputes and dispensing justice, maintaining local infrastructure, and overseeing the welfare of the village. In the nineteenth century, many of the Russian elite pointed to the commune as proof of the naturally cooperative and communal nature of the Russian peasant and idealized the commune as a haven of equity in an otherwise hierarchical and corrupt Russia, but more recent studies have shown that the village elders used their power ruthlessly to their own advantage. The more powerful families in the village could easily dominate the commune, and the older generation—the heads of households who usually composed the commune—dominated the younger generation, preventing adult sons from forming their own households, which would have given them more independence and a voice in the commune. As long as sons lived in a household with their father, the father was the head and the sole representative in the commune. One historian has calculated that three-quarters of the labor obligations in a village were carried out by one-third of the village population who had reached adulthood but were not yet heads of households.[5] The commune also controlled conscription, a very serious matter for the village. By law, conscripts were supposed to be chosen by lottery of men from every 20 households, but the most powerful men in the commune would protect their own families from the draft and would use exemption from conscription as a patronage or extortion mechanism. Although some landlords took a more active role in governing their serfs, villages usually took care of their own internal disputes and dispensed rough justice against those who broke laws or transgressed village tradition, and the commune could manipulate these aspects of village government as well. People who challenged the authority of the commune or who questioned its decisions could be disciplined, even exiled to Siberia if they presented enough of a threat

Group of Russian peasants posed at an outdoor table with samovar and balalaika, early twentieth century. Library of Congress, Prints & Photographs Division, LC-USZ62-43049.

to those in power. The most usual threat for a younger man who caused trouble was conscription, which had the advantage of not only removing a troublemaker from the village but also of fulfilling the conscription requirements. Land distribution was abused in the same way, so that the picture of the commune is not one of natural egalitarian principles but one of a vicious power struggle in which the richer and more powerful preyed upon the young and the weak.

Village size varied considerably depending on the region: in the north, villages tended to be smaller, sometimes only a few households; villages were larger in the central regions, and villages on the open steppe might have several hundred households. The structure of villages varied, but most consisted of their households and a church built along a waterway, surrounded by the land that the village farmed, although smaller communities might not have a church. After the fifteenth century, Russian peasants adopted a three-field rotation, dividing their land into one field for the spring crop (oats, barley, or wheat), one for the winter crop (rye), and one to lie fallow, possibly serving as pasturage. Russian peasants practiced strip farming: they divided the three fields into strips and divided the strips up among the householders. After Peter I instituted the poll tax, the land was, at least in theory, divided up according to the number of taxpayers (male souls) in the family, although in many villages it was divided by the number of labor teams (husband and wife) in the household. Different villages redivided land at different intervals, ranging from every 20 years to every 3 years or whenever the village elders thought it was necessary. As we have seen, the elders of the village commune frequently manipulated the division of land to their own advantage and would do their best to foist most of the responsibility and hard work onto weaker families or the younger generation. Families received scattered strips of land from each field to ensure that everyone received a roughly equal proportion of good and poor land. Each family also had a garden plot where they grew vegetables. The village usually held grazing and forest land in common. In addition to their own land, the villagers often had to work their landlord's estate for a set number of days every week. The economic relationship between serf and landlord varied by region—in highly fertile areas, the landlord held as much land as he could and squeezed as much labor, known as *barshchina,* as possible out of his serfs. In areas with less rich soil, the landlord might rent all of his land out to his serfs and simply

Russian peasants, early twentieth century. Library of Congress, Prints & Photographs Division, LC-DIG-ggbain-17495.

collect monetary payments, or *obrok*, from them. Many landlords required a combination of *barshchina* and *obrok* from their serfs.

AGRICULTURAL METHODS

Most Russian peasants continued to use the *sokha*, the light wooden plough with iron tips, throughout the imperial period. Because they farmed in scattered strips, no advantage would be gained by investing in heavy machinery, and in much of Russia, the soil was very light; heavy machinery would cut too deep and lead to erosion and moisture loss. Because the strips were periodically redivided, there was no incentive to invest in fertilizer beyond manure from their grazing animals. With all of the peasants' strips adjacent to one another, the peasants all had to farm the same crop and plant and harvest at the same time, but they did not work together. Each family took care of its own strips. The system was inherently conservative—no change could occur without the agreement of the entire village. Peasants, or more often landlords, who wanted to try new-fangled ideas, fertilizers, or hybrid seeds were simply ignored while work continued the same way it had for

Peasants sitting on cart, early twentieth century. Cabinet of American Illustration, Prints & Photographs Division, Library of Congress.

hundreds of years. For these reasons, Russian agriculture remained highly labor-intensive and changed little after the fifteenth century; the agricultural revolution that preceded the industrial revolution in the rest of Europe did not affect Russia. No revolution occurred, in fact, until Stalin forced collectivized agriculture on the peasants in the 1930s.

Despite the drawbacks of the Russian system of farming, peasants had good reasons to resist change. In general, peasants were less interested in profit than in survival, and the village system had enabled them to survive for many generations and had a number of highly practical safety nets built into it. The practice of dividing the land into strips did not maximize the land's productivity, but until the mid-nineteenth century, land was abundant, and there was no need to maximize its use. Furthermore, the strip method helped to ensure that each family would produce enough to survive. If one field was destroyed by flood, for example, each family would still have strips in other fields to fall back on. By scattering their strips within fields, peasants also hedged their bets against the very real danger that part of a field would suffer damage. If family holdings were consolidated in one area of each field, damage to one area would leave certain families destitute; the scattered strips meant that isolated damage would affect several families, but there was a good chance that these families would have other strips in the undamaged portion of the field.

Peasants also had rigid rituals and traditions that dictated when and how farming cycles would occur. Although these rituals might inhibit a highly motivated peasant from trying a new innovation, it also prevented unscrupulous or unwary peasants from activities that would harm the rest of the village. For example, animals were not allowed out to graze until the first of the two St. George's Days, April 23 (or in more northern regions, the first of the two St. Nicholas Days, May 9), when the peasants would use the switches blessed by the priest on Palm Sunday to drive their livestock to the fields. A special service in which the priest blessed the animals with holy water was followed by a communal feast. By surrounding the release of livestock into pasture with such rituals, the village ensured that no family released its animals early, thereby stealing first spring grass from their neighbors.[6] Such ritual commanded all of the major agricultural events in the village, although the content and timing of the rituals varied from region to region.

CONSCRIPTION

Conscription was a serious business. Until the Petrine reforms, soldiers taken from the peasantry were conscripted by lottery and for indeterminate lengths of service—some might return at the end of a campaign; others might move from one campaign to another for the rest of their lives. These men often had wives and children who were left to the mercy of their in-laws. The *soldatki*, or soldiers' wives, were at the very bottom of the village social structure. In their homes, they were often seen simply as extra mouths to feed given that the household had lost the labor of the soldier. They and their children were abused and dominated by their in-laws. Other women in the village looked on the soldatki as potential rivals; with her husband gone, the soldatka had no legitimate outlet for her sexual desires and was widely believed to be on the prowl for love affairs with other women's husbands.

The soldatka's best hope was that she would get official confirmation of her husband's death, so that she might remarry and escape her in-laws, hopefully with her children. The life of the soldier was, of course, even worse. Soldiers in the Russian infantry could expect deprivation and hardship, stern discipline, and all manner of physical abuse from their noble officers. The life expectancy of the soldier was low, given the frequent wars and the dangers from hunger and disease.

MILITARY COLONIES

Alexander I was the only pre-emancipation ruler to make a concerted effort to improve the lives of soldiers and their families with his disastrous experiment in military colonies. The idea behind the colonies was to make the life of the common soldier more comfortable and to enable the army to supply itself. In the wake of the Napoleonic Wars, over 750,000 men were in the Russian army in 1815, which put a huge strain on the budget; the army could not be completely demobilized because so many former serfs would constitute an unstable element in society. In order to meet this budget crisis and in hopes of providing soldiers with something of a family life, Alexander's advisors developed a plan to combine army units and their families with villages of state peasants. During peacetime, the soldiers would help with farming, and when the soldiers were away, the village would support their families. In the long run, it was hoped that the colonies would eliminate the need for conscription because all male children born in the colonies, except for the oldest son, would automatically become soldiers themselves. The idea looked good on paper but was disastrous in its execution. Villages were removed to border lands to keep the troops close to their deployment areas, forcing the state peasants to abandon their homes to begin new farms far away from, and often agriculturally quite different from, their traditional lands. The villages were run along military lines with a highly regimented routine complete with uniforms for all peasants and a military timetable for sleeping, eating, and working. The fact that the village could not know whether its soldier population would be present at the crucial times of planting and harvesting made planning virtually impossible. The colonies became nightmare settlements populated by starving and angry peasants. Alexander, however, was impressed by their regimentation and was shown only the positive reports, so the colonies lasted throughout his reign, finally being dissolved in 1831.

THE PETRINE REFORMS AND PEASANT LIFE

Daily life changed for almost all of Russia in the eighteenth century. Peter I wanted to transform noble life and enacted reforms specifically to do so; throughout the rest of the eighteenth century, his cultural and social as well as political and military reforms continued to shape the nobility into a reasonable facsimile of European nobility. The changes for other levels of society were more a by-product of reforms directed at other issues than a desire to change them. Although daily activities did not change much for the peasantry during the eighteenth century, their obligations to state and landlord rose enough to have a clear impact on their quality of life. The most striking change was the division in culture between the urban and gentry elite and the rest of the population. As the elite adopted Western dress, education, culture, and entertainments, the vast majority of the Russian population continued to follow Russian traditional practices in their dress, diet, rituals, and attitudes. The gap that this created in Russian society is sometimes overstated, but it contributed substantially to the social problems that emerged in the nineteenth century.

Russian peasants outside a peasant home, early twentieth century. Library of Congress, Prints & Photographs Division, LC-DIG-ggbain-23997.

TAXES

Peter's change to the tax system has a very controversial place among historians, but all agree that the peasants believed that it made their lives much harder. Before Peter, Russian taxes were confusing in the extreme. Basically, in the beginning of Peter's reign, taxpayers—serfs, state peasants, and lower townsmen—were responsible for a variety of both fixed and extraordinary taxes every year, collected by a variety of government agencies. All taxes were calculated based on the number of households in a community, and villages were collectively responsible for paying their taxes. Peter tried various means to raise revenue and to get the tax money to the military where he really needed it but finally decided on a poll tax instead of the household tax. This necessitated a census and a reorganization of the bureaucracy so that the first poll tax (calculated on the number of males) was not collected until after Peter's death in 1724. There is much debate among historians as to how the new tax system affected the peasant economy, but it is certain that it placed great hardship on many peasants because it was calculated strictly on the number of male souls, regardless of their health, age, or ability to pay. Regardless of how it affected the peasant economy, the poll tax stayed as the main tax in Russia until 1887. Peter also levied indirect taxes on almost anything he could think of—livestock, bathhouses, cheese, barrels, cups, spoons, oak coffins, playing cards, and so on—and placed a government monopoly on distilled liquor, which proved such an effective source of revenue that it lasted throughout the imperial period.

The consequences of the poll tax on peasant life have been very controversial among historians because it is difficult to say whether the tax substantially increased the burden on the individual peasant. Anecdotal evidence indicates that the peasants felt more strapped by the new system than they had by the old, but it is almost impossible to separate the impact of the new taxes from other economic events that adversely affected the peasantry at about the same time. Four years of poor harvests hit Russia in 1721, just before the poll tax went into effect, and this certainly had an adverse effect on the peasant economy. In theory, the poll tax should have been somewhat more equitable given that all taxable male souls simply owed the tax, but the tax was allocated by community, not collected from individual families, and this allowed the stronger families in the village to shift more of the burden onto the weaker and poorer members of the community; complaints both to landlords and to the government strongly suggest that it was quite common for poorer families to pay more than their fair share of the burden. Because the poll tax counted all male souls regardless of their age or abilities, families with injured, elderly, or very young males were subjected to higher taxes than they could readily afford. Given that the new tax system came after decades of increased extraordinary taxes and labor and military conscriptions, the peasantry already felt increased pressure from the state and expected that the new tax system would bring more misery.

RELATIONSHIP TO THE ELITE

The new lifestyle of the elite did have a negative impact on peasant life because the new fashions and the parties were expensive, and the landowners needed more money to support their new luxuries. As the peasants were being hit with higher taxes and increased labor and military levies, their landlords were also squeezing as much as they possibly could out of their serfs in order to purchase new clothing and Western-style furniture as well as to throw the elaborate parties that the emperor now required everyone to have. The more elite nobles were also required to build homes in St. Petersburg. These homes had to be built in the Western style according to Western architecture. In addition to the more expensive and larger buildings, the homes had to be decorated and furnished with imported Western furniture, carpets, tapestries, and artwork. They also had to be heated and lit, both heavy expenses in the cold, dark Russian winter. So while the peasants already found themselves conscripted into labor gangs to build the new city, they also had to provide their landlords with enough money to build and maintain their new expensive homes. As time went on, and the upper classes more fully embraced the Western style of living, giving several parties a season, attending theaters, concerts, and other amusements, their expenditures went up. Western carriages, gowns from Paris, imported artwork, tutors, furnishings, china, crystal, exotic foods, and so on all sent the cost of living for the elite higher and higher, and their demands on their serfs rose accordingly.

In addition to the added economic and labor burden that Peter's reforms placed on peasants, he is often accused of creating a gap between serf and landowner that had not existed before. This accusation is true but is often overstated. As the upper classes became more educated and adopted Western-style dress and manners, they did begin to look and think differently from the peasants who retained traditional Russian values, culture, Orthodoxy, and lifestyle. But the gap was not insurmountable. Although nobles had to learn to speak French and German to be considered cultured, it is not true that they forgot how to speak Russian—almost all noble children had Russian nannies and grew up in homes staffed by Russian serf servants; they learned to speak Russian in order to communicate with the people around them from birth. They listened to bedtime stories from Russian nannies, who told traditional folk tales and sang traditional Russian lullabies. Although later education did not center on Russian culture, it was a part of the lives of the elite from the cradle. Orthodoxy also remained as a common tie for all classes of Russian people and provided much of the basis for values, morals, and the worldview that Russians of all levels shared to a certain extent. The gap between elite and peasant certainly existed but in the eighteenth century was not much more pronounced than in most other European countries where education and culture came first for the nobility and only slowly penetrated into the lower orders of society. The most devastating change came from the fact that most nobles, even by the end of the century, spent very little time on their estates, and this widened the gap between noble and serf. When noblemen returned to their estates and tried to take control of their management, they looked very much like conquerors to their serfs, who had no personal ties to their landlords.

PEASANT REVOLTS

Given the uneasy relationship between peasants and nobles, it is not surprising that Russian history is littered with peasant revolts. Indeed, the uprisings that occurred during the Time of Troubles were in many ways peasant revolts that found leadership and became huge armies. The Stepan Razin revolt under Tsar Alexei had been only the largest of a series of revolts that occurred on a regular basis in Russia. In general, peasant rebellions were small and short-lived. Peasants usually destroyed property and less often killed or wounded their landlords or their families. Revolts often occurred during times of hardship and were almost always localized for the simple reason that peasant villages were often very isolated, and travel was slow and difficult. It was nearly impossible for peasants to gather widespread support before the rebellion simply burned itself out. Although the authorities and the upper classes deplored rebellion, it rarely presented any sort of real danger to the throne.

Two large-scale rebellions occurred during the eighteenth century—one at the beginning and one at the end. The Bulavin revolt, 1707–1708, was in direct response to the pressures created by Peter the Great's changes, particularly the increased conscription burden. As mentioned earlier, conscription was not new, but under Peter it became much more widespread and changed from conscription for a single campaign or war to conscription for life. From 1700 to 1710, about 300,000 men were conscripted into the regular army from a population of 14 million. Labor conscription fell heavily on the peasantry as well, particularly in the south in the beginning of the century, when conscripts were required to build a fleet at Voronezh, fortifications at Azov, and a naval station at Taganrog. The Cossacks also felt threatened by the new technology and tactics of warfare, specifically the bayonet and the flintlock musket, which could stop a Cossack cavalry charge much more effectively than older weapons had been able to do. The decline of the streltsy also led to much unrest as these formerly elite units found themselves depleted, scattered, and considered archaic. Combine all of this with higher taxes, Peter's attack on the Church, traditional dress, and beards, and his reliance on a virtual army of foreign experts who were in charge of many of the new military units and construction sites, and it was easy to convince people, especially Old Believers, that he might be the Antichrist. As the central government began to tighten its grip on the Don Cossacks, the revolt started and quickly gathered support among all the disaffected groups in the area. By the end of 1708, peasants had rebelled in 43 districts throughout the country. The revolt went well for several months, and Bulavin managed to take and hold the fortress at Cherkassk, and even after Bulavin himself was killed, it took several more months to put the rebellion down completely. The government then set about cleaning up all vestiges of the rebellion, hunting down all those who might have taken part. One historian estimates that over 14,000 men, women, and children were executed; several new villages on the Don and upper Donets Rivers were destroyed and their inhabitants forced to return to their old masters from whom they had fled.[7]

The Pugachev revolt in 1773–1774 began for reasons similar to the Bulavin revolt—the Russian central government was exerting increasing control over the Cossack population. Led again by a Cossack, Emelian Pugachev, the revolt began among the Cossacks along the Yaik River over the high levels of conscription and taxes needed to fight the Seven Years' and First Turkish wars. Pugachev claimed to be Peter III, who had been very unpopular with the nobility but quite popular with the lower classes. He had been a clearly legitimate male heir to the throne and had raised the hopes of the serfs by freeing Church peasants. His emancipation of the nobility had also led to speculation that this was only the first step to freeing the serfs—after all, Peter I had clearly stated that serfdom was necessary to enable the nobles to serve the state; if the nobles were freed from service, it logically followed that the serfs would be freed as well. Pugachev charged that the nobility had tried to kill Peter III and replace him with the evil German, Catherine II, in order to prevent his vision of freedom for the peasantry to be realized. Pugachev promised freedom to the Cossacks and then issued customized manifestos to various other groups: Old Believers, nomadic peoples, factory workers, and peasants. His troops began to take over nearby areas, and Catherine sent a wholly inadequate army to suppress his revolt. Pugachev escaped and continued his war. He moved into Russian territory and gathered support from the peasantry, promising freedom from conscription and taxes and control of the land. He ordered peasants to execute their landlords, and many did so: 1,572 nobles (of which 474 were women and 302 were children), 1,037 officials, and 237 priests were murdered.[8] The rebels tortured and killed anyone who stood in their way. Finally, Catherine was able to send troops from the Turkish front and suppress the rebellion, and Pugachev was eventually turned over by his own men. He was publicly hanged and then quartered.[9]

The Pugachev revolt led to the provincial reforms because it demonstrated to Catherine that she did not have adequate control over her realm. It spread quickly because it had leaders who understood something of organization, warfare, and propaganda and because it followed a long period of high taxes and conscription. It failed because a handful of experienced Cossacks could not lead a poorly armed mob of peasants to victory over the huge and battle-hardened Russian army. This was the last great Cossack uprising; the new administrative arrangements prevented any such large-scale rebellion from occurring again. The high levels of violence of this rebellion, however, testified to the increasing alienation of the peasantry and poor urban workers from their gentry landlords and provincial authorities.

THE ROAD TO EMANCIPATION

The wars of the early nineteenth century had a profound effect on all aspects of Russian life. The Napoleonic Wars were particularly devastating for the Russian peasantry. The Russian economy suffered under the Continental System, the invasion of 1812 cut a swath of destruction along Napoleon's path to Moscow, and the huge conscriptions of soldiers depopulated the countryside throughout Russia—between 1811 and 1815 about 436,000 peasant men were drafted into the already swollen Russian army;[10] in the battle of 1812 alone, Russia's casualties numbered between 250,000 and 300,000.[11] The Crimean War also drained Russia of resources and manpower, with another 470,000 peasants recruited into the army for that war.[12] In addition to the hardships caused by the wars, a cholera epidemic broke out in January of 1848: 1 of every 28 Russians contracted cholera, and 1 in 70 died. In some areas the ratio was much worse, as in Novgorod, where 1 in 9 died.[13] The summer of 1848 was particularly dry, resulting in far more fires than usual and one of the worst famines of the century. The Ministry of the Interior reported that the harvest for 1848 yielded less than half of the grain planted.[14] The low harvest was exacerbated in some areas by the cholera, which killed the peasants and left the grain standing in the fields and by the government's inability to transport grain to the hardest-hit areas. At the same time, both Alexander I and Nicholas I tried to ease the plight of the peasants. Alexander passed his Law on Free Agriculturalists, which permitted noblemen to free their serfs as long as they provided the freed peasants with land. Although very few landlords availed themselves of this opportunity, it was finally legally possible to be a free farmer, neither serf nor state peasant. Nicholas began to codify serf-landlord obligations. He forbade landless nobles from buying serfs without land and placed limits on the punishments that landlords could impose on their serfs. Serfs could purchase their freedom if their landlord went bankrupt and gained the right to buy unpopulated land for their own use. State peasants were given title to their lands and right to own property, make contracts, obtain education, and enter the civil service. Nicholas's new Ministry of State Properties administered the state peasants, built village schools, provided fire and crop insurance as well as medical care, and promoted modern farming methods. These small steps preceded the final emancipation of the peasantry in 1861.

POST-EMANCIPATION

The social group most directly affected by the emancipation was the peasantry. After more than three centuries of legal oppression, the peasantry was finally freed from personal domination by the landlord. Unfortunately, that is about all that they were freed from. The terms of the emancipation left them under the control of their village communes, which had a vested interest in maintaining the status quo. Because the commune had to collect taxes and redemption payments, its primary concern was to ensure that the village produced enough to make those payments and survive for another year. Peasants who wanted to branch out or try new methods were met with suspicion. Peasants who wished to leave the village were often prohibited from doing so in order for the village to retain their labor. As we have already seen, the commune tended to be dominated by the stronger families and was often corrupt; this did not change with the emancipation.

In general, village life remained much the same after the emancipation, although slow changes began to emerge. The commune continued in its role of dividing up the land among its members and overseeing the daily workings of the community. The main change in the countryside was the establishment of the zemstvos, which eventually brought schools and a certain degree of medical care to the countryside. For peasants who participated in the new governmental structure, the zemstvo could be a valuable political experience, but most peasants were not directly involved in the workings of the zemstvo, and they mostly resented the economic drain it imposed in the form of increased local taxes. Peasants had a mixed reaction to education. On the one hand, it was clearly an advantage to be able to read and cipher. On the other hand, peasants needed their children's labor and feared that too much education would result in rebellious youth who would challenge tradition and endanger the welfare of the community with new-fangled ideas and experiments. As the century wore on, the literacy levels among the younger generation steadily increased, with female literacy rates remaining at about one-quarter that of males. By 1897, over 40 percent of peasant males between 10 and 19 were literate as opposed to about 10 percent of females in that age group.[15] Far fewer peasant men or women went beyond basic literacy and ciphering.

The change in military service affected peasant life because it meant that young men no longer left the village for life but could be expected to return after their six-year obligation. This meant that the soldatka was no longer such a divisive figure in village life, and this certainly alleviated a great deal of pain and suffering for that segment of the population. It also undermined the power of the village elders who could no longer use the threat of conscription to keep younger men in line. Rather than leaving the choice of conscript up to the elders, conscripts were now chosen by ballot. The fact that most of the conscripts returned after six years meant that conscription was no longer as much of a threat. Finally, as more young men returned from military service, the elders found themselves faced with a more worldly younger generation whose members were less likely to allow themselves to be ordered around by the older generation. This also contributed to the breakdown of the extended peasant household, as returning soldiers demanded to be allowed to set up households separate from their fathers' domination. By and large, the peasantry remained isolated from the other groups in the population and did not benefit much from the other reforms because they continued to have their own court system that operated outside of and differently from the new judicial system and because they could not send their children to university.

For the first few years after the emancipation, village life was virtually indistinguishable from the pre-emancipation village. The family continued to be the basic economic unit of the countryside, and marriage continued to be the most important event in a peasant's life—a successful and fruitful marriage was essential to a family's survival. The fact that a landlord no longer had any voice in the marriage practices of the peasants meant that young people had a little more freedom in their courting practices, but their parents still arranged most marriages. The high infant and child mortality rates did not abate in the post-emancipation period, with 432 deaths per 1,000 live births between 1887 and 1896.[16] As zemstvo doctors tried to introduce modern hygiene and health practices, they ran up against not only the implacable wall of peasant traditional practices and centuries of folk wisdom, but also the practical realities of peasant existence: women could not take time off from agricultural labor to nurse infants or watch children and continued to rely on the *soska* (the peasant pacifier, see chapter 6) and other potentially harmful or deadly methods for comforting infants while their mothers worked. Physical abuse of women and children continued in the peasant household, contributing to the high mortality rates for both groups.

If anything, peasants felt that their economic position was much harder after the emancipation because they had the added burden of the redemption and because they often had to lease pasturage, waterways, and such from their former landlords, who often retained control of this type of land. As the nineteenth century progressed,

however, the peasants' position changed. Even as industrialization expanded, peasant women continued to engage in putting-out
work—the practice, widespread throughout preindustrial Europe,
of receiving raw materials from a travelling contractor, finishing
them in the home, and returning them to the contractor who would
then move them to the next level of production or sell them. Common forms of putting-out work included winding thread on bob-
bins, making lace, sewing gloves, or rolling cigarette tubes; other
women worked in the textile factories that sprang up near peasant
villages to take advantage of the pool of cheap labor.[17] Overpopu-
lation in the countryside meant that communes were more likely
to allow young people to leave and move to industrial centers to
take jobs, on the condition that they send a portion of their income
home to help with taxes and redemption. At first, only a trickle of
peasants left the village, and these individuals often left only during the winter when the village workload was light and returned
to help out during the busy summer months. These workers were
often family men, who went into the factories to supplement the
family's income and who returned to the village every season and
continued to think of themselves as peasants. Slowly, as the population growth placed more strain on the land, younger, single men
and women began to move to the cities to work in the developing
industrial sector. These young people began their work lives with
the expectation that they would eventually move back to their villages to marry, but many of them ended up marrying in the city
and making their home permanently in the city. Over the course
of the nineteenth century, more young people removed to the city
and began to view themselves less as peasants and more as urban
workers, adopting the urban style of dress and adapting to urban
culture. We discuss this new working class later, but the flight from
the stifling and increasingly poverty-stricken countryside increased
steadily from 1890s to World War I. Those who returned brought
new clothing and habits to the village and were often blamed for
such things as the spread of syphilis to the countryside.

PEASANTS ON THE EVE OF WAR

The peasants were frustrated by the government's apparent lack
of concern for their plight. In the years leading up to 1905, many
peasants found themselves in desperate circumstances. The famine years hit the peasantry hard, and by 1905, most villages were
several years in arrears on their redemption and tax payments. The

peasantry believed that the solution to their problems was for the nobility to turn all of the land over to the peasants, but the upper classes generally felt that the peasants needed to update their farming methods in order to meet the rising demands of the Russian population for food and export grain. The issue of land was the main stumbling block to unity in the first two Dumas as politicians from across the spectrum debated how to increase agricultural production. Needless to say, the large landowners were opposed to distribution of their land among the peasants, and they were supported by constitutional liberals, who believed that private property was sacred and could not simply be taken from its owners. They were opposed by the radical parties, who believed that the peasants had a right to the land and proposed a variety of solutions ranging from simply giving the land to the peasantry to forcing landowners to sell land to the peasantry. Neither of the first Dumas made any headway on the issue, and the Third and Fourth Dumas did not debate the issue.

Stolypin's "Wager on the Strong and Sober" did not make much headway with the peasants either. Stolypin wanted to transform the Russian countryside into consolidated family farms, liberating the peasantry from their commune, consolidating strips of land into family farms, and forcing the peasants to embrace modern farming methods in order to use their land more efficiently. He believed, in other words, that the traditional peasant way of life had to be completely eradicated and replaced with a new farming culture that would resemble the American family farm. This new culture would improve the land; embrace new technologies, seeds, and practices; and have a stake in a stable government. Unfortunately for Stolypin's plan, the peasants were not eager to radically alter their way of life, dispense with their traditions, and destroy the safety nets of their communal system. Few peasant families had the means to force a consolidation of their strips, and the pressure from the village to continue in the traditional manner was enormous—any family that insisted on leaving the village with a consolidated plot could expect to receive the worst land as their portion. There were exceptions: very powerful peasant families were able to force a favorable consolidation, and some villages, particularly in areas that had not lived under the communal system before the emancipation, opted to dissolve their communes entirely. Although Stolypin's reforms freed peasants from the legal tyranny of the commune, very few villages consolidated plots or dissolved themselves into independent family farms. The vast majority of peasants continued to work within their traditional village structure and to use traditional farming methods well into the Soviet period.

NOTES

1. Natalia Pushkareva, *Women in Russian History from the Tenth to the Twentieth Century,* trans. Eve Levin (Armonk: M. E. Sharpe, 1997), 220.

2. George Vernadsky, *Kievan Russia* (New Haven: Yale University Press, 1973), 301–302.

3. Catherine Evtuhov, David Goldfrank, Lindsey Hughes, and Richard Stites, *A History of Russia: Peoples, Legends, Events, Forces* (Boston: Houghton Mifflin Company, 2004), 176.

4. Paul Avrich, *Russian Rebels, 1500–1800* (New York: Schocken Books, 1972), 6.

5. David Moon, *The Russian Peasantry, 1600–1930: The World the Russian Peasants Made* (London: Longman, 1999), 231.

6. Moon, 140.

7. Avrich, 135–177.

8. Evtuhov et al., 288.

9. Moon, 237–254.

10. Moon, 30.

11. Michael Adams, *Napoleon and Russia* (London: Hambledon Continuum, 2006), 407.

12. Moon, 30.

13. W. Bruce Lincoln, *Nicholas I: Emperor and Autocrat of All the Russias* (Bloomington: Indiana University Press, 1978), 274.

14. Lincoln, 271.

15. Moon, 348.

16. Barbara Alpern Engel, *Women in Russia 1700–2000* (New York: Cambridge University, 2004), 91.

17. Engel, 94.

5

The Church
and the Towns

The Church and towns were both important institutions throughout the imperial period. The clergy and the urban residents formed very small yet important segments of the social structure. The Church served as a powerful force for unity and dictated morality, values, and behaviors for most Russians in the imperial period. Towns and cities housed only a fraction of the overall population of Russia, but the work of trade and manufacture were vital elements of the Russian economy. The urban population exploded at the end of the nineteenth century as the professional and working classes grew by leaps and bounds and gave the urban centers a renewed importance that they had not experienced since the Kievan period.

THE CHURCH IN KIEVAN RUS

Christianity came to Kievan Rus in 988 under the reign of Grand Prince Vladimir. The story as recorded in the *Primary Chronicle* states that Vladimir was visited by envoys from the four major faiths of his region, Catholicism, Judaism, Islam, and Orthodox Christianity, who all wanted to convert the Rus to their faith. The Muslim delegation's descriptions of paradise appealed to Vladimir "for he was fond of women and indulgence...but circumcision and abstinence from pork and wine were disagreeable to him. 'Drinking, said he, is the joy of the Russes. We cannot exist without that pleasure.' " He listened to the Catholic delegation but refused their notions of fasting as well, saying, "Our fathers accepted no such principle." Vladimir rejected the Jewish faith on the grounds that "If God loved you and your faith, you would not be thus dispersed in foreign lands." He was more accepting of the Orthodox emissaries, saying, "Their words were artful and it was wondrous to listen and pleasant to hear them." Finally he sent his own emissaries to investigate the various faiths. After denigrating the other three faiths, the emissaries reported their experience in the Greek Church: "[While there] we knew not whether we were in heaven or on earth. For on earth

Vladimir I, Grand Prince of Kiev. Eon Images.

there is no such splendor or such beauty and we are at a loss how to describe it."[1] This account was recorded at least two hundred years after the adoption of Christianity and therefore reflects the biases of the writer, an Orthodox monk, rather than the actual events, but it is indicative of how the Russians conceived of their own history and national character.

In the Kievan period, the Church helped the princes to administer their lands, provided some cultural unity through monasteries and churches, and began to educate the lower classes (particularly in cities where the churches were first located) on this new religion. But the peasants continued in their pagan beliefs and practices for the entire Kievan period—churches emerged slowly in the countryside. For a time, the countryside evinced symbols and rituals from both the old pagan beliefs (household idols, fertility festivals, and reliance on village witches for all types of potions and amulets) and the new Christian faith (using the shape of the cross, for example). The early pagan beliefs had deified natural forces but had not been organized enough for institutional development, so Christian priests did not have to fight with pagan institutions for the loyalty of the people. In some ways, this may have slowed the conversion process, given that there were few clear opponents in the form of temples or religious organizations for the Christian priests to target. The pagan religion had been largely local, and Christianity slowly displaced traditional practices and beliefs.

IMPACT OF THE MONGOLS AND THE RISE OF MOSCOW

The Church gained much authority during the time of Mongol domination. In addition to the collection of wealth, the Church's moral authority in Russia became absolute. As the only institution not directly associated with Mongol rule, the Church preserved the unity of the Russian people and became the sole authority in matters of marriage, divorce, birth, death, morality, and, of course, salvation. The Church was seen as the protector of the Russians and provided the first real cultural unity in the area—the distinction between Russian Christians and Mongol pagans (or later, Muslims) bound Russians of all social and economic classes together much more fully than had been true during the period of Kievan Rus and facilitated the development of the new kingdom under the princes of Muscovy. With Christianity constituting the main unifying identity against the hated Mongols, the Church grew much more influential in the countryside during the Mongol period. The Muscovite princes were highly aware of the importance of Church support in their bid for power and expressed their devotion to the Church by building cathedrals and churches, founding monasteries, and actively and publicly participating in all Church rituals. Thus, the Orthodox Church emerged from the Mongol period much strengthened both in terms of its relationship to the crown and in the prestige and respect it commanded among the lower classes, who during the Mongol period had turned to the Church for comfort and consolation as the only universal institution that survived from the Kievan past. After the metropolitanate, the highest Church office in Russia at this time, moved to Moscow, the princes and the metropolitans worked together to unify the lands under the rule of Moscow. Unification was certainly in the Church's best interest. During this time, the metropolitans were struggling against Lithuanian bids for a separate metropolitanate for the Orthodox under their control. The metropolitan of Moscow traced his office's heritage back to the metropolitan of Kiev and was, naturally, unwilling to lose the southwestern portion of his flock to a new office. This conflict over the Church hierarchy was part of the larger effort of the emerging Lithuania to spread further east into Russia. For both the metropolitan and the grand prince, Catholic Lithuania was a distinct threat, seeking as it did to expand its borders into Russian territory. Although the Lithuanians, unlike the Poles, did not force conversion to Catholicism, the idea of Orthodox Slavs being ruled by a Catholic prince was unpalatable to the metropolitan. The more unified the Russians were, the better they could fend off the Catholic/Lithuanian threat, and thus, the metropolitans believed that it was in the best interests of the Orthodox to unite under one grand prince. The support of the Church for the supremacy of Moscow was cemented during the early years of Grand Prince Dmitrii Donskoi (1359–1389), who ascended to the title when he was nine years old, positioning Metropolitan Alexis as the de facto ruler of the principality. Later metropolitans not so closely associated with the Muscovite family continued to support the Muscovite efforts to unify all of the Russian lands in pursuit of a unified Orthodox nation. The hope that the entire east could be governed by one metropolitan was eventually defeated, and in 1448 Moscow and Kiev separated into two metropolitanates. Just a few years later, in 1453, Constantinople fell to the Ottoman Turks, and Moscow remained as the only major state whose government and people were both Orthodox. The Church's most powerful influence, however, came from its control over the calendar and over the values, morals, rituals, and traditions that governed the everyday lives of people of all ranks, from the lowest slave to the tsar himself.

CHURCH STRUCTURE

The Orthodox Church had its own social structure and hierarchy in Russia. Orthodox clergy are divided into two types: The white clergy is comprised of village priests. These men could marry and have families but could not move up in the Church hierarchy. The

St. Basil's Cathedral, Moscow. Maxim Kulemza/ Dreamstime.

black clergy were monks from whose ranks the Church leaders emerged. The highest Church office was that of patriarch. In Kievan times, the patriarch was in Constantinople, but under Boris Godunov, the Russian Church obtained its own patriarch, appointed by the tsar. Under the patriarch were metropolitans, and under them, bishops oversaw priests and the lesser Church hierarchy in their diocese. Men of any rank could, in theory, join a monastery and potentially move up in the Church hierarchy. Village priests, though not able to move up in rank, constituted something of a closed caste because their sons tended to go into the priesthood as well. The village priest was frequently a local man (son of the previous priest) who had to support himself and his family through agriculture in addition to his spiritual duties. The Church had its own courts that governed violations of religious law, crimes committed by clergy, and crimes against Church property.

THE SCHISM

In addition to establishing the new social structure, the early Romanov tsars faced and easily defeated the only challenge to the tsar's authority that the Orthodox Church ever presented. Under Mikhail, the position of patriarch became exceedingly powerful and influential, largely because Mikhail's father, Filaret, was patriarch during his son's reign. Not surprisingly, the young tsar relied heavily on his father's guidance, although scholars are divided on how completely Filaret dominated his son. It is clear, however, that Mikhail valued his father's opinion and that Filaret wielded a great deal of power in his own right: he took the title Great Sovereign and received foreign embassies in his own court. It is likely that Filaret was a very valuable advisor to Mikhail—Filaret had been one of the contenders for the throne during the Time of Troubles and was politically very astute. This cooperation between ruler and patriarch set an example that future patriarchs sought to emulate. At the same time, the Church was undergoing an internal reformation that led to heated debates over the proper way for Russian Orthodox to worship. The reformers wanted to purge the Church of all inaccuracies and impurities that it had acquired over the years and to improve public morality by closing shops and taverns on Sundays and banning strolling musicians who sang bawdy songs. In addition to the new restrictions, however, the Church revised some of its rituals and practices in order to come into line with the other Orthodox religions: Russians would now make the sign of the cross with three fingers instead of two fingers, priests would wear Greek-style vestments, and some details of the liturgy were revised with new prayer books published to reflect these changes. These few changes led to a deep schism in the Church between those who called themselves "Old Believers," who insisted on using the old symbols and liturgy, and the rest of the Orthodox, who adopted the changes.

These conflicts came to a head under the leadership of Patriarch Nikon, appointed by Alexei in 1652. Nikon continued reform of the Church, and under his guidance, with the full support of the tsar, the changes became mandatory. This angered many Russians, who rebelled and refused to adopt the new practices. At the same time, Nikon himself made many enemies in the Church and among the elite because of his arrogance and vengeful attitude toward any who opposed him. He also angered Alexei by assuming more power than Alexei was willing to bestow upon him, even taking the title "Grand Sovereign" in imitation of Patriarch Filaret Romanov. Eventually, the tsar and patriarch had a disagreement, which sent Nikon in a huff from the city. Alexei had him tried in an ecclesiastical court for abandoning his post and exiled Nikon to a distant monastery. The tsar was acknowledged as the undisputed leader of both Russia and the Orthodox Church. Never again would a Church leader openly defy the tsar.

OLD BELIEVERS

The problems in the Church continued, however. The Old Believers were a constant thorn in the side of Romanov Russia. They were declared schismatics by a Church council in 1666 and ordered to return to the official doctrine. Many refused and were arrested, the most famous of these being the Boyarina Morozova, who refused to accept the new practices and died of starvation with her sister in prison in 1675. Entire villages locked themselves in their churches and burned them down, preferring to die in the purifying fire of earth rather than suffer the eternal fire of hell. From 1666 on, Old Believers formed an opposition community in Russia that was sometimes persecuted and sometimes tolerated. For the most part, Old Believers were sober, hardworking peasants and merchants, and the state left them alone. In times of crisis, however, Old Belief could form a rallying point for civil disobedience and draw the wrath of the crown.

The Old Believers occupied a volatile position in eighteenth-century Russia. Old Believers had, of necessity, their own clergy who retained the traditional Russian liturgy and rituals. Old Believers could not cut their beards, don Western clothing, or use tobacco. Although his father had persecuted the Old Believers for their refusal to fall in with the new teachings, Peter I did not seem to find them particularly troubling. He forced them to pay a double tax and a beard tax and to wear special clothing to mark their belief but refused to make them into martyrs. Over the course of the eighteenth century, their fortunes changed with the emperors: Elizabeth proved herself to be the most avid persecutor of Old Believers and exiled many of them from Russia, Peter III invited them back, and Catherine II operated on the Enlightenment principle of religious toleration and permitted Old Believers to practice their faith along with the other minority religions in Russia. The schism in the Church created more opportunities for disgruntled people to find justification for their dissatisfaction and, in extreme cases, to join the two large rebellions of the eighteenth century, the Bulavin and Pugachev revolts.

THE PETRINE REFORMS

Peter I targeted the clergy in his reforms, which culminated in the Spiritual Regulation of 1721. As with all of his other reforms, Peter's goal was to ensure that the Church supported the state. Peter believed that priests performed a necessary service, but monks did not—monasteries and nunneries, in Peter's view, were simply a place for people to waste their lives in idle and useless contemplation and to hide from their obligations. He therefore restricted the number of monastic institutions in Russia and forbade anyone other than monks or nuns to live in monasteries. He forced the Church to produce recruits for the army from its estates and exacted taxes from the Church to fund his wars. He prohibited the construction of new churches and limited the number of priests. Although Peter believed that priests were necessary, he wanted Russia's priests to be better educated and to focus their efforts on creating good subjects who would obey their superiors. Peter also refused to appoint a new patriarch when Patriarch Adrian died in 1700.

Peter and his successors also attacked monastic life and the Church hierarchy. Peter believed that the black clergy (monks and nuns) contained many idlers who were simply trying to avoid their service and financial obligations. Furthermore, Peter charged that the Church absorbed too many of Russia's resources, in terms of both land and labor. To limit these evils, Peter closed and combined many monastic institutions and insisted that they engage in socially useful work, such as running hospitals and schools. He forbade young healthy people from entering monastic life, legislating that no women under 40 could take vows and that no able-bodied young men could enter a monastery. He forced "extra" monks to join the army or to enter the bureaucracy. His successors seem to have agreed with him; over the course of the century, they continued to limit the number of monasteries and their landholdings as well as the number of people allowed to take vows to the Church. Peter III finally removed all productive lands from the Church and converted them into state lands, an act later confirmed by Catherine II, leaving the Church with no income other than the subsidies it received from the state budget. The Church also lost much of its legal jurisdiction during this century; even its control over marriage was challenged by Peter, who objected to the Church's prohibition against remarriage for widows and widowers. Peter wanted all people of childbearing age to marry and reproduce, and he expected the Church to support this position. He was also perfectly willing to ignore religious teaching that interfered with his other plans; both the cutting of beards and the use of tobacco were strictly forbidden by the Church, but Peter actively promoted both, punishing those who did not comply with the new fashions with taxes and ostracism.

Before the Petrine reforms, the white clergy (priests) were widely regarded as a drunken group of men who had little understanding of their spiritual duties. Most village priests inherited their jobs from their fathers, who had overseen the sons' education—few had formal seminary education—and this perpetuated ignorance. Peter required priests to attend Episcopal schools before they could be ordained. He tried to harness the power of the pulpits, ordering priests to give sermons that emphasized useful values, like submission to authority, and to report treasonous confessions to the police. Peter even forced churches to melt down church bells for weapons and collect taxes to fund his wars, and he insisted that many sons of priests go into the army rather than the priesthood because he believed that Russia had more priests than it needed. Furthermore, the Spiritual Regulation of 1721 laid down rules of conduct for priests and parishioners with stiff punishments for anyone who violated them: drunken priests were subject to corporal punishment and defrocking, and parishioners who disrupted church services could be beaten or fined. Peter also hoped to make priests more useful by requiring church schools where gentry sons could begin their education, but these were a failure because most nobles preferred to educate their children privately. Later in the century, Catherine II set up provincial schools for the same purpose, preferring secular teachers and curriculum and liberating the Church from any educational duties other than training its own clergy.

NINETEENTH-CENTURY DEVELOPMENTS

Under Alexander I, Russia experienced a spiritual revival of sorts. As in the rest of Europe, mystical religion came into fashion. The Orthodox Church spawned sects who practiced self-flagellation and one whose members castrated themselves. In addition to Orthodox mysticism, Western writers on mystical religion were highly popular, and the Masonic Lodge experienced a revival. All of these groups came under government suspicion later in Alexander I's reign, and most were disbanded or shut down. Throughout the remainder of the imperial period, the Church continued in its role as religious supporter of the state. Despite Nicholas I's emphasis on Orthodoxy as the first component of his Official Nationality, the Church did not regain any institutional power during his reign. Nicholas believed in the importance of religious education but beyond that made no changes to the status quo. Well aware that the independent religious societies that had been tolerated for so long under Alexander I had created space for the discussions that led to the Decembrist uprising, Nicholas had a great distaste for anything but official Russian Orthodoxy. The last three emperors did nothing to improve the position of the Church, although they continued to rely on its teaching to support their policies; Alexander III and Nicholas II increased the number of Church schools with the idea that these schools could be expected to support the regime more reliably than the zemstvo schools, increasingly mistrusted as hotbeds of subversive activity. The Church drew much criticism as social and economic conditions worsened in the early twentieth century because it was viewed as a staunch supporter of the status quo. The negative impression of the Church was only exacerbated by the antics of Gregory Rasputin, the famous ex-monk who manipulated Nicholas II through Empress Alexandra. Rasputin's hold on the royal couple stemmed from his purported ability to stop their hemophiliac son from bleeding; the empress believed that he had been sent from God to guide Russia and relied on him absolutely, with disastrous results for Russia during World War I.

THE ROLE OF THE CHURCH

The Church remained a strong influence on Russian culture throughout the imperial period, but its power and position were undermined over the course of the eighteenth century as religious considerations were firmly subordinated to the interests of the state. Although it had always been the policy that the emperor was the head of the Church, the patriarch had also wielded a certain amount of independent power and moral authority; Peter's father had been unsuccessfully but publicly challenged by Patriarch Nikon, resulting in the Great Schism and leading to Peter's decision to do away with the position of patriarch. The eighteenth-century rulers harnessed the power of the Church to their own ends and firmly subjugated the Church to the state; however, this shift in influence should not be interpreted as the secularization of society or as an attempt to secularize Russia. Although rulers and nobility were motivated by secular concerns, they remained firmly committed to the Orthodox faith. The vast majority of the Russian population continued to be profoundly influenced by their religious beliefs, which dominated their view of morality and justice and shaped their daily activities through the practice of religious rituals, fasts, and festivals. Even among the elite, Orthodoxy vied with the new Enlightenment ideas and continued to play an integral role in the elite's daily existence, informing their values, determining their daily and yearly routine, and shaping the seminal events in their lives through religious domination of the rituals governing birth, marriage, and death. The Church no longer possessed any institutional ability to challenge a ruler, but it continued to play the dominant role in the lives of most Russians.

TOWNSPEOPLE

Towns played an important role in Russian history. Kievan Rus was a much more urban society than was western Europe at that time—one scholar has calculated that 89 towns existed in the eleventh century, with an additional 134 developing in the twelfth century, culminating in about 300 by the time of the Mongol invasion.[2] These towns varied in size depending on importance and proximity to trade—Kiev is believed to have contained between 36,000 and 50,000 people (as many as London or Paris at this time), and Novgorod had about 30,000 by the thirteenth century.[3] The size of towns descended from these large cities down to mere fortified posts. Princes lived in the largest cities with their retinues, but they formed a relatively small part of the population. Most of the people were laborers, skilled craftsmen, artisans, and tradesmen, with slaves at the very bottom of the social scale. These people lived in different sections of the city depending on their economic level. Homes were made of wood around courtyards where the livestock were housed. Refuse was simply thrown in the courtyard and covered with dry twigs. The Kievan urban economy was dominated by trade along the river routes and eventually attracted foreign merchants to travel to Kiev. The princes imposed transit fees and custom duties and even sales taxes on some items, such as salt, and in exchange, they accepted responsibility for policing the marketplace to ensure fair weights and discourage fraud. They collected fines and fees for any disputes that ended up in court as well. The princes used this money to maintain their military retinues, which kept the trade routes relatively secure. The Rus exported furs, wax, honey, and slaves and imported luxury fabrics, jewelry, glassware, wine, olive oil, naphtha, combs, and marble. The Rus also traded with their steppe neighbors, exchanging grain, clothing, and weapons for horses and other livestock. Novgorod conducted her own trade with Scandinavia and Bulgar, importing wool, weapons, pottery, and salt from Scandinavia and trading them for silk, spices, gems, jewelry, and silver coins from the Bulgars and Kiev. Later, in the twelfth century, Novgorod began to trade with Germanic merchants, adding European silver to her list of imports.

Not all merchants were engaged in the lucrative but hazardous foreign trade; many engaged in the somewhat safer domestic trade among the cities of Kievan Rus. Novgorod supplied most of the furs that went through Kiev to the Byzantine trade and received olive oil and wine in exchange. Glassworks, pottery, tiles, jewelry, and enamel work were traded. Artisans, craftsmen, and laborers traveled as well, selling their skills in the big building projects in various cities. Artisans and craftsmen engaged in the many trades one would expect in a medieval city: leatherworking, carpentry, pottery, blacksmithing, and weapons making. As warfare relied increasingly on mounted cavalry, the demand for sabers, swords, armor, shields, and protective equipment for the horses rose considerably, given that the Kievan Rus fought frequently either among themselves or with the surrounding steppe nomads and the Byzantines. The huge building projects that princes undertook to display their glory also employed many of the artisans and craftsmen as well as a significant number of the unskilled laborers who inhabited the larger cities.

MONGOL IMPACT

As the region slowly recovered from the initial devastation of the Mongol invasion, urban life revived as well. Most cities suffered from the depopulation occasioned by the Mongol invasion and by the Mongol practice of seizing artisans and craftsmen to work for the Great Khan. It took several generations for towns to recover from the loss of skilled labor. The areas that continued to engage in trade—Novgorod, for example—prospered under the Mongols, who protected trade routes and merchants, although they levied taxes on much of the trade. By 1600, Russia had about 170 cities, growing to 226 by 1650, many of them along the rivers that had been more heavily populated before the Mongol invasion.[4] Cities were far apart, which inhibited communication and control from the center and also inhibited trade. Most of the cities grew as military centers to govern border regions, others as commercial and administrative centers. Cities were built around a kremlin—a fortress of stone, wood, or earth enclosing the government of the city, the arsenal, the homes of the city leaders, and the cathedral. Around the kremlin was the *posad*, the area outside the kremlin but inside the earthen wall that surrounded the entire city, where the residences and businesses of the city were located and which was considered the property of the tsar.[5]

THE URBAN SOCIAL STRUCTURE

Most of the inhabitants of the cities during this time were service people, which meant that they were not taxable inhabitants of the city; some were craftsmen, but most were soldiers. The more commercially oriented cities of the far north and the center contained a lower percentage of service people and more residents who engaged in crafts and trade, who paid taxes instead of rendering service. As cities grew larger, and more people engaged in trade who were not registered as taxpaying residents, the population of the cities became more complex and difficult to define. Instead of paying taxes, the group of tax-exempt people—boyars, pomeshchiki, state servitors, soldiers, clergy, and the wealthiest merchants—rendered service to the state. The wealthy merchants were probably the smallest portion of the tax-exempt group, numbering only a few hundred in the entire country in the seventeenth century. Their service to the tsar consisted of not only advising the tsar on foreign trade but also engaging in foreign trade to both the tsar's advantage and their own. They also helped the government with economic and fiscal administration. The *posadskie liudi* were the tax-paying citizens of the city: artisans, craftsmen, and family merchants who paid the urban residents' tax, known as the *tiaglo*. Finally, there were the people who were registered taxpayers in another community but lived and worked in the city: artisans, merchants, or craftsmen who were peasants, serfs, Church peasants, or household servants.

This last category was probably the most worrisome for the posadskie liudi because peasants who were not registered taxpayers in the town competed with the artisans, craftsmen, and merchants who were subject to the tiaglo, undercutting their business yet not contributing to the community's tax rolls. Russian artisans and craftsmen did not have such tightly controlled and regulated guilds as their west European counterparts, and this permitted increased competition as well. In addition, most heavy production during the seventeenth century took place not in cities, but on estates held by the Church or by noblemen. As the tax burden increased with the rise of Muscovy, urban taxpayers would sometimes indenture themselves to a nobleman or to the Church, agreeing to work for their benefactor for a certain number of years to fall under their protection and become exempt from taxes. This practice eroded the taxpaying community and increased the burden on those who remained in it.[6]

STABILIZING THE TOWNS

Town life continued in much the same way that it had since the Mongol invasion. Although towns were less important than they had been in the Kievan period, they housed around 185,000 people in the 1670s.[7] Towns still lacked paved streets, and almost all buildings were still constructed of wood, which explains the frequency of fires that plagued Russian towns. Moscow was distinguished from the provincial towns only by its size and its many fine cathedrals and churches as well as the Kremlin itself, but its social composition did not yet resemble capital cities in the West with their new professional classes of people and emerging civil society—doctors, bankers, lawyers, scholars, and so on. In the wake of the Troubles, the problem of posadskie liudi leaving the posad for the tax protection of the Church or the nobility became even more acute; the new dynasty desperately needed its taxpayers. Just as the pomeshchiki petitioned for the right to enserf their peasants, the posad leaders petitioned for the right to reclaim taxpayers who had abandoned the posad. Finally, the Law Code of 1649 came down on the side of the posad leaders, forbidding the nobility and the Church from granting posadskie liudi refuge from taxes and requiring all those who had escaped their taxpaying status to return to it. The Law Code also gave the posadskie liudi a monopoly over trade in the cities—peasants and serfs were no longer permitted to engage in crafts and trade in the cities at will; they were only permitted to trade on bazaar days and were forbidden to occupy shops or stalls. Posadskie liudi were to be registered in the city rolls and were forbidden to leave in much the same way that serfs were forbidden to leave their lands. The Law Code helped the posadskie liudi by ensuring that their taxes would be more evenly spread among all those who were supposed to be paying them; on the other hand, it bound them and their children permanently to their estate.[8]

EIGHTEENTH- AND NINETEENTH-CENTURY SOCIAL CATEGORIES

By the eighteenth century, the policies of the early Romanovs had divided Russian society into categories known as *soslovie:* gentry (nobility), clergy, merchants, peasants, and a loosely defined group known as *meshchanstvo*, a term that replaced the earlier posadskie liudi to describe all those town dwellers, usually artisans, craftsmen, and lesser merchants, who were subject to the tiaglo. Under Catherine II, merchants were separated from the meshchanstvo into their own category with their own stratifications based on wealth. These legal categories were highly porous, and the soslovie became increasingly muddled as time went on and new opportunities for education, manufacture, and government service allowed people to move in and out of these categories. Even serfs could operate in a sphere of life far removed from the village, appearing in the royal theater, in shops, and in manufacture.

Peter I's imposition of the poll tax meant that the government needed to categorize everyone in order to determine who would pay the tax. The poll tax was supposed to be levied on all male souls of the non-free (taxpaying) population. There is no easy answer to who composed the taxpaying population—most people paid taxes because most people were peasants—but there were many other categories in society, and some did and others did not pay the poll tax. Gentry were exempt from the tax; they gave service instead. Certain professions were exempted from the tax—for example, drivers of official post horses were exempt, as were retired soldiers and state employees. By the end of the eighteenth century, the government finally determined that the only groups exempt from the poll tax were nobles, clergy, merchants, officials, and military servitors.[9] In these efforts to categorize all people, a new group, the *raznochintsy*, emerged as a category in which to place those people who did not easily fit into any other group; the term is best translated as "people of various ranks." The definition of who was in the raznochintsy evolved over the course of the century and was never clearly delineated, although it encompassed minor government officials, teachers in national schools, and retired soldiers who did not settle on land inhabited by state peasants and who were not enrolled as merchants. Basically, anyone who did not fall easily into one of the other categories became raznochintsy, and most of them had to pay the poll tax. Despite the inadequacies of the soslovie, we will continue to use these categories in our discussion because they provide the most accessible framework for understanding the way that the Russians themselves viewed their social structure into the nineteenth century.

Catherine II made further refinements in the urban social structure. She wanted to create a "middling sort of people" between the nobility and the peasantry, and her 1785 Charter to the Towns was in part an effort to encourage the development of this new estate. Catherine divided the urban population into six fluid groups: those who possessed property in the city, merchants of all levels, artisans, foreigners conducting business in the city, honorary citizens (artists, scholars, officials, bankers, and anyone worth over 50,000 rubles), and the posad people (those who lived by manual labor, industry, or crafts). The merchants were removed from the poll tax and instead paid taxes based on their wealth, leaving the meshchanstvo deprived of its wealthiest members and increasing their relative burden.[10]

Alexander I also embarked on moderate social reform and began to break down the old soslovie. He permitted state peasants, merchants, and the meshchanstvo to purchase land and allowed landlords and eventually peasants to engage in foreign trade, previously reserved exclusively for the merchants. This created more fluidity in the social structure of Russia, allowing people of different categories to engage in economic activity once reserved for specific soslovie. To further break down social barriers, Alexander created more parish and local schools and founded provincial universities, allowing far more non-noble people access to a university education.

THE POST-PETRINE URBAN POPULATION

Cities and towns grew enormously during the eighteenth century, a result of Peter I's emphasis on manufacturing and his successors' desires for increased trade. Aside from the capitals, Moscow and St. Petersburg, towns were usually small and composed mostly of poor artisans and merchants. By the end of the century, most cities had a particular product associated with them—Moscow was dominated by textile production, for example—although all towns housed a variety of artisinal occupations, and many towns remained devoted exclusively to agricultural production. Cities continued to be composed of complex groups of people as well, given that many of the inhabitants of any given city or town, particularly the capitals, were often not registered as inhabitants but were instead registered as peasants, soldiers, clerics, or government officials. As discussed previously, these people were not taxpayers in the town even if they lived and worked there but either were exempt from taxes as nobles or soldiers or were registered elsewhere, in a village commune, for example. Problems with peasants and serfs trading in towns and undercutting the meshchanstvo continued to generate much discontent among the town dwellers. In Moscow in 1730, for example, out of 138,792 people, only 23,707 were part of the urban estate (meshchanstvo). Of the remaining, 35,959 were house serfs (who were registered in their home communes), 32,475 were nobles (who were tax exempt) and raznochintsy (who may or may not have paid urban taxes), 18,310 were state peasants (registered in their home communes), 15,348 were officers and soldiers, and 5,456 were clergy (all tax-exempt categories). St. Petersburg had an even lower percentage of meshchanstvo because the court was there, housing even more nobles and their house serfs.[11] The relatively low percentage of urban taxpayers placed an extraordinarily heavy burden on that group, making it difficult for any of them to grow into more prosperous merchants or manufacturers.

The urban population occupied an odd place in the Russian social hierarchy, far below the gentry and only slightly above the peasantry. At the lower end, the meshchanstvo deeply resented the fact that they were in the same category as peasants with regard to

Peasants selling bread, milk, eggs, and so on, early twentieth century. Courtesy of the Library of Congress, LC-USZ62-36538.

the poll tax and conscription. The meshchanstvo considered themselves a cut above the peasantry, but the new laws did not make this distinction. At the high end of urban society, those wealthy merchants who were exempt from taxes and conscription by virtue of their service to the state still bore the stigma of trade. The gentry closely guarded their ranks and regarded even the wealthiest merchants as tradesmen, lower on the social scale. Those few very successful merchants who could work their way into nobility, either by educating their sons and sending them into state service or by obtaining a grant of nobility from the emperor, could escape the stigma, but these routes to nobility became increasingly difficult to follow as the century wore on. In Catherine's Charter to the Nobility, she affirmed the nobility's exclusive right to own populated estates, which not only emphasized the nobility's higher privileges but also made it very difficult for the non-noble urban population to get labor; this would have a profound impact on Russia's ability to industrialize in the next century. Catherine also permitted anyone to engage in trade, believing that this would strengthen the economy. For the urban population, however, it seemed to give others an unfair advantage; once again, the nobility could compete with the wealthy merchants, and the peasantry could compete with the lesser merchants and meshchanstvo, but the urban population could not cross into either of the other estates.[12]

EIGHTEENTH-CENTURY TRADE

Most Russian merchants were not involved in particular lines of trade—they sold whatever they were able to acquire. For the large-scale wealthy merchants, imports were the most important item, and the development of westernization over the course of the eighteenth century made luxury items increasingly valuable. From 1780 to 1790 the most valuable items imported into St. Petersburg were raw sugar, silk items, wool, broadcloth, liquor, tobacco, coffee, clothing, cotton, English beer, lemons, fresh and dried fruits, oysters, and anchovies. In domestic trade, agricultural products were the most prominent. Import trade was centered in the merchants' court in each city. Confining the most valuable trade to one area allowed the merchants to control prices and the government to collect its tariffs and customs duties. Trade fairs, held yearly, also constituted an important venue for all levels of merchants, to include serfs and peasants who traveled to the fairs to sell their wares.[13]

GUILDS

Both Peter I and Catherine II took an interest in the guild system. Apprenticeship had been regulated in the seventeenth century along much the same lines that existed in western Europe: Masters were supposed to supply food and clothing, train the apprentice, and sometimes pay the apprentice. Apprentices had to be obedient and sober and behave properly. Peter endeavored to expand the guild system and mandated that craft guilds should be created and regulated. Catherine set down specific guidelines regulating guilds in her Charter to the Towns, even stipulating the details of hours of rest, meals, and work for apprentices, but guilds and the apprentice system remained weak throughout the eighteenth century; they were not permitted the same kind of exclusivity and self-regulation that guilds in western Europe enjoyed, nor were they able to create monopolies in their towns. Peasant, serf, noble, and raznochintsy entrepreneurs continued to practice crafts and to trade freely in spite of the guilds.

TOWN GOVERNMENT

Peter I and Catherine II also both tried to improve the conditions of towns, and both believed that government institutions could force towns to be clean, spacious, law-abiding places to live. Peter's charge to the police stated,

[The police] dispenses good order and moral admonitions, gives to all safety from robbers, thieves, ravishers, tricksters, and similar persons, drives away disorderly and indecent living, and compels each to work and to honorable industry, makes good householders, careful and good servants, looks after the correctness and the construction of homes and the conditions of the streets, prevents high prices, and brings satisfaction in all that human living requires, stands on guard against all occurring illnesses, brings about cleanliness in the streets and in the houses, forbids a superfluity of domestic luxuries and all manifest sins, looks after the poor, the sick, the crippled and other unfortunates, defends widows, orphans, strangers, according to God's commandments, educates the young in chaste purity and honorable sciences; in short, over all these things the police is the soul of citizenship and all good order, and the fundamental support of human safety and convenience.[14]

This was a tall order for any organization to meet—and one that apparently was not realized considering that Catherine II passed similar legislation in her reign. Catherine also decreed that any free person could engage in trade or manufacture without any interference from the central government, which had tended in the past to harass small producers in order to protect the larger manufacturers, who had much influence over the College of Commerce. She affirmed the right of urban inhabitants to their lives and property, stating that no one could be relieved of either without due process.[15] The Police Statute of 1782 divided towns into districts of 200–500 households and then into quarters of 50–100 households under the supervision of police boards. The police were given a myriad of duties to ensure the well-being of towns, similar to those listed by Peter I. She created foundling homes and orphanages that were supposed to raise and train abandoned children to be productive subjects, but they were so poorly funded that they did not succeed very well either, earning the name "angel factories" because of their high death rates.[16] Catherine wanted to clean up the towns and to turn them into well-ordered, healthy communities; despite her humanitarian efforts, she believed that regulation was the best way to achieve her ends.

URBAN PROBLEMS

Eighteenth-century Russian towns were made of wood, making them highly vulnerable to fire. Cities and towns were also subject to various outbreaks of infectious diseases that seemed to grow more common toward the end of the century. Catherine II was particularly concerned about the recurrence of plague in the capitals and invested much time and effort trying to safeguard herself and her son as well as making vain attempts to limit the spread during the outbreaks. In 1770–1772, Moscow was subjected to a particularly virulent outbreak of plague, resulting in somewhere between 100,000 and 200,000 deaths in that city alone, with death tolls at their peak reaching as high as 900 a day.[17] Urban life was difficult even in the absence of great disasters, especially for women and girls who were not protected by a family. There was no respectable employment for a woman outside of a family business. Women who migrated to the city without a husband found themselves forced into prostitution in order to make ends meet. The state blamed prostitutes for the spread of venereal disease and, until 1843, did its best to stamp out prostitution by severely punishing women believed to be engaged in the business. After 1843, the state legalized prostitution and regulated its practitioners in an effort to curb the spread of disease.

URBAN PLANNING

The first concerted attempt at urban planning was Peter's construction of St. Petersburg, his new capital on the Baltic. Peter called it his paradise and forced his nobles to move to the new city and to build appropriate housing there. He oversaw much of the planning and construction himself and conscripted tens of thousands of serfs and Church and state peasants to work on the construction. Construction was difficult given the swampy land and the extremes of weather—hot, humid, and plagued by mosquitoes in the summer; dark and terribly cold in the winter. Peter began the city in 1703 and slowly moved the government from Moscow. Nobles who were ordered to build homes in the city had to follow Western-style architecture and decorating schemes and were supposed to build a home in keeping with their status—the most prestigious families had to construct near palaces as their contribution to realizing Peter's dream of a modern, Western city. Peter also built Peterhof, his answer to Versailles, a few miles outside of St. Petersburg, also an incredibly costly and labor-intensive project. Elizabeth continued construction of the very beautiful and expensive Winter Palace in St. Petersburg.

After St. Petersburg was built, with its broad, stone-paved avenues and orderly rows of stone or brick homes facing the street, new towns began to follow that model. Catherine continued the efforts to improve the appearance of towns by constructing government buildings of stone rather than wood and encouraging town planning. She favored a grid pattern of streets and preferred to build new government buildings on town squares. She encouraged the construction of private homes by tax exemptions as long as they were at least two stories high and built of brick or stone. Houses were traditionally built sidewise to the street rather than facing it, and traditional urban homes had consisted of three rooms all on the ground floor; by the end of the century, more two-story homes that faced the street were constructed. For the wealthier classes, glass windows, tapestries, wooden floors, artwork, and a greater variety of furniture became the norm. Catherine II addressed issues of public health in her provincial and town reforms, founded a hospital in Moscow, and imported doctors from the West in an attempt to make her cities healthier.[18] Town planning also included sanitation with water pipes and drainage ditches and placement of factories, stables, and cemeteries on the outskirts. Of course, these new plans could be applied only to new towns or to towns that had to be rebuilt after a fire; although the development of provincial government facilitated the construction of new towns, many old towns continued to follow the old patterns of development, and aside from the capitals, towns were small and dirty with unpaved streets laid out in a concentric pattern.

THE PROFESSIONAL CLASS

The Great Reforms and rapid industrialization at the end of the nineteenth century and beginning of the twentieth spawned two important new urban social classes: the professionals and the workers. The attempt to modernize Russia led to a demand for professionals of all kinds; some of them worked in the countryside, but the professionals' education and many professionals' occupations were in the towns: The zemstvos required medical services, teachers, and engineers to provide education and medical care to the peasantry and to maintain and expand local infrastructure. Technical experts of all kinds were needed in the growing industries and in government service as the state rapidly expanded its network of railroads, roads, and canals. The new court system required not only lawyers and judges but also court clerks, secretaries, and a variety of support personnel. As literacy grew in Russia, the publishing business also grew, and young people might find work in newspapers, journals, or magazines. The demand for editors, translators, and tutors grew as well. The new industries also created new white-collar positions—managers, secretaries, assistants, accountants—that opened up more opportunities for the educated classes. The growing demand for professionals meant that more technical schools, universities, and other institutions of higher learning opened in Russia, creating a demand for teachers at all levels. Students at university took degrees in mathematics, the sciences, medicine, and law in addition to reading revolutionary literature and debating the future of Russia. For many of these young people, the new professions offered a practical means to help the lower classes; by getting a degree that was in demand for zemstvo work, young people could move to the countryside and actively work to improve the lives of the former serfs. This calling was very powerful for the post-emancipation generations as they struggled to find a way to atone for generations of living off the oppressed peasantry. The new professions usually paid very poorly, particularly for those who went to work for the zemstvos, but they did provide at least a meager livelihood for those whose families found themselves increasingly impoverished after the emancipation. The sons and daughters of the nobility, gentry, clergy, and merchant classes all flocked to institutes and universities in order to attain a degree that would enable them to support themselves and to further modernization in Russia.

These new professions had an even greater impact on the lives of young women. Although not all of the professions were open to them, medicine and teaching provided new avenues for women who needed to earn a living. The first midwifery courses for women had begun in the mid-eighteenth century and had been supplemented by obstetric courses later in the century, but the steadily increasing demand for nurses and midwives led to more schools. In the late 1860s and 1870s, courses of higher education became open to women, and women began to attend lectures and labs at the universities even though they could not obtain university degrees. Impoverished noble and gentry women had never before had such opportunities; in the past the only respectable work for an educated young woman was to become a governess, but even this was a difficult job to get because higher-ranking families preferred French or German governesses so that their children could become fluent in one of those languages. The governess position was also highly vulnerable, as were all domestic service positions—young women were isolated from their own families and sources of protection and frequently found themselves harassed, abused, and even raped by the men in the family they served. Although being a zemstvo nurse, midwife, or teacher was hardly a glamorous job, these professions allowed young women a certain amount of independence and opened new educational opportunities to them.

WORKERS

Although Russia had industry before the emancipation, it was scattered around the empire and often employed serf labor. The industrial boom that Russia experienced after 1880 resulted in the shift of a sizeable amount of the population from the countryside to the new industrial centers, particularly Moscow and St. Petersburg. This migration began very slowly and at first did not change the orientation of the peasants, who migrated to industry to find better wages but remained very much tied to their villages through family connections and who returned to the village for the peak agricultural seasons. The increasing demands of industry meant that workers, particularly skilled workers, were in high demand. Factory owners welcomed the shift in the workforce because the migratory peasant labor on which they had been relying was not particularly conducive to industrial growth. The peasants who worked seasonally in a factory did not adapt well to the rhythm of factory life and were not usually interested in advancing in the factory because they were there for only a few months of the year. Even peasants who spent most of their time in the factory still considered it to be a temporary job and identified the village as their home. As time went on and industry grew, more peasants moved permanently to the cities and adopted the city lifestyle. As more workers flocked to the industrial centers, all of the problems with rapid urbanization hit Russia—poor sanitation, lack of housing and infrastructure, and so on all contributed to the development of urban slums with the attendant rise in crime rates and infectious diseases. By the turn of the century, huge worker slums had sprung up on the outskirts of the major industrial centers, and a generation of people who identified themselves as factory workers had emerged. Still a tiny proportion of the population, the new workforce was of great concern to the government, which perceived in industrial workers a threat to the status quo and deplored all of the urban problems that the new industrial class created.

In the absence of legislation governing industry, most factories ran long shifts that prevented workers from having much leisure time to pursue other interests. Factories were dangerous, dirty, and overwhelmingly male spaces with a strict hierarchy that governed worker life. Semen Ivanovich Kanatchikov's account of his life as a young apprentice gives a vivid picture of how the hierarchy operated.[19] When he was 12 years old, his father took him to the city and placed him under the supervision of a man from his village in an *artel*—a group of workers who lived together and shared living expenses—of men from their region of Russia. Kanatchikov worked in a pattern shop as an assistant to a skilled worker, running errands, fetching materials, and doing the grunt work while trying, in his spare time, to learn the skills of a master. They worked 11-hour shifts, often with overtime added.

Kanatchikov described the workshop as a highly stratified place with different cliques of workers: The skilled pattern-makers had apprentice helpers and ran the shop but often drank heavily during work hours or showed up to work drunk or hungover. One of the jobs of the apprentices was to ensure that they warned their masters when a supervisor approached to ensure that the master was working hard whenever a boss appeared. The men would distill spirits from varnish and drink it throughout the day, particularly on Monday mornings, when almost all of the workers suffered from terrible hangovers. The boy apprentices were not supposed to drink but of course stole sips from the cans of liquor whenever they had the opportunity. If an apprentice failed in any way to satisfy his master, he could expect to be beaten and sworn at for his failures. Another group of workers were the peasant workers—the men who still had strong ties to the countryside, who sent much of their money home, and who continued to dress in the peasant style with high boots, cotton blouses with a sash, and long beards. These men were also skilled workers but kept themselves isolated from the other workers who dressed in urban fashion—tucked-in shirts, long trousers, lace collar fastenings, bowler hats, and short-cropped hair—and who often ridiculed the peasant workers for their style of dress and their strong religious convictions.

Not all workers lived in artels. Many large factories had worker dormitories to accommodate their employees, often located far from the actual factory. In general, these dormitories were barracks-like and lacked basic amenities such as heat, running water, or cooking facilities. Workers lived in large rooms lined with bunks, often having to share their bunk with one or two other workers who were on different shifts. These rooms provided no storage for worker belongings, which had to be confined to a box under the bed. Workers had no way to wash themselves, their clothing, or their bed linen, and in these unhygienic conditions, disease ran rampant. Workers often kept food under their beds as well, contributing to the vermin problem. Workers who married often could not find another place to live, so husband and wife lived in their separate dormitories until they could find alternative housing. Workers with families often occupied small, one-room apartments usually on the bottom floor of a building.

WOMEN WORKERS

As the nineteenth century drew to a close, the number of women who migrated to the cities rose steadily. The growing economy created more of a demand for service personnel as a consumer economy began to develop in the rapidly expanding cities. Impoverished young women of good breeding might find work in an elite shop, whereas daughters of the merchant class might work in less affluent shops or work as waitresses in the new restaurants and cafes that sprang up to meet the demands of the urban population. Domestic work continued to be the largest employer of young women throughout the nineteenth and early twentieth centuries. The expansion of industry, particularly in textiles, increased the demand for low-paid, unskilled female labor. In patriarchal Russia, women workers were at a particular disadvantage in the new industrial slums. At work, women were harassed, abused, and raped by male foremen and supervisors and treated with scorn by their male coworkers, who sometimes treated female workers as prostitutes. The fact that women tended to populate the lowest-paid and least-skilled echelons of workers meant that they were easily replaced, so a woman who refused sexual advances or stood up in any way to abuse could easily be fired. Domestic workers had even less protection and privacy: only the most elite Russian homes provided bedrooms for their servants, and most domestic workers slept on cots in kitchens or hallways; domestic servants were highly vulnerable to the sexual advances of the men in the families where they worked.

A woman who lost her job or who was paid too little to support herself might be forced to turn to prostitution. Prostitution was regulated after 1843, but many women engaged in casual prostitution, exchanging sex for money only when they were desperate. These women ran the risk of arrest because they were violating the laws that regulated prostitution, but the oversupply of labor combined with very low wages left many with no alternatives to selling their bodies. Women in these circumstances did not want to register as prostitutes, which would require them to carry a yellow passport that would identify them forever as "public women." The state's regulation of prostitution was inspired by the desire to limit the spread of venereal diseases, which the government felt was reaching epidemic proportions in the mid-nineteenth century, particularly among soldiers and sailors. For those women who did register as prostitutes, the police required regular physical examinations in an effort to control the spread of venereal disease; male clients were not required to have the examinations. The police knew that many women operated outside the system of legalized prostitution and conducted periodic roundups of lower-class women in the working-class slums of the cities, around barracks and factories, and in bars. Any unmarried woman who was found to have a venereal disease was forced to register as a prostitute.[20]

Despite the dangers that urban life presented women, many peasant women who moved to the city enjoyed far more independence than village life would ever afford them and chose to stay in the city. It was possible for women, particularly those who were literate, to obtain training in skilled work and make a reasonable living outside the restrictions of the peasant family. In the years before World War I, new respectable amusements became more available to women—public gardens, worker theaters, and even inexpensive movie tickets could provide entertainment for women workers who had the leisure and the means to enjoy them. Women also sometimes became involved in the socialist and union movements that began underground in the 1890s but exploded into legal activity after 1905. Most women workers did not have the time for political or union activity, which concentrated on the concerns of male workers without considering the special problems women faced, but still, the opportunity for involvement existed, and some women took an active role in organizing workers and spreading radical propaganda among their coworkers.

CHANGES IN URBAN LIFE

Throughout the imperial period, Russian urban centers housed very diverse populations. The merchant classes did not experience a great deal of change in their status or lifestyle with the Petrine reforms or with emancipation but continued to live in much the same way that they had in the previous centuries. The biggest change in urban life came with the ever-increasing influx of workers and professional people generated by industrialization. Worker slums developed in the suburbs and brought with them the problems that rapid industrialization always brings. This changed the character of Russian urban life as cities expanded in new ways and the population shifted to the suburbs. Working-class life differed from that of the other urban groups and also from peasant life in many ways, but workers retained many of the habits of the village. Whereas some historians have suggested that workers became far less religious than peasants, others argue that workers manifested the same deep belief in Orthodoxy even if they attended church less regularly. The Church continued to control marriage and divorce, and most children were baptized. The Church also dictated the calendar, which designated holy days and holidays for the workers. The traditional family hierarchy with the man as patriarch and the woman responsible for the housework remained unchallenged. Alcohol consumption continued to be very high among workers and was an important part of the male worker social scene, just as it was in the village.

NOTES

1. Thomas Riha, ed., *Readings in Russian Civilization, vol. 1: Before Peter the Great, 900–1700* (Chicago: University of Chicago Press, 1969), 7–8.

2. Janet Martin, *Medieval Russia, 980–1584* (Cambridge: Cambridge University Press, 1995), 60.

3. George Vernadsky, *Kievan Russia* (New Haven: Yale University Press, 1973), 61.

4. J. Michael Hittle, *The Service City: State and Townsmen in Russia, 1600–1800* (Cambridge: Harvard University Press, 1979), 21.

5. The word *kremlin* simply means fortress; all urban centers had a kremlin in the early modern period; "the Kremlin" refers to the fortified center of Moscow where the tsars lived and built their most important cathedrals.

6. Hittle, 23–61.

7. Catherine Evtuhov, David Goldfrank, Lindsey Hughes, and Richard Stites, *A History of Russia: Peoples, Legends, Events, Forces* (Boston: Houghton Mifflin Company, 2004), 176.

8. Hittle, 62–69.

9. Elise Kimmerling Wirtschafter, *The Structures of Society: Imperial Russia's "People of Various Ranks"* (DeKalb: Northern Illinois University Press, 1994), xii, 22, 165 n. 33.

10. John T. Alexander, *Catherine the Great: Life and Legend* (New York: Oxford University Press, 1989), 191; Hittle, 221.

11. Janet M. Hartley, *A Social History of the Russian Empire, 1650–1825* (London: Longman, 1999), 164.

12. Hittle, 162–163, 201.

13. Hittle, 100–101.

14. Quoted in Hittle, 88.

15. Hittle, 221; Alexander, 191.

16. Alexander, 80.

17. Alexander, 156–160.

18. Alexander, 149–161.

19. Reginald E. Zelnik, trans., ed., *A Radical Worker in Tsarist Russia: The Autobiography of Semen Ivanovich Kanatchikov* (Stanford: Stanford University Press, 1986).

20. Barbara Alpern Engel, *Women in Russia 1700–2000* (New York: Cambridge University Press, 2004), 64–65.

6

Lifestyle, Traditions, and Rituals

Daily life in Imperial Russia varied enormously depending on time, place, and social status. Some of the customs and traditions of Kievan times survived into the imperial period, but many others did not. Russian culture was also affected by its interactions with other cultures—steppe peoples, Byzantium, Poland, and Lithuania were among the most important of these contacts for the early period. Some aspects of Russian culture transcended social divisions—Orthodoxy, for example, formed an important part of daily life for all Russians. Of course, Russia's expansion added many non-Russians to the empire, and their lives were often regulated by other religious traditions; the most numerous of these people of other faiths were the Jews and the Muslims. These cultures fall outside the scope of this book, but it is important to note that Russians often lived in close proximity to people of other faiths, particularly Russians who lived closer to the borders of the empire. Although the observance of Orthodox traditions might vary from town to country, elite to commoner, all Russians were baptized, married, and buried within Orthodox tradition. All Russians were subject to the moral, liturgical, and ritualistic demands of the Orthodox faith. Within this framework, however, the changing political and economic context had profound consequences for the way that Russians of all social groups lived. In this chapter, we explore changes in diet, clothing, and housing as well as the beliefs, rituals, and traditions that surrounded the common experiences of marriage and family life and developments in Russian education and culture, some of which created deep divisions among the different social groups in Russia.

DIET

The Kievan Rus were a remarkably healthy people for the time, and this is partially due to their diet. The Kievan diet was much healthier than the later diet, and the Rus were meticulous about keeping bread and water clean and out of the reach of their animals. The Rus consumed mostly bread (wheat in the south and rye in the north) and meat—beef, mutton, pork, goose, fowl, duck, pigeons, cranes, and every kind of game.[1] For the Orthodox, Wednesdays and Fridays were supposed to be meatless, as were three periods of fasting (fish was acceptable). Eggs, dairy products, and vegetables were also eaten, and for the poorer families, millet or oat porridge was an important part of the diet. In the sixteenth and seventeenth centuries, imported spices—pepper, ginger, cloves, saffron, and coriander—became more common. No distilled liquor was made during the Kievan period, but *kvas* (a mildly alcoholic beverage usually made from rye bread), mead, and beer were common. The Church imported wine from Greece for use in Church rituals, and the prince also sometimes imported wine. Although gold and silver dishes, spoons, and goblets were used in the prince's house on state occasions, most people ate from pewter or wooden dishes, cups, and spoons. At banquets, men and women dined separately.

Before the Petrine reforms, the nobility ate the same food as the peasantry, albeit in greater quantity. Along with Western fashion, however, came Western food, and those who could afford to do so hired European chefs to prepare their food. New foods for the elite included cheese, foreign wines and liquor, and sugar. Elite households ate in courses, beginning with soup, fish or fowl, vegetables, and roasted meats, although foreign visitors still reported much use of onion and garlic in the eighteenth century. One visitor observed that Russians ate raw garlic throughout the day and considered it to have strong medicinal purposes. Local fruit such as melons, apples, cherries, and plums—and eventually imported pickled lemons—were important parts of the diet.[2] By Catherine II's day, Russians had built hothouses where they could grow more exotic fruits such as oranges for elite consumption. Of course, the separation of the sexes at banquets ended; large, elegant dinners became important social events and could take hours to finish. By the nineteenth century, sumptuous dinners with several meat and fish courses began at four in the afternoon and were the main meal of the day.

In contrast to the changes in the diet for the elite, the peasant diet became more restricted to grains and vegetables during the imperial period. Meat was usually relegated to feast days, although lard and butter were often used to flavor the cabbage or beet soup and the porridge (*kasha*) that most peasants ate on a daily basis. Fat was an important part of the peasant diet, and when lard or butter was not available, or during fast days, peasants flavored their soup and *kasha* with vegetable oil. Dairy products were also used sparingly, largely because dairy animals were expensive to raise; milk, sour cream, and butter were used as seasonings in various dishes, although small children and infants were frequently given milk to drink. Fish was a more common form of protein for those who lived near rivers but was not consumed on a daily basis by most peasants. Salted or pickled fish was often consumed in small quantities, and dried fish could be used to thicken soups or porridge. Vegetables from peasant gardens formed an important, although not very large, part of their diet, and this varied from region to region depending on what would grow in the soil. Pickled vegetables were popular, particularly cucumbers, cabbages, mushrooms, and beets. Cabbage was the most widely available vegetable and was the main ingredient in the most common soup in much of Russia. Russians also ate turnips, radishes, and onions. Berries were the main fruit but were consumed in very limited quantities and were usually preserved. Rye bread constituted the largest proportion of the peasant's diet; rye was slowly replaced by wheat in the southern parts of the empire over the course of the nineteenth century. The most common bread was a sourdough black rye bread. The potato was introduced to Russia by the seventeenth century but was not widely cultivated until the 1840s, when the government made a concerted effort to expand potato production in the wake of poor harvests. In 1840 the Ministry of State Domains required state peasants to plant a certain amount of potatoes on their common lands. This decree sparked riots in 10 provinces that were serious enough to require troops to suppress. The peasants resented the decree, which required them to restructure their traditional farming methods for this new and, from the peasant point of view, highly uncertain crop. Old Believers called the potato the "devil's apple" and refused to cultivate or eat them. The violence of the peasant response prompted the government to repeal the decree, but production of potatoes had increased five times by 1843, and potatoes had become a staple in peasant diets by the late nineteenth century. One historian has estimated that grain and potatoes constituted from 60 to 80 percent of the peasant diet by the end of the nineteenth century.[3]

Orthodoxy affected the diet of all Russians. Fast days, during which no meat or milk products could be eaten, constituted from 196 to 219 days a year. The Church also disapproved of certain kinds of meat such as squirrel (because it was vermin), beaver and horsemeat (because they were unclean), and any meat from an animal that had been strangled or trapped rather than slaughtered, which would include hare, grouse, duck, and goose. This was particularly limiting for the peasantry, given that the hunting of larger game was a privilege restricted to the nobility.[4] This is not to say, of course, that Russians followed the restrictions all of the time; the prohibition on meat from strangled animals seems to have been widely ignored, but for peasants who followed the rules, options for meat were severely limited. Peasants could not usually afford to keep livestock for slaughter because of the enormous amount of fodder required to maintain them over the long winters. Peasants kept draft and more rarely dairy animals if they could. Those who did raise cattle did so for the market, so that beef became an urban luxury—indeed, in merchant households that could afford it, meals centered on meat on a daily basis. Feast days on the Orthodox calendar, weddings, and funerals called for special foods. During these times, peasants who could manage it ate meat and fish—this was often the only time peasants ate beef, but pork and lamb were more common—as well as special pies called *pirogi* filled with meat, fish, cabbage, cottage cheese, or fruit; thin pancakes rolled around fruit or cottage cheese called *blini*; or cream-filled puff pastries called *knyshi*.[5]

VODKA

Of course, no examination of the Russian diet is complete without a discussion of vodka. There is some debate among historians as to when vodka—distilled spirit—arrived in Russia, but it was sometime between the fourteenth and sixteenth centuries. We know that Ivan IV permitted the establishment of eight "strong drink houses" in Novgorod in 1544.[6] The sale and distribution of vodka was regulated by the government, which made a good portion of its revenues from vodka. The manner of regulation varied over time from selling licenses to drink houses or vodka farmers to sell distilled spirits to an outright government monopoly on the trade in vodka by the early twentieth century; after 1840, it became the single largest source of revenue for the state. The fact that it was so lucrative had to be weighed against the problems it presented to public health and safety, so that the imperial government had a love-hate relationship with the libation. The ideal solution was to teach the peasantry to drink regularly and in moderation, but this directly opposed traditional Russian use of distilled spirits, which remained stubbornly conservative despite all attempts of the state and the gentry to change peasant drinking patterns. Traditionally, vodka was not an everyday drink for Russian peasants. Instead, it was a vitally important part of village feasts and celebrations, during which peasants drank huge amounts of vodka. Vodka was also used to mark other solemn occasions—to seal a business deal or a marriage contract, for example. At these times as well, vodka was consumed to great excess. Anecdotal evidence strongly suggests that everyone drank—men, women, teenagers, and even young children partook of vodka on appropriate occasions. Vodka was also used as a part of the village patronage system and as a bribe to village officials or to swing votes a certain way within the village commune. Until the nineteenth century, most Russians did not drink vodka often, but when they did drink it, they did so to get drunk.

Over the course of the nineteenth century, Russia moved slowly toward a cash economy, and more taverns appeared, providing peasants more opportunities to drink, but their pattern of drinking vodka to get drunk did not change; more people were drunk more often. As access to vodka became easier, drunkenness increased, and associated problems rose as well—abuse of spouses and children, alcohol-related illness and death, crime, and public violence to name only a few. Peasant families afflicted with a drunken patriarch fell deeper into poverty. Most villages had a couple of families afflicted with a chronic drunk, and those families were often the poorest in the village. As peasants moved into urban industry, they took their drinking habits with them; drink constituted a real problem for factories as workers came to work drunk or hungover, drank on the job, or failed to show up to work altogether. For the emerging working class, the city offered little in the way of leisure-time amusement other than the local tavern, and workers flocked to bars in droves. Wives of workers would sometimes wait outside the factory gates on payday to be sure that their husbands did not drink all of their wages. Both men and women drank, but women tended to drink at home or in the homes of friends because women who appeared in taverns were considered little better than prostitutes. By the twentieth century, several temperance movements had begun both among the affluent and among peasants, but the problem of drunkenness was not solved, even with the institution of prohibition at the beginning of Word War I.[7]

CLOTHING

Clothing in Kievan Rus was simple and warm. The lower classes dressed in the same style as the upper classes but used cheaper materials and decorated their clothing with embroidery rather than jewels or precious metals. The poorest women wore sheepskin cloaks in the winter, but wealthier women wore fur—sable or beaver for the very wealthy elite, marten or squirrel for the less wealthy. Both men and women wore fur caps made of sable or beaver. Peasants from the forest regions wore woven bast shoes of willow, birch, or oak bark. Men usually wore linen shirts and pants in the summer and put woolen caftans or cloaks over them in the winter. Princes and very wealthy boyars sometimes wore silk or brocaded clothing. Coats or cloaks made of sheepskins, bear, wolf, or marten served as outer garments during the winter. For state occasions, princes and princesses wore Byzantine dress—ornate robes for the prince trimmed in gold with leather boots and a long dress with wide sleeves and gold accessories (belts, earrings) for the princess. Both men and women wore elaborate headdresses: a prince might wear a fur cap with a crown of fabric or a high fur cap; a princess would certainly have her hair covered with some sort of kerchief or shawl. For everyday circumstances, women usually wore linen blouses and woolen skirts in the summer or sleeveless dresses covered by the blouse. Wealthy women might substitute silk for linen and brocaded materials for the skirt. Later, in the Muscovite period, women often wore a belted underdress with long embroidered sleeves and substituted a *sarafan* or sleeveless robe for the overskirt. In the winter, women might wear a fur cloak with slits for the hands. Married women covered their hair, sometimes with a scarf or kerchief or with an elaborate headdress for ceremonial occasions. Men usually wore felt hats with high crowns in the summer, and women wore headbands in the shape of an open

Antique dress of a peasant woman from Olonetskaia Province (Starinnyi kostium krest'ianki Olonetskoi gub). Library of Congress, Prints & Photographs Division, Prokudin-Gorskii Collection, LC-DIG-prok-01958.

crown. Wealthy ladies would decorate the front of their headbands with jewels. Wealthy men wore leather boots dyed in bright colors or low leather shoes. Wealthy men and women wore jewelry, particularly belts, which were the most important accessory for men, decorated with gold and silver or jewels. Women wore necklaces and earrings made of silver, gold, or pearls.

Russian elite women were also noted for their use of makeup, which was used to enhance a healthy appearance—round rosy cheeks, white skin, and bright eyes. To this end, they used powder to whiten the skin, applied very red rouge to their cheeks, and put drops in their eyes to make them more lustrous. They plucked their eyebrows and drew in thin arched brows in black soot. Women often lined their eyes with soot and wore eye shadow out to their temples.

A group of Russian nobles called boyars, the Kremlin in the background, 1600s. North Wind Picture Archives.

Western observers were particularly shocked by the practice of blackening the teeth. It is not clear why women blackened their teeth, but it is not unlikely that it was to conceal discolorations and rot. Russian women did not wear corsets under their voluminous dresses—thinness was seen as a sign of ill-health and not valued—so foreign observers often commented that Russian women were fat, even though they could not have known how heavy women were under their loose clothing.

Peter forced the Russian elite to abandon their traditional dress and adopt the styles of western Europe. Before the eighteenth century, Russians of all classes dressed in the traditional manner, the distinctions of wealth appearing only in the quality of materials, the ornamentation, or the variety of clothes a person might possess. Peter the Great hated traditional Russian clothing. He saw it as a symbol of Russia's backwardness and her separation from western Europe. He also believed that for men especially, it inhibited work.

Tzar Peter I cutting the long sleeves of the boyars symbolically reducing the nobles' power. North Wind Picture Archives.

For boyars, caftans often included very long sleeves that kept hands warm but that also made working with their hands difficult. Boyars also wore high hats and long robes that Peter also believed inhibited movement and restricted their ability to work. As soon as he returned from his Grand Embassy, Peter immediately began to cut off boyars' beards and to insist that the Russian elite adopt Western clothing; for men this meant a uniform in the Western style—a three-cornered hat, knee-breeches, waistcoat, and tunic. Peter attempted to color-coordinate his army regiments, but this proved nearly impossible to achieve during his reign, although the elite units had designated colors: the Semenovskys wore dark blue, the Preobrazhenskys wore dark green, and the artillery units wore dark red.[8] For women, Peter introduced Western-style dress with corsets, bare arms, low neck-lines, and uncovered hair dressed in elaborate coiffures. In order to enforce his changes in dress, Peter instituted taxes on beards and on traditional clothing among the elite and for all who lived in or entered towns. These were radical changes for the upper class because the new costumes for men and women were designed to display the figure rather than to conceal it, but these changes were limited to the aristocracy and to the urban population. In the late nineteenth and early twentieth centuries, more people adopted Western-style dress, particularly in the cities, and these fashions

Russian noble and ladies in summer dress, 1700s. North Wind Picture Archives.

Peasant girls (Krest'ianskīia dievushki), Russian empire, early twentieth century. Library of Congress, Prints & Photographs Division, Prokudin-Gorskii Collection, LC-DIG-ppmsc-03954.

followed the changes in fashion in Paris, becoming more ornate and cumbersome in mid-century when hoopskirts and tight corsets were in vogue and giving way to a sleeker silhouette by the end of the century. Merchant women wore an interesting combination of Western fashion and traditional Russian hairstyles and headdresses. Working women favored simpler costumes, often wearing a simple *sarafan* with a matching blouse or a plain calico skirt.[9] Peasants, who constituted the vast majority of Russians, continued to dress in their traditional manner throughout the imperial period.

HOUSING

Throughout Russian history, elite houses in both the cities and the countryside were almost always made of wood. A typical Kievan-period urban house had three parts—one main room with a large clay or brick oven used for heating and cooking and on top of which the family slept in winter, a hallway, and a smaller, unheated room for storage. The wealthiest people might have larger houses, but most could not afford to heat more than one or two rooms adequately for the winter. Each house had a "beautiful corner" where the icon stood surrounded by wreaths and candles. Around the house would be barns, stables, and a bathhouse. Windows were made of mica, and at night clay lamps, candles, or, for the very poor, wooden splinters provided light. All of the furniture was made of wood. The only exceptions to this type of housing were the princely palaces, made of stone and containing a large hall for the retinue and the terem where the women of the palace lived.[10] Cities were healthier in the Kievan period than later because they were not overcrowded, although occasionally epidemics struck the urban centers—people assumed that they were a result of God's wrath. The northern Russian custom of frequent use of the bathhouse also resulted in a cleaner population than was common in western or southern Europe. Bathhouses were a part of every northern Russian homestead. These were steam baths where Russians would sit and sweat, beating themselves with reeds and birch branches. After this, they rolled in the snow or doused themselves with cold water, repeating the process two or three times. These bathhouses were not as common in the south, but a large public Roman bath appeared in Kiev in the eleventh century.

Elite housing changed little until the time of Peter. As the elite embraced the cultural changes, they also had to change the way they built their homes because the traditional Russian houses could not hope to accommodate the large parties, balls, and salons that became an integral part of upper class life. These homes had to be decorated with Western art and furnished with Western furniture, and Peter imported foreign architects, artists, musicians, and actors not only to help develop the Russian skills in these areas but also to tutor Russians in Western taste. He insisted that nobles build Western-style mansions in St. Petersburg. Peter's sister, Natalia, and his closest associate, Alexander Menshikov, worked together to develop and plan certain parts of St. Petersburg to ensure that it reflected modern Western ideas of architecture and landscaping as well as urban planning in the form of sewers and paved roads. Elizabeth was also keenly interested in Western architecture and hired the Italian architect Count Bartolomeo Rastrelli to build the Winter Palace. Catherine II continued building in the new capital and encouraged her nobles to do the same. The demand for Western

The Hermitage (The Winter Palace in St. Petersburg). Marek Slusarczyk/ Dreamstime.

furniture and decorations led to the development of the decorative arts in Russia, particularly during the reign of Catherine II. By the end of the eighteenth century, the elite sections of the capitals closely resembled the elite neighborhoods of other European cities, with wide boulevards, well-tended English-style gardens, and huge mansions that could not only provide room for entertaining but also house a bevy of serf servants to run the household. The very wealthy nobility also built large mansions in the countryside, complete with extensive gardens.

MARRIAGE

For most people, daily life was dictated by the season of the year and was varied only by feast days, weddings, funerals, and births—all controlled by the Church. Although many of the Church holidays required fasting, fasts were followed by days of feasting. Other types of celebrations—weddings, harvests, and even funerals—included feasts, drinking, music, and sometimes dancing. Such festivals varied from region to region and from urban to rural settings. Weddings provided the most common reason for a holiday. Women in the upper classes, particularly princely families, could marry very young to cement alliances—one was recorded to have been married off at age 8—but for most people, marriage came later; Church law dictated that girls could marry at 12 and boys at 15.[11] From the eighth to tenth centuries, marriage was usually performed by a ritual abduction, with the consent of the bride, and sanctioned by the marriage god, Lado. With Christianity, new rituals were added, although many villages retained the old customs long after the adoption of Christianity. The Church dictated that children could not be married against their will. Marriages could be made only within the faith, and no marriage could be made between relatives to the sixth degree (second cousins), and usually only two marriages were allowed. The parents of the couple made a marriage contract, which, after the thirteenth century, had to be signed by the bride and groom as well. As a part of the betrothal, the priest would place a gold ring on the groom's right hand and an iron ring on the bride's to symbolize the union. The contract was celebrated by a feast, after which the groom could not back out of the marriage without paying a heavy fine. The couple then could not see one another until the wedding. Wedding days had to be chosen carefully because no wedding could occur on a holy day or a fast day (Wednesday and Friday) or during one of the penitential periods before Christmas or Easter. The traditional time for a wedding was spring or summer. The day before the wedding, the bride's parents would send the dowry to the groom's house, and gifts from the groom were sent to the bride's parents. The groom would often send the bride a small chest of pins and needles to ward off the "evil eye" and a small whip, symbolizing the husband's authority over his wife (in pagan times, it had been believed that lashing the wife with the whip would increase her fertility). On the night before the wedding, the bride took a ritual bath, and the water was saved because tradition held that its magical powers would excite love in her husband. Then the bride's hair was restyled from the single braid of a maiden into two braids crowned by a wreath. These rituals were overseen by the bride's female relatives and friends and could last all night.

On the day of the wedding, the women of the bride's family baked round loaves of bread decorated with figures of birds. These were given to the bride, and coins were scattered on the floor as wishes for a rich life. The bride dressed in her wedding clothes and was sprinkled with hops, which symbolized joy, and grain which

Russian peasant girls in holiday attire, early twentieth century. Library of Congress, Prints & Photographs Division, LC-DIG-npcc-20189.

symbolized prosperity. Fur coats, guaranteeing wealth and frightening evil spirits, and straw mattresses, promising an easy childbirth, were brought. Then the bride rode to the wedding ceremony and walked over fur rugs into the sanctuary. After a mass, the couple joined hands and exchanged rings; the priests placed wedding crowns on their heads, blessed them with incense, and prayed for a peaceful, long life with children and grandchildren. The wedding party then moved to the groom's house, shouting and cracking whips the whole way to ward off evil spirits. After being greeted with salt and bread for prosperity and happiness, the couple walked on fur rugs while being showered with coins, grain, and hops. The rest of the day was filled with traditional games to determine who would be the boss in the house—the first over the threshold, the first to break a wine goblet. The wedding feast consisted of kasha, pies, cold meat, and a chicken divided between the bride and groom; only the groom and his guests could drink alcohol. After the feast, the couple was escorted to the marriage bed made of straw mattresses, which were supposed to ease the bride's pain when the hymen broke. The Church levied fines against women who lost their virginity before marriage, and dowries reinforced the notion that female virginity was a necessary commodity in the marriage market. Marriage was the most important event in a woman's life, signifying her freedom from her parents. Even though she would now be subject to her husband, the position of wife carried with it many new privileges and responsibilities that only married women could enjoy.

Marriage rituals did not change much from those of Kievan times, although the advent of serfdom meant that most marriages had to take place within a village because landlords were reluctant to allow their female serfs to marry into a family belonging to another estate. Most landlords required that women who wished to marry into another estate ask for permission, and some landlords arranged for their villages to exchange brides. This could be a particular problem for small villages because of the Church's prohibition against marriage to relatives to the sixth degree, including those related through in-laws and through godparents. Marriages were usually instigated by a matchmaker, often a married female relative of the prospective groom, who would approach the prospective bride's mother to open negotiations. If the initial discussion was promising, the two families would work out the dowry and the bride-price. On the rare occasions that the groom moved in with the bride's family—which occurred only when the bride's family had no male heirs and needed the labor of a son-in-law—her family would pay a groom-price. After the agreements were made and the contract sealed by drinking vodka and clasping hands, it became binding. The groom and his family then visited the bride's house to inspect her to be sure that she was healthy and not pregnant; a feast followed. In much of Russia, the groom still "abducted" the bride on their wedding day, "bribing" the family with vodka and money before her family released the bride to go to the church. After the wedding, the party would then remove to the groom's household for a celebratory feast, where the bride's father presented the groom with a lash, symbolizing her transfer from her father's control to her husband's. The newlyweds were then bundled off to bed to consummate their marriage while the guests continued to celebrate, toasting the new couple into the late hours. The bride then moved into the household of her husband's family.

BIRTH

For all levels of society, children were an important part of survival. For the elite, children not only perpetuated the lineage but also provided valuable connections through marriage even after the system of mestnichestvo was abandoned. In lower-class and peasant families, children provided much-needed labor and security for parents in their old age. Although the Church applauded the birth of children as the fulfillment of God's desire to populate the earth with Orthodox Christians, children came from sex, and sex came from the devil. As a result, Church rules and rituals displayed a highly misogynistic attitude toward all the aspects of womanhood associated with sex and childbirth—sex, menstruation, and childbirth itself were all seen as unclean and potential pollutants to the purity of the church and of men. The exception to this was, of course, the virgin birth of Jesus. Because Mary had not experienced sex, the birth of Jesus was painless and proceeded from Mary's ear, rather than from her vagina. Since birth was painful as a punishment for original sin, it was unclean, as were all aspects of womanhood that contributed to it. Therefore, women were forbidden to enter the church while menstruating and for 40 days after birth until after they had ritually purified themselves. Although sex during menstruation and after birth were both prohibited, it was worse in the eyes of the Church to have sex during menstruation than to have sex after birth; menstruation indicated a failure to conceive, whereas the successful birth of a child showed a woman's worthiness—in fact, some churchmen argued that it was fine to have sex just 8 days after birth, even before the ritual purification that occurred after 40 days. Thus, the prohibition of sex during menstruation was linked less to the fear of female bleeding and more to the perception of a woman's failure to conceive a child. The emphasis on the impurity of childbirth could work in the woman's favor: women who were impure and isolated from family could not perform household tasks or penance, and this gave a woman the chance to recover from childbirth before returning to the myriad of duties that awaited her.

Peasant women usually gave birth in the bathhouse, with the aid of either a midwife or female relatives and friends—no men were permitted. These views and practices isolated women and cast their reproductive capacity in a negative light but also gave women control over their reproductive functions as husbands, fathers, brothers, and priests kept away from women who were menstruating, heavily pregnant, giving birth, or with a new baby. The bathhouse, the woman, the child, and the attendants all had to be ritually purified after the birth before they could resume their normal activities. In addition, no one was permitted to eat in the presence of a new mother until after she was ritually purified. To preserve a newborn infant from feeding from the impure mother, a wet nurse could be hired, or the baptism of the child could be delayed until the 40th day, when the mother would be purified, thereby liberating the infant from the rules regarding eating in the presence of its mother. The afterbirth was usually buried under the house or placed in a casket in the "beautiful corner" of the house in order to dedicate it to the Virgin. Some midwives believed that ingesting a part of the placenta would either help a woman to conceive or prevent conception. The cradle was blessed before the infant was placed in it. The infant was christened on the eighth day and usually baptized and welcomed into the community of believers on the fortieth day, right after the ritual purification of the mother.[12]

The point of marriage was to have children—the Church, state, commune, landlords, and householders all agreed on that point. Childbirth practices changed little from the pre-Petrine era—throughout the eighteenth and nineteenth centuries, childbirth continued to be viewed as a time of pollution, shrouded in mystery and hidden from view, usually in a bathhouse or a barn. The village midwife, who had no formal training, and older women of the household would assist in childbirth, but all of the traditions and rituals were geared toward warding off evil spirits, not toward creating a clean and hygienic environment. The locations chosen for birth were unsanitary and provided excellent conditions for infection and illness. Childbirth was a very dangerous time for women at all levels of society and all over Europe because the connection between hygiene and infection was not recognized until the mid-nineteenth century; for peasant women, childbirth was particularly dangerous because they often entered into it undernourished and overworked. The rate of infant and child mortality was very high. The earliest statistics available are from the last third of the nineteenth century, when 25–30 percent of all children born in European Russia died before age two, and almost half of all children died by age five.[13] There is no reason to believe that the death rates in the eighteenth century were any lower, and they certainly may have been higher. Children died from a variety of illnesses caused by the highly unhygienic conditions of the overcrowded peasant household and the means by which busy and often undernourished peasant women tried to calm hungry infants. The peasant pacifier, or *soska,* made from grain or bread that was chewed up and bound in an often dirty rag, was stuffed in the hungry baby's mouth. Infants were also fed solid food as soon as possible, again by the caregiver chewing bread soaked in water or milk and then feeding it to the baby. Babies suffocated in beds, and although sometimes this happened by accident, sometimes mothers practiced infanticide when an infant was sickly. Girls were more likely to die in this fashion than boys. Many women died during childbirth or as a result of complications during birth, and the impurity of the situation presented special problems for funereal rites. Priests were prohibited from entering the building where a woman was giving birth, so if a woman was dying, she had to be washed and taken to another building for communion and last rites. The body of a woman who died after giving birth could not enter the church; her funeral had to take place outside or in the entryway to the church. Newborns in danger of dying were baptized as soon as possible. Special ceremonies existed for baptizing even partially born infants who were expected to die as well as twins and triplets who were expected to die. In all cases, the baptism or last rites had to be performed outside the church and in the manner that would spread the contamination of childbirth to the least number of people.

As more of the population moved into the cities in the late nineteenth century, the rituals surrounding childbirth necessarily changed—urban working women did not have access to bathhouses and usually had to give birth in their homes if they did not do it on the shop floor; before 1912, no provisions existed for maternity leave for women workers, and most simply worked until they gave birth and then returned to work immediately, taking the baby to the factory in a basket. After 1912, women were entitled to two weeks leave before and four weeks leave after giving birth at one-quarter of her salary if she had been working for 26 weeks, but few women could afford to take the leave with so little pay, and even fewer actually knew about the law.[14] The religious taboos and rituals that surrounded childbirth in the countryside had to be abandoned under these conditions. Working-class infants suffered extraordinarily high mortality rates as well; working mothers had to stop nursing much sooner than peasant women and had less access to fresh milk. In one working-class St. Petersburg district in 1912, 400 of every 1,000 children born died within a year. Working-class women had very little access to contraception and used traditional folk remedies to limit pregnancy—withdrawal, taking hot baths, or drinking chamomile.[15] After the turn of the century, various groups began to debate issues of sexuality, contraception, and abortion from a medical and social rather than a religious point of view. Abortion was illegal throughout the imperial period, but the number of abortions increased two and a half times between 1900 and 1914.[16] Women's groups introduced the idea that women should have the right to decide whether or not they bore children and argued that many women were forced into motherhood against their will. Medical conferences discussed women's sexuality along with other issues concerning women's health, removing that discussion for the first time from the purview of the Church.

DISEASE AND DEATH

Although infants and small children may have been particularly susceptible to infectious diseases, diseases were a problem for everyone. In the Kievan period, people who got sick or wanted help conceiving or aborting a child often turned to village "witches" who would provide them with a potion or an amulet. This practice was very widespread and very much condemned by the Church, even when done to achieve a laudable goal, such as conception. The Church viewed these as pagan practices and as the work of the devil and fought long and hard to convince people that obtaining help from such women was hazardous to their souls and their very salvation. People who confessed to using such potions or charms were given severe penances, as were the providers of such services. Despite the Church's efforts, old rituals lingered, although often with Christian overtones. Peasants viewed epidemics as God's punishment for sin, and many of their rituals that were meant to appease God spread the disease. Priests would lead villagers in a ceremonial procession from house to house, visiting all of the infected people to bless them, effectively exposing the entire village to the disease. Mothers would distribute a dead child's clothing to her neighbors as a blessing, again spreading disease. The coffins of those who succumbed to illness were left open, and mourners would often kiss the corpse. Although Russian doctors kept up with medical discoveries in the West, they could not implement them effectively, particularly in the vast rural areas of Russia. Catherine the Great introduced the smallpox vaccine to Russia in 1768, but less than half the population had been inoculated by 1850.[17] Other common causes of illness and death were diarrhea, dysentery, influenza, measles, syphilis, and typhus as well as fungal diseases caused by eating moldy rye. Most deaths occurred in the spring and summer, when the warm weather helped to spread infectious diseases and gastrointestinal problems increased.[18]

Funerals also followed traditional patterns. When possible, last rites were given by the village priest. After death, the body was laid out in the house with its head under the icons, and an older woman would read the Psalter over the body. The older women of the village would wash and prepare bodies for burial, closing the eyes and the mouth and following careful rituals to give them protection from the (spiritually) unclean dead. Bodies were often buried with food, tools, and coins to assist the dead during their 40-day journey from this world to the next. After interment, the family would hold a wake. During the next 40 days, special services and feasts were held to help the dead with this journey. One historian has noted that Russians associated death with women—women cared for the dead, and the image of death was a woman with a scythe—arguing that they viewed the afterlife as the world stood on its head, as women took revenge on the patriarchal world.[19] All funeral rites, of course, were dominated by the Church. Cemeteries were laid out near churches for the ordinary people, whereas princes were placed in sarcophagi in the crypt of the cathedral of the prince's capital. Prayers were said for the dead, and in some cases, professional mourners might be hired for the occasion. The wealthy would often bequeath a portion of their property to a monastery to ensure that prayers would be said for their souls, but others had to rely on relatives to continue praying for them. The village church would offer up a list of names at every Mass for the departed souls of the parish. For the lower classes, women sometimes became the heads of households when their husbands died, and all women had the right to inherit substantial portions of their husband's property. Among the elite, a widow could become very wealthy depending on her husband's will. On the other hand, a woman could enter a convent upon her husband's death. Convents could be havens for elite women who wanted to escape direct male control, but they could also be prisons—men could send unwanted wives or mothers into a convent to get rid of them, and unmarriageable daughters were sometimes consigned to the convent as well.

SEXUALITY

Family life as described by canon law and the writing of churchmen prescribed a household led by the father—"the man is the head of his wife; the prince is the head of the man; and God is the head of the prince." Various biblical passages that emphasized the wife's subordination to the husband were to guide the couple

through life. Women were supposed to be quiet, humble, and submissive, and husbands were supposed to firm—beating a wife was
acceptable as a form of control. Evil women manipulated their husbands, according to the Church, creating weak men. A good wife
was "God-fearing, ascetically chaste, indifferent to her own welfare, and ready to fulfill any task for her husband."[20] Marriage for
the Church was seen as a necessary compromise for most people;
the celibate life was better, but the Church recognized that most
people could not aspire to such a life. The best form of marriage
was the chaste marriage—again a state that most people could not
hope to maintain. As a result, sex within marriage was seen as a
necessary evil both to produce children and to allow the natural
human weaknesses to be honorably satisfied—but not too often
and in very limited ways. Lust and love were seen as unconnected
emotions; lust and sex came from the devil, love from God. On the
other hand, spouses were discouraged from refusing sex to their
partners on the theory that this might drive the partner into more
sinful activity such as masturbation, adultery, rape, or sex with animals. Having fully acknowledged that most people were incapable
of escaping the sin of sexual activity, the Church sought to control it
within marriage. Having children justified marital sex, but Church
law regulated when and how married couples could engage in sex
even for the purposes of procreation. Sex was forbidden on days
of religious observance (Sundays or holy days) or bodily purification (Saturdays and the day before other holy days, which occurred
often throughout the year). Wednesdays and Fridays, which were
fast days, were also taboo, as were the four annual Lents: before
Easter, Christmas, Feast of Saints Peter and Paul, and St. Philip's
Week. Sexual activity was forbidden while a woman was menstruating and for 40 days after giving birth—although sex during pregnancy was not prohibited. One historian has calculated that couples
who scrupulously followed the rules above would be unable to
have sex 300 days of the year.[21] The only acceptable method was
vaginal intercourse in the missionary position with the husband
on top (sex with the woman on top was viewed as a violation of
the divine order of the universe and carried as strict a penance as
incest or adultery). Any other time or position was sinful and had
to be confessed and repented. The Church was clearly very concerned about sexual behavior considering that most of the penitential questions (questions asked by the priest during confession)
involved sex. Anyone who violated the many prohibitions on sex
was forbidden communion and often even entry into the church

until they had performed the appropriate penance, which might consist of a fast (no meat or milk products on Mondays, Wednesdays, and Fridays) of a few weeks, months, or years; special prayers; prostrations; abstention from communion for a period; or exclusion from the church for a period. Even couples who had engaged in the right kind of sex at the right time were forbidden to enter the church until they had bathed. A wife's primary job was to produce children and raise them to be good Christians; therefore, contraception, abortion, and infanticide were all serious sins and virtually analogous in terms of their seriousness.

DIVORCE

Sexual pleasure was not important to the Church, but marital happiness was. The Church believed that marriage was an important and necessary institution—it produced new Christians, created structure for the society, and allowed an outlet for sexual desire. On the other hand, marriages were made for economic and political reasons, not for love or sexual attraction; therefore, it is not unlikely that many spouses welcomed the opportunity to limit sexual contact by following the restrictions that the Church imposed. Because marriage was important, the Church permitted divorce only for limited reasons—a man could divorce (in fact was required to divorce) an adulterous wife, and adultery was defined broadly to include any type of unseemly interaction with outside men (eating or drinking with them) or attending amusements outside the home without the husband's permission. Both husband and wife could divorce for impotence, infertility, or financial impairment or if one of the couple wished to take monastic vows. By the fourteenth century, a woman could divorce her husband if he sold himself into slavery without telling her or if he accused her of witchcraft or murder or made insinuations about her chastity without cause. Because divorce was difficult to get and involved a lot of red tape, most unhappy couples simply stopped living together rather than going through the trouble of a divorce. Of course, without an official divorce, remarriage was not permitted. For women whose husbands went off to war and simply disappeared, the issue of remarriage was a real problem until a law in the fourteenth century allowed divorce after three years of non-communication by a spouse. Men who abandoned their wives were supposed to pay a fine to the Church and a large sum to the abandoned wife to compensate for her shame. Princes sometimes shipped wives off to convents against their will in order to remarry, but the Church did not permit divorce for blindness, deafness, lameness, or chronic illness.

THE PEASANT HOUSEHOLD AND FAMILY LIFE

After marriage, the bride moved in with her husband's family. The peasant household usually consisted of several generations: a husband and wife and their grown male children along with their wives and children. The head of the family, the *bol'shak,* controlled the household, deciding how to allocate work and consumption; he had absolute authority in his home. Of course, traditions also governed who did what work—women were exclusively responsible for the home, the children, cooking, sewing, the garden, and small livestock. Men were responsible for the fields, buildings, and large livestock. Women often worked with men. For example, women routinely helped with the harvest and cared for the livestock; when men were away, at war for example, women would take over all of the farm work. Men almost never did women's work. Preparing fields and planting were considered to be male tasks, although the increasing military and labor conscriptions of the eighteenth century meant that fewer men were in the countryside, and women often had to undertake even the tasks believed to be exclusively male. With the advent of the three-field system, harvesting came to be increasingly done by women because men were often busy preparing or planting the next crop. Men and women both worked all day to keep the household running. Water had to be carried in, flour had to be ground, bread had to be baked, and grains, vegetables, and meats had to be properly processed and stored so that they would not spoil. Women spun thread, wove cloth, and sewed and mended clothing. Men and women both tended to farm animals and kitchen gardens. Child care was the purview of the women of the household, but particularly during harvest season, children were often left to fend for themselves. The main goal of child rearing was to teach the children how to do the tasks necessary to keep a household running. Girls began helping the women as soon as they were old enough; it was not uncommon for a five- or six-year-old girl to be left in charge of the smaller children while the older girls and women worked in the fields. As soon as boys were old enough, five or six, they would begin to go to the fields with the men, learn the skills needed to farm, and begin helping to care for livestock. Peasant children were not educated, except on very rare occasions, nor was it thought necessary to allow children to play—a very modern notion, not in vogue for the lower classes in most of Europe until the nineteenth or even twentieth centuries. The purpose of child-hood was to learn to be an adult, with all of the duties that required. Corporal punishment was the preferred method of correction, the popular biblical phrase "spare the rod and spoil the child" forming the sum total of most peasants' notions of discipline.

The village was composed of peasant households, and it controlled the pattern of life for its inhabitants. Household size and composition varied over time and space—hardly surprising in a country as large as Russia—but overall, households continued to be multigenerational and patrilocal (newlyweds moved in with the husband's family). Peasant homes remained unchanged from the pre-Petrine period, centering on the large stove in one corner, upon which the family, particularly the older generation, would sleep in the winter, and the icon in the corner directly opposite. Peasants married early—on average, the peasant woman married between the ages of 16 and 18, and peasant men married between 18 and 20. Early marriage increased the chances of fertility, leading to more workers for the fields. Landlords, communes, and heads of households all insisted on early marriage—more births meant more workers, which spread the burden of taxes and conscription and also allowed more land to come under production. For the household, the more male souls they had, the more land they received, so the bol'shak would insist on his sons marrying as early as possible. The high levels of infant and child mortality and early death rates encouraged families to produce as many babies as possible in order to maintain the workforce and to help to care for the older members of the household.

In the extremely patriarchal peasant household, the newest daughter-in-law would find herself at the bottom of the family hierarchy, subject to the authority of her new mother-in-law, who ruled over the females in the household and assigned work as she saw fit, and her new father-in-law, who dominated the entire family. The bol'shak wielded absolute authority in the household, even in demanding sexual favors from his daughters-in-law, a practice common enough to have its own word in the Russian language, *snokhachestvo*. The new daughter-in-law's status was dependent on her husband's relationship with his father and on her success producing children, preferably male children. Violence was common in the peasant household: parents beat their children as a disciplinary measure; husbands beat wives whenever they felt it necessary or when they were drunk. Wives occasionally beat their husbands, and physical fights between brothers or in-laws were not uncommon. In such cramped and overcrowded conditions, peasant families easily got on one another's nerves, contributing to the high levels of violence. Traditional values and even the Church encouraged men to beat their wives in order to maintain discipline and order. Particularly in the nineteenth and twentieth centuries, high levels of drunkenness also contributed to violence against both women and children and among the various members of the household and community. As long as the violence was contained to a household, the commune would likely ignore it. When violence began to disrupt village life, the commune might step in to restore order. The most vulnerable people in any village were the soldatka and her children. Without the protection of her husband, a soldier's wife had no defense against the whims of her in-laws and was often subject to sexual and physical abuse and sometimes was forced to take her children and leave the household entirely. This was not a change from the pre-Petrine period, but the higher rates of conscription spread the misery of the soldatka to many more families and resulted in increasing resentment toward them as useless extra mouths to feed and uncontrolled sexual predators competing with the other women of the village.

IMPACT OF THE PETRINE REFORMS

For the peasant household, Peter I's new conscription practices were not a great change from former times, but they were far more frequent and heavy than had been usual under previous tsars. Peter was at war so much of his career that the army needed a constant supply of new recruits. It seems that the heavier conscription rates offset one of the probable results of the poll tax, the breakup of the multigenerational household. For a long time, historians believed, based mostly on complaints registered by nobles, that the poll tax led to more households breaking up into smaller units. This was based on the assumption that the earlier practice of taxing households had contributed to more multigenerational households to avoid taxes and that the poll tax, which taxed all males equally regardless of their household, would allow the multigenerational households to break up. More recent scholarship, however, has indicated that the multigenerational household survived the tax changes. One explanation for its survival is that the heavy military conscription that occurred throughout the eighteenth century discouraged peasants from setting up smaller households that could not survive the loss of a man to conscription. The multigenerational household had definite drawbacks—the almost total power of the bol'shak over the lives of the other members, the crowded conditions, and difficult interpersonal relationships might all encourage young families to strike out on their own, but the dangers of breaking away from the parent household were serious enough to prevent most peasant families from breaking up. In addition, the bol'shak often went to great lengths to prevent his household from breaking up because that would undermine his control over his family and might enable his sons to challenge him in the commune. That is not to say that families never split apart, but the split was far more likely to occur in a household that had grown larger than necessary. Then an older son with nearly grown or adult sons might begin a new household on vacant land. Households also sometimes split up when the bol'shak died, but more often, one of his sons would take his place. If no adult males survived the bol'shak, his widow would become the head of household until one of her sons reached adulthood. Because households did not split up every generation, each village would have a combination of households of different sizes at any given time.[22]

MERCHANT HOUSEHOLDS

In terms of family life, merchant households tended to be somewhat smaller than peasant households, and nuclear families were more common than the multigenerational household. Wealthier urban households tended to be larger than poor ones, partly because their households might include servants, laborers, or apprentices in addition to their families. In order to retain their respectability, merchant families endeavored to keep their wives and daughters isolated from the public. Although a wife and even daughters might help in the family business, whenever possible they worked behind the scenes. Courting rituals for the merchant classes followed the traditional Russian pattern in that the young couple rarely chose one another. In an account of his marriage preparations in 1773, a young merchant wrote that at the behest of his father, he went to Moscow to "view" his prospective bride, and three days later, the fathers came to an agreement on the marriage. Mothers of girls of the merchant class in Moscow showed their daughters off by walking along a certain lane in the park so that matchmakers and prospective suitors could view the eligible girls.[23]

Merchant life changed little in the nineteenth century. Merchants rose early and spent the day at work. Wives of petty merchants helped in the business, but the wealthier merchant wives ran the home. Those who could afford to hired servants to do the actual work, but many of the less wealthy women did the work on their own. Merchant families with the means had summer homes outside the city with gardens that provided vegetables for the family. Merchant sons went to work with their fathers as soon as they were old enough and had received sufficient education—the most prosperous might send their sons on to higher education at a university. Merchant daughters spent their days in idleness, engaging in fancy needlework and visiting one another to gossip. Merchant families enjoyed an active social life, usually revolving around food and drink.

WORKER LIFE

The growing working class had a lifestyle very different from the merchants. Until the early twentieth century, the vast majority of industrial workers were single men or men with families back in the village, and therefore, they did not live in family households. Peasants who went to work in industry often followed earlier workers from their region to the same factories. Peasant-workers often formed artels in the city, living associations where a group of peasants from one region would share living quarters; they would pool their money to pay the rent and pay a woman to do basic cleaning, laundry, and cooking for them. The more skilled and prosperous workers in the artel would pay more and get more space, perhaps even a room to themselves in the house. The poorest paid workers would pay the least and share cots with one another. The older, more experienced workers were supposed to help look out for the younger workers—take them to church, oversee their education in the factory, and keep them out of trouble. Parents felt more secure leaving their sons and sometimes daughters in these artels, hopeful that older workers would keep their children in line. Most of the young people who went to the city expected to return to the village—young women often planned to earn their dowry in the factory; young men hoped to be able to expand the family's farmland. But sometimes the young people would enjoy the freedom of the city and begin to adopt an urban lifestyle; they might meet their future spouse in the city and decide not to return to the village. As time went on, more young people decided to marry and settle in

Laborers awaiting work at the Hill of Idleness. Types of Russian working people at Tumen (i.e., Tiumen), early twentieth century. Manuscript Division (George Kennan Papers), Library of Congress, LC-USZ62-123369.

the city, breaking their link to the countryside and developing into a class of true workers.

In his artel of about 15 men and boys, Kanatchikov was one of the lowest-paid workers and so shared with another apprentice a cot infested with bedbugs and fleas. The artel paid a woman to shop for them and to cook their noon meal:

All fifteen men ate from a common bowl with wooden spoons. The cabbage soup contained little pieces of meat. First, they would ladle out only the soup; then, when the soup was almost all gone, everyone tensely awaited a signal. A moment later someone would bang his spoon against the edge of the soup basin and say the words we were waiting for: "Dig in!" Then began the furious hunt of the spoons for the floating morsels of meat. The more dexterous would come up with the most. Avdotya, the cook, her sleeves tucked up and the hem of her calico-print dress pulled back, would look steadfastly at the bottom of the soup basin, saying: "Is there anything left, fellows, to dig out of there?" "Go ahead, Duniakha, dig away!" several voices would sing out in unison. Avdotya would carry the basin to the oven, refill it with cabbage soup, and return it to the table.

After the soup came either buckwheat gruel with lard or fried potatoes. Everyone was hungry as a wolf; they ate quickly, greedily.[24]

After eating and a brief rest, the men all rushed back to the factory for the afternoon shift. They were paid every other Saturday, and then they caroused. The older men would usually go out drinking while Kanatchikov and the other boys from his factory would brawl with boys from neighboring factories; his favorite amusement was watching the fires that plagued Moscow. His "guardian" was supposed to make sure that Kanatchikov did not deviate from his father's strict upbringing but instead confined himself to questioning the boy on his church attendance. Life for Kanatchikov was far less constricted than it had been in the village, except for his long hours in the factory.

Courtship among urban workers differed markedly from the countryside for the simple reason that parents were usually back in the village. For those men and women who did not have a spouse back in the countryside, new opportunities for love and marriage arose. For women workers, courtship in the city could be dangerous without the protection of her family and the pressure of the village. Male workers had more freedom to toy with unprotected women, and the rate of illegitimate births rose accordingly—in Moscow and St. Petersburg, illegitimate births outnumbered marriages in the working-class sections of the cities by the early twentieth century.[25] Working-class couples in the city did not have to go through matchmakers or traditional betrothal rituals. Married women of the working class stayed home if they could, but almost all continued to work in some way—some worked in the factories, but more married women earned money in other ways, such as taking in laundry or boarders. As in the early days of industrialization in the West, many women took their small children to work with them and found employment for them in the factory—girls as young as 10 worked in factories. Other women tried to find someone to watch their children while they worked, and still others simply left the children at home with no supervision.[26] Working-class women were responsible for all of the cooking, cleaning, laundry, and child care in addition to their paid labor. This was not a change from the village, but the extended family that had made this possible in the countryside only rarely existed in the city. Urban housing rarely included running water, which had to be carried in buckets to the apartment for cooking and cleaning. Bathing took place in the neighborhood bathhouse, if one was available, but only rarely because the bathhouse cost money to use. Urban women often had to do laundry in the city canals, which meant that they did not do it at all during the winter months. Refuse was simply tossed into the courtyard or stayed for days in the house until someone could remove it. Even though women managed the finances, working-class men expected to act as bol'shak in their family; while women worked and maintained the family, men worked and socialized at the local tavern.[27]

ELITE LIFE

Elite life centered on the capitals, Moscow and St. Petersburg. Over the course of the eighteenth century, the elite embraced Peter's social reforms so that they eventually lived in much the same way their European counterparts lived: Russian nobles attended parties, concerts, balls, and banquets. By the end of the century, the salon had appeared in Russia, adding to the social scene. All of these changes affected the way that the noble family raised its children and viewed family life but did not supplant all earlier notions of proper behavior. Although noblewomen were no longer confined to the terem, they were still supposed to exhibit chastity and submission with the goal of making a good marriage.

Part of the new emphasis on socializing was to encourage more interaction between men and women, which Peter hoped would lead to happier marriages and, therefore, more children. Peter was concerned about the population of Russia and expected all women to do their duty by bearing children. Men were expected to serve the state through military or civil service, and women were expected to serve the state as well by bearing and raising the next generation. To this end, Peter prohibited young women from entering convents, encouraged social interaction between young people, and decreed that no one could be forced into a marriage without consenting to it—parents could no longer present a young man with his bride sight unseen. The young couple had to be allowed to meet before the wedding, and both had to consent to the union. Although Peter's law prohibited forced marriage, most elite marriages were arranged, and almost all took place between older men and younger women. Noblemen who entered into state service very young often put off marriage until they had established a good career. It was not unusual for men to wait to marry until their late twenties or thirties or even later, particularly widowers whose first wives had died in childbirth. Women, on the other hand, married as early as 12, and noble parents usually tried to get their daughters married in their early teens, before they became willful. Because women married so young, it was unlikely that they had any real choice in the matter, instead just meekly obeying their parents' wishes as they had been brought up to do. Peter's desire to have all of his subjects marry put him at odds with the Church's preference for widows and widowers to live out their years alone and chaste. Peter ordered that young, marriageable widows were to be married off so that they could produce more children. Peter was not concerned about the happiness or rights of women, just in their usefulness as reproducers of population. That he was not particularly concerned about equity between the sexes is demonstrated by the legal position of women during his reign: Peter reinstated the practice of punishing women who killed their husbands for any reason by burying the murderess up to her neck in the ground and leaving her there until she died. A man who killed his wife, on the other hand, was punished by a beating with the knout. The punishment for rape was to pay the husband or father of the victim a certain amount based on the husband or father's status; the woman received nothing. Peter believed in hierarchy and discipline in the family, and women remained subservient to their husbands and fathers.

THE LESSER ELITES

Most of the gentry were not wealthy enough to live the life of the elite. Only one in five noble families owned the requisite one hundred serf families to pay for a lifestyle that included a house in one of the capitals and the whirlwind of social events enjoyed by the very wealthy.[28] The vast majority of noble families had far fewer serfs or none at all and had to struggle to survive on the meager salary that the state paid for noblemen's services or scratch out a living on a small estate. These noblemen made up the vast majority of middle-ranking officers and government servitors, particularly at the provincial level. Whereas the elite nobility had an active social life in the cities, engaged French or German tutors for their children, and traveled abroad, most gentry families could not afford such luxuries; their best hopes for the future lay in making good marriages for their children or in advancing their sons' careers in service. These families would educate their children as well as they could, sinking much more into their sons' education than their daughters'. For many of these families, the father would spend much of his time away from home, leaving his wife to manage the home and children while he was away serving the state.

Most noblewomen could expect to spend their lives isolated on distant provincial estates, managing the household on their own or with a few servants and struggling to raise their children. For this level of nobility, the Petrine reforms made life much more difficult and expensive; as husbands were forced to travel, their wives struggled to make ends meet and endeavored to scrape together enough money to educate, train, and dress their children to move into a better station in life.

Differences in the gentry lifestyle persisted in the nineteenth century, but more and more gentry fell into genteel poverty as they struggled to keep up with the financial requirements of the gentry lifestyle and increasing education requirements for state service. Many nobles mortgaged their estates or more commonly their serfs in order to meet their routine expenses. This practice was so widespread that at the time of the emancipation, one-third of all estates and two-thirds of all serfs were mortgaged to the state.[29] As the century wore on, the economic problems affected marriage patterns for both men and women. More and more of the lower-level nobles did not marry until very late in life because they could not afford a family. The lives of noblewomen and girls were affected by the economic problems in that the poorer noble families even in the capitals were less likely to be able to afford to launch their daughters into society to find a good husband.

MORALITY

The eighteenth-century changes in elite culture, particularly in the education and social duties of women, led to a great deal of concern over women's morality. Many conservatives felt that educating girls led to romantic notions of life and marriage that would ruin them as good wives and challenge their religious faith. There was also a good deal of concern over sexual morality, particularly in the second half of the eighteenth century, as social critics asserted that elite women used the social whirl to take lovers and have affairs almost as a sport. No concern was expressed for male morality because, as in the earlier period, the assumption was that women—in this case modern women—lured men into sinful behavior and that men simply had less control over their sex drives than did women. Social critics argued that women's reading should be carefully monitored and stressed that young girls should avoid novels and other romantic literature that would give them false notions of love and marriage. The ideal of the good Russian noblewoman continued to be that of a chaste, pure, meek wife who could efficiently run a large household but who could, if necessary, also be a charming and well-informed hostess, capable of impressing her husband's associates at all sorts of social gatherings with her wit, beauty, and talents. It is not surprising that few seemed able to live up to both sides of this ideal.

The Petrine changes had little effect on the activities of the lower classes, but the onslaught of industrialization and the increasing presence of working women caused a great deal of concern. We have already discussed the problems that working-class women faced, including the lack of protection from unscrupulous men and the assumption that any working-class woman might be a prostitute. The changes in education and the rising number of women in the new professions and in the service sector led to concerns over the morality of these women as well. Often from the impoverished gentry or the raznochintsy, the appearance of these women as teachers, midwives, or office workers generated a great deal of concern over their ability to protect themselves and their ability to be good mothers when exposed to these public environments. A high-ranking official remarked, "Can a woman be a good mother and a good housekeeper if she spends half the day in a bureau or an office filled with men, where liaisons are inevitably formed and demoralization occurs?"[30] Concerns of morality may have slowed the acceptance of gentle-born working women but could not stop it; women's involvement in the professions continued to rise steadily throughout the last years of Imperial Russia.

CONCLUSION

The changes caused by the emancipation and industrialization affected each of the social categories very differently, and we have already explored those changes in the chapters on the individual groups. Rituals and traditions, however, remained largely unchanged by these great events and continued to be practiced by gentry, merchants, and peasants much as they always had been throughout the imperial period, and the growing working class found new alternatives to the traditional rituals. Changes in lifestyle affected different groups at different times; the nobility's day-to-day existence was altered radically by the Petrine reforms, but the peasants and urban classes experienced far more change in the late nineteenth century. Despite these events, on the eve of World War I, many Russians' daily lives looked remarkably like they had at the beginning of the imperial period.

NOTES

1. Further information on clothing and diet for the Kievan period can be found in George Vernadsky, *Kievan Russia* (New Haven: Yale University Press, 1973), and for the later period in R.E.F. Smith and David Christian, *Bread and Salt: A Social and Economic History of Food and Drink in Russia* (Cambridge: Cambridge University Press, 1984), 8–9.

2. Smith and Christian, 8–9.

3. Smith and Christian, 251–287; Janet M. Hartley, *A Social History of the Russian Empire, 1650–1825* (London: Longman, 1999), 185–187.

4. Smith and Christian, 10–12.

5. Smith and Christian, 260.

6. Smith and Christian, 88–89.

7. Smith and Christian, 300–326.

8. Lindsey Hughes, *Russia in the Age of Peter the Great* (New Haven: Yale University Press, 2000), 73.

9. Natalia Pushkareva, *Women in Russian History from the Tenth to the Twentieth Century,* trans. Eve Levin (Armonk: M. E. Sharpe, 1997), 242–247.

10. Vernadsky, 300–303.

11. Details on wedding rituals are based largely on Pushkareva, 31–34.

12. Most of the detail on childbirth is taken from Eve Levin, "Childbirth in Pre-Petrine Russia: Canon Law and Popular Tradition," in *Russia's Women: Accommodation, Resistance, Transformation,* ed. Barbara Evans Clements, Barbara Alpern Engel, and Christine D. Worobec (Berkeley: University of California Press, 1991), 44–59.

13. David Moon, *The Russian Peasantry, 1600–1930: The World the Russian Peasants Made* (London: Longman, 1999), 25.

14. Pushkareva, 238.

15. Barbara Alpern Engel, *Between Fields and City: Women Work and Family in Russia, 1861–1914* (New York: Cambridge University Press, 1996), 216, 218.

16. Pushkareva, 239.

17. Nancy M. Frieden, "Child Care: Medical Reform in a Traditionalist Culture," in *The Family in Imperial Russia: New Lines of Historical Research,* ed. David L. Ransel (Urbana: University of Illinois Press, 1978), 237.

18. Moon, 26.

19. Christine D. Worobec, "Death Ritual among Russian and Ukrainian Peasants: Linkages between the Living and the Dead," in *Cultures in Flux: Lower-Class Values, Practices and Resistance in Late Imperial Russia,* ed. Stephen P. Frank and Mark D. Steinberg (Princeton: Princeton University Press, 1994), 11–13.

20. Pushkareva, 36–37.

21. Eve Levin, *Sex and Society in the World of the Orthodox Slavs, 900–1700* (Ithaca: Cornell University Press, 1989), 178. Most of the detail on sexual mores comes from this work.

22. For a detailed analysis on the structure of peasant households in this period, see Moon, 156–198.

23. Barbara Alpern Engel, *Women in Russia 1700–2000* (New York: Cambridge University Press, 2004), 60.

24. Reginald E. Zelnik, trans., ed., *A Radical Worker in Tsarist Russia: The Autobiography of Semen Ivanovich Kanatchikov* (Stanford: Stanford University Press, 1986), 9.

25. Engel, *Women in Russia,* 101.

26. Pushkareva, 225.

27. Engel, *Between the Fields and the City: Women, Work and Family in Russia, 1861–1914* (New York: Cambridge University Press, 1996), 206–214.

28. Engel, *Women in Russia,* 27.

29. Roberta Thompson Manning, *The Crisis of the Old Order in Russia: Gentry and Government* (Princeton: Princeton University Press, 1982), 9.

30. Quoted in Pushkareva, 237.

7

Conclusion: Radicals and Revolution

In the course of this book, we have examined the structure and lives of the various segments of the Imperial Russian population, but we have not yet touched on one of the most important developments of the late nineteenth century—the radical movement. This group constituted a tiny yet very important proportion of the population that focused attention on the problems that continued to plague Russia after the emancipation, and it posed a real challenge to traditional political, economic, and social structures as well as to the basic beliefs of the Russian people. It is important to note that the radical movement gained supporters from all segments of the population but was dominated and led by men and women of the gentry and professional classes. Their goal was to liberate the lower classes from the domination of the autocracy and the propertied classes. They saw themselves as the leaders of the peasants and workers and had many of the same paternalistic attitudes toward those groups that their ancestors had displayed. In spite of this, their desire to empower the lower classes sets them apart from all the reformers and rebels who preceded them. The emergence of this group was largely a response to the problems of daily life that we have covered so far—the huge disparity between the tiny wealthy minority and the huge impoverished majority, the oppressed condition of women, and the exclusion of the vast majority of Russians from political power. Ultimately, the radicals would spawn a group of revolutionaries that changed the lives of all Russians and put the country on an entirely new path with the Bolshevik Revolution of 1917.

THE INTELLIGENTSIA

The nineteenth century saw the emergence of a distinctive Russian intellectual movement that developed along with Russia's Golden and Silver Ages in literature and the arts. Although it may seem that the oppression that characterized Russia from 1815 to 1855 should have eclipsed any independent thought, it was precisely during this time period that Russian intellectuals and artists began most seriously to challenge the ideals of the government. This tension between official and traditional ideology and the emerging Russian intelligentsia created one of the most vibrant cultural and intellectual communities in Europe and led to the development of the revolutionary movement in the second half of the century.

The roots of the Russian intelligentsia can be found in the gentry who left government service in the aftermath of the Napoleonic Wars and to avoid the oppressive government of Nicholas I. As already noted, many of these men retired to their estates and immersed themselves in the Western philosophies of liberalism (which emphasized individual rights, rule of law, and the inviolability of private property and which generally hailed the progress of industrialization) and romanticism (which suggested that industrialization was destroying man's organic connection to nature and emphasized the importance of shared histories, cultures, and languages). By the 1840s, some of these men or their sons had begun to write philosophical treatises of their own, questioning the autocratic system in Russia. A schism quickly occurred in the young Russian intellectual movement, generated by the question of Russia's destiny. Two groups emerged: The Westernizers believed that Russia needed to continue on Peter's path of westernization. They believed that in order for Russia to continue to be an important force in Europe, she needed a constitutional government (opinions varied as to what kind of constitution), rule of law, freedom for the serfs, and industrialization. This group believed that Russia was backward and that she had no past to be proud of and no future to look forward to unless she quickly reoriented herself to follow the path of western Europe. The Slavophiles, who developed from the Romantic movement, believed that Russia had a special destiny that was connected to her role as the defender of Orthodoxy.

This school of thought idealized the Russian peasant commune as a uniquely Russian institution that proved Russia's superiority to the rest of the world. The commune showed that the Russian peasantry, the purest and least touched by westernization of all social groups, was naturally communal and cooperative. The Slavophiles feared industrialization, which would undermine the countryside and the commune, and believed that constitutions and laws merely inhibited the organic connection between tsar and people. Within these two very broad categories, there was much disagreement as to exactly how Russia should realize her greatness and even over what that greatness actually was, but over the course of the nineteenth century, these two broad frameworks shaped political and philosophical debate and would eventually shape the revolutionary movements as well.

It would seem on the face of it that Nicholas I's doctrine of Official Nationality would fit in well with the Slavophile stance, but Nicholas viewed the Slavophiles with as much suspicion as he did the Westernizers. Many Slavophiles advocated emancipation of the serfs and freedom of speech, two courses of action that Nicholas greatly feared. Much Slavophile literature resembles nationalism as conceived in the West, but Official Nationality differs from nationalism in that it bears no active role for any Russian other than the autocrat—the sovereign alone dictates action; the people must obediently carry out that action. The people do not need to understand their sovereign's will; they need only to submit to it, secure in their unquestioning faith in the knowledge that the sovereign, like a loving father or like God, knows what is best for his children. Whereas European nationalists argued that legitimacy emanates from a particular people and limits the body politic to those who share an ethnic, linguistic, or cultural heritage, Official Nationality assumes that legitimacy comes from the government and limits the body politic to the emperor who governs all those loyal subjects, regardless of origin, who share the bond. Although many Slavophiles would agree that the tsar should be the absolute autocrat of Russia, most disagreed with Nicholas's methods and yearned for a free society where the peasants would be able to pursue their own interests without the cumbersome bureaucracy that the nineteenth-century autocracy had become.

Over the course of the nineteenth century, the Russian intellectual movement continued to grow and to explore new directions: the "woman question" was part of this discussion, as were emancipation, industrialization, education, religion, and political development.

Alexander II's opening of the press to discuss emancipation added a new dimension to the discourse by inviting Russians to discuss a volatile political issue openly—before and after this brief period of limited freedom, all discourse took place either in foreign journals or in veiled language designed to bypass the censors. The failure of the emancipation to result in a prosperous peasantry or an independent gentry served as a catalyst for more vitriolic debate. The vast majority of peasants felt that their burdens had increased with the assumption of redemption payments and all of the responsibilities that the commune bore. The gentry struggled to maintain itself with much reduced income from their estates. At the same time, the philosophical struggles that had emerged during the time of Nicholas I began to coalesce in the universities. The children of the men of the 1840s who had been brought up to believe in a variety of progressive Western philosophies—and who felt themselves to be indebted to the former serfs whose labor had provided for the gentry not only a relatively luxurious lifestyle but also an education—began to believe that reform in the context of the Russian autocracy was not possible.

NIHILISTS

As they watched the emancipation unfold and saw how little it actually freed the peasants and how much it often hurt their own families, these young people began to look for more radical ways to effect change. The emancipation was a failure from their perspective and was proof that reform was not possible. A variety of groups emerged with different ideas on what should replace the autocracy, but all of the radicals strongly believed that the autocracy itself must be destroyed. At first, many of the radicals thought only in terms of destruction. The nihilists, as they were called, believed that the autocracy and all of the old political and social structures should be eradicated; out of the crucible of destruction, a new society would emerge. The nihilists did not have a plan for the new society, but they generally had vague notions that the peasantry would retain its communal tradition and that some sort of loosely connected communal structure would emerge. But their only real aim was to destroy the Russia that existed in order for a new and better society to be born. Nihilism was popular among students during the 1860s and is most famously portrayed by Ivan Turgenev in his novel *Fathers and Sons*, in which the main character, Bazarov, is a nihilist. Nihilists tended to be interested in science and to regard Romanticism as fluff and emotion as one of the defects of the human character. As the 1860s wore on, however, nihilism became less popular. The radicals still believed that the old society had to be destroyed, but they became more interested in empowering the peasantry to create revolution themselves. These groups were heavily influenced by Mikhail Bakunin, a Russian anarchist who lived in exile abroad. Bakunin argued that the peasantry was a tinderbox of revolution; light the match, and the countryside would explode.

THE WOMAN QUESTION

The radicals also rejected traditional social roles, dress, and occupations in favor of new ideas of what life should be like, particularly for women. The "woman question" had been a topic of discussion in Russia since the middle of the nineteenth century, when the heroic efforts of women nurses in the Crimean War inspired the surgeon Nikolai Pirogov to write a treatise praising women's capabilities and arguing that women could be far more useful members of society if they were educated and allowed to use their talents for the greater good. This, along with a spate of literature in western Europe at about the same time on women's emancipation, variously defined, inspired a heated discussion among the educated elite in Russia on the proper roles for women in Russian society. Although many stuck to the traditional notions that women should be submissive helpmates to their husbands, a variety of other proposals began to emerge, ranging from those who followed Georges Sand and argued for emotional, intellectual, and sexual freedom to those who saw women as the ultimate symbol of Russian political and economic oppression and argued that women should be treated in all ways as equal to men. This discussion, naturally, took place among a very small proportion of the population, but the "woman question" had a significant impact on the Russian radical movement. As they rejected the luxurious lifestyle of the nobility, they also rejected the idea that women served primarily ornamental and reproductive functions; Russian radicals believed that women must be productive members of society and sought to create equality for men and women in their own circles.

RADICAL LIFESTYLES

A highly influential book from 1863 by Nicholas Chernyshevskii titled *What Is to Be Done?* suggested an alternative to the traditional

Russian patriarchal family. In this book, the main character, Vera Pavlovna, escapes from an unwelcome marriage arranged by her tyrannical mother by contracting a fictitious marriage with a radical medical student. In this new form of marriage, the young man helps a young woman escape from the bonds of her only legally viable roles in Russia—daughter or wife—by marrying her and giving her control over her passport, which allows the woman to travel, live, and work wherever she chose. The young man also agrees that the marriage is entirely fictitious and will never be consummated. In the book, Vera lives with her "husband" in an apparently platonic relationship while setting up a sewing cooperative with women from the working class. The workers live in the commune, work together, and share all of the profits. Vera eventually falls in love, and her husband obligingly fakes suicide, leaving Vera free to marry. Meanwhile, the sewing cooperative has grown more and more prosperous, and Vera goes on to get an education, have children, and become a doctor.

The plot of this book is worth retelling here because it had an enormous impact on the radical youth of Russia. The values it espoused—selfless devotion to the causes of individual liberty (freeing women from paternal tyranny), economic cooperation, and radical change for Russia—became the espoused values of the radical youth of the 1870s and 1880s. Revolutionary chastity was an important value of the radical movement through World War I and allowed young men and women to work together toward their rather hazy goals of freeing Russia from the autocracy and serfdom. Fictitious marriages became a common way for young gentlewomen to escape their homes and embark on independent lives—and it is important to note that these marriages constituted a real sacrifice on the part of the young men involved; in conservative Russia, the couple could not divorce, which meant that neither could hope to contract a real marriage unless their fictitious spouse died—or successfully faked suicide. Cooperative economic enterprises were also popular, although few were successful. Communal living, not only as a radical statement of morality but also as a practical necessity for impoverished students cut off from family funds, became the norm for radical youth. Young female revolutionaries rejected traditional feminine roles and clothing, feeling that ornamenting themselves with fashionable clothing, makeup, or jewelry simply perpetuated their subordinate status in society, and many adopted a simple uniform of plain dress and hair and blue glasses to hide their eyes. Young male revolution-aries adopted a variety of dress, many preferring to sport tradi-tional peasant blouses and trousers instead of the fashionable suits of Petersburg or Moscow society. Although most of the radi-cal youth were far more puritanical in their sexual relationships than the mainstream youth, given that they shunned flirting and marriage as distractions from the larger cause, their unortho-dox and scandalous communal living arrangements made the rest of society very uneasy and spawned rumors of their sexual depravity. Their distinctive dress made them highly visible and encouraged all manner of speculation about their activities and goals and drew much unwelcome attention from the authorities as well as from conservative elements in society. Students were closely watched by the police and by their neighbors for any signs of illegal activity. This meant that universities came under increas-ing fire for harboring such radical elements, and students who were not involved at all in radical movements came under suspi-cion as well, as the government began cracking down on universi-ties in an effort to break the radical movement.

Although both male and female radicals rejected traditional gen-der roles, they still tended to fall into them. Many communal living arrangements were single-sex, but in those that involved both men and women, women tended to do the majority of the housework. Men tended to do the intellectual and theoretical writing while women did the tedious work of typesetting. Gentle-born women who became radicals often had more difficulty adjusting to the aus-tere rigors of the communal existence; life in the cooperative often sounded romantic, but the day-to-day drudgery of shopping for food on a very restricted budget, cooking and eating the same sim-ple and monotonous food, and struggles over cleaning and laundry with the other members of the household all without the help of servants turned out to be more work and less fun than it sounded in theory. Radical women had less freedom of movement and fewer economic opportunities than did the men. Although these women had rejected the frivolous existence of upper-class life, they often missed the amenities and the cosseting they had enjoyed at home, and some found that they missed the flirtations and roman-tic attachments they had so despised in their former lives. Finally, some found it very difficult not to depend on men; however much they might have believed that women could be fully independent, a lifetime of training to rely on men for protection was very hard to overcome. Women who found the new life difficult responded in a variety of ways: some adapted, some went home, and some stayed but became disruptive influences in their groups if they could not acclimate to the new lifestyle.[1]

RADICALS INTO REVOLUTIONARIES

Paradoxically, most young radicals, despite their living situations and appearance, engaged almost exclusively in reading and arguing about revolutionary philosophies. They read Mikhail Lavrov, and many agreed with his conclusion that their main purpose in life was to educate themselves as thoroughly as possible and then to educate the lower classes so that the lower classes could then take over the movement. Others read Bakunin and ached to get the peasants to begin a revolution. In the summer of 1874, at least 2,500 young radicals, known as Populists, took to the countryside to raise the peasantry.[2] They fanned out, handing out pamphlets and exhorting the peasantry to rise up and throw off the chains of their servitude by overthrowing the tsar and Church. The peasants failed to react. Most saw these excited youngsters as upper-class troublemakers who blasphemed both God and tsar, and a few even turned the students in to the police. Few peasants could read the pamphlets, and fewer still were moved by arguments about evils of sacred institutions. The authorities reacted with dismay and violence. Hundreds of students were rounded up beaten, tortured, and imprisoned. The movement was not very highly organized and had taken few security precautions, which meant that one student could name dozens of others. The lack of security and organization meant that it was relatively easy for the authorities to identify hundreds of the radicals. They also stood out in the villages they visited, despite their attempts to adopt peasant attire. By the end of the summer, several hundred young people were tried and sentenced to imprisonment or hard labor. Although the "Go to the People" movement, as it was called, failed in its revolutionary goals, it served as a valuable learning experience for the revolutionaries—if they were to survive, they would have to go underground. Many also reacted to the government's heavy-handed response to their peaceful activities: if handing out pamphlets resulted in heavy prison sentences or exile, there was no reason not to up the ante. Some of the revolutionaries rejected peaceful means as futile and embraced for the first time violence and terror.

POPULISTS

After the 1874 debacle, the movement split into two organizations, the Black Repartition, named after the practice of repartitioning land on the peasant commune, and the People's Will. The Black Repartition continued to espouse Populism: a broad-based, albeit more secret, movement to propagate their goals among the peasants. Members of this group often trained as schoolteachers, engineers, midwives, or doctors and then obtained employment from the zemstvo in order to infiltrate the countryside. They hoped then to be able to combine their occupational service to the peasantry with revolutionary agitation. Most of them found, however, that their professional duties were too heavy and exhausting to allow them to engage in much agitation. Zemstvo professionals, particularly midwives and teachers, were overworked and underpaid. Teachers found that their students were often uninterested and that the parents sometimes resented their attempts to teach even basic literacy and ciphering to their children. Teachers spent weeks on the alphabet in overcrowded classrooms and then faced the resentment of the community when it came time to collect their salaries. Midwives and medical professionals found it necessary to travel long distances to serve their territories and faced even more resentment than teachers when they attempted to teach basic hygiene practices that conflicted with their patients' customary practices. Both teachers and medical professionals were regarded with deep suspicion by many peasants, so that even those who found the time to attempt to "enlighten" the peasantry as to their potential political power often found themselves denounced to the authorities as troublemakers. Despite the difficulties in the lives of the zemstvo professionals, many radicals found their work to be rewarding because they believed that they were finally helping to improve the lives of the peasants. Only a fraction of the new professionals would consider themselves radical or actively engaged in radical activity. Still, the fact that radicals used the zemstvo system to infiltrate the countryside placed all zemstvo professionals under the deep suspicion of the authorities, making their lives that much more difficult.

TERRORISTS

The other group, the People's Will, was a small, tightly controlled underground group dedicated to terror. The experience of 1874 led them to the conclusion that in a society as oppressive as Russia, it was not possible to agitate peacefully for change without danger of arrest. The failure of the Great Reforms taught them that reform in Russia was not possible; the autocracy would never allow for changes that would threaten its power. Therefore, the only way to fix Russia was to bring down the government, which could be accomplished only through violence. The group idolized the legendary Vera Zasulich, a young student who, in 1878, shot and injured the Governor-General of St. Petersburg, Trepov, in his office in retaliation for the brutal treatment of a young male radical. Zasulich simply walked into his office one day and shot him. He was not killed, but Zasulich was instantly arrested and brought to trial. The government seized on her case as a good way to show its subjects the evils of the radical movement and opened the trial to the public, certain that it would rouse public sentiment against the student movements. Ironically, Zasulich proved so ladylike and articulate in her defense of her crime that the jury acquitted her while the press ran her impassioned critique of the police state verbatim. The emperor, shocked by the outcome, ordered her to be arrested again, but Zasulich had immediately gone underground and was successfully smuggled out of the country to Zurich where she joined the ex-patriot revolutionaries and worked with Georgii Plekhanov and Vladimir Lenin.

Zasulich eventually denounced terror and regretted her foray into violence, but to the People's Will, she was an icon of a successful revolutionary who took action and galvanized public opinion against the system. It is important to distinguish this group's ideology of terror from twenty-first century notions of terror. Whereas modern terrorists target civilians on the theory that they can frighten entire populations into submission, the People's Will targeted only government officials whom they deemed to be guilty of specific crimes against the Russian people. Although they did kill some innocent bystanders in their assassination attempts, they attempted to limit the damage to certain officials and their immediate circles. It is instructive to note the open letter sent by the remnant of this organization to the American people after the assassination of President Garfield. The group deplored the assassination and argued that in a free and democratic society such as the United States, assassination and terror were crimes. Because it was possible to remove government officials through legal means, killing them was unconscionable. In Russia, they argued, the government did not allow the people to make any changes, and this oppression forced them into violence against those officials who maintained and benefited from the oppressive government. Thus, they articulated a clear definition of when terror was permissible: only when all peaceful means were unavailable. In their eyes, no matter how evil the assassin believed Garfield to be, the fact that he had been freely elected and could be replaced by another election meant that terror was immoral and insupportable.[3] Throughout the end of the 1870s, this group successfully assassinated several high-ranking government leaders, but their main target was the tsar. After several unsuccessful attempts, three of the members successfully killed Alexander II in 1881. The death of Alexander opened a new chapter in the revolutionary movement in Russia by showing most of the radicals that assassination alone was useless. The People's Will had hoped that the assassination either would provide a window of opportunity during which the masses of peasants would rise up and overthrow the system or would at least frighten the government into granting more freedoms to the Russian people and allowing for more change. But although they managed to kill Alexander II, no mass uprising followed; his son, Alexander III, immediately assumed the throne and proved to be a vicious reactionary, in part, no doubt, as a response to the assassination of his father.

MARXISM

After 1881, radical activity was severely curtailed inside Russia. The "Temporary Regulation" made agitation all but impossible, and most revolutionary-minded radicals found themselves in prison or exile. This did not stop radical thought, however, and over the course of the 1880s and 1890s, radicals in exile kept up a lively discourse on how to change Russia. By the mid-1890s, this discourse had become increasingly dominated by Marxists. Led initially by Georgii Plekhanov, the Russian Marxists debated the proper application of Marxism to the Russian situation.

Karl Marx had developed his theory of history in the mid-1800s. In his study of European history, Marx concluded that the human environment and all human behavior were governed by economics and that history moved forward through stages as a result of the struggle between the dominant class and the oppressed class. The countries that Marx observed—England and the Germanic states in particular—presented a dreadful picture of working-class life. Governments had not yet begun to enact much in the way of labor legislation, nor was there any indication that workers would be allowed to vote or affect government in any legal way, because nineteenth-century liberals believed that only men of property should have the vote; Marx identified the emerging liberal governments as bourgeois democracies—democracies dominated by the wealthy segments of the middle class who were allowed to vote and hold office. Bourgeois democracies did not admit workers into the workings of government, but did tend to extend education and grant civil liberties to all, enabling even the oppressed workers to organize, propagandize, and easily communicate with one another. As the numbers of workers in industrial slums grew, Marx expected that eventually these millions would rise up and destroy the few thousand people who controlled not only the industry and government but also workers' lives. Marx believed that, based on the past pattern, the new society that would emerge after the workers' revolution would be the first truly egalitarian society that the world had seen. Because the vast majority of people would be workers, this new society would be ruled by the majority rather than a minority and would reflect the interests of most of the people. Furthermore, because these people understood the value of work and had never experienced much leisure, this new society would value work as well, and those who wanted to survive in this society would engage in productive labor (rather than pushing paper or living lives of leisure as some of the upper classes had done). Because work would form the highest value in this society, everything would be based on a person's productive labor: "from each according to his ability, to each according to his work." Over time, Marx believed that the remnants of the older society, the capitalist parasites who did not work, would die out or be eliminated. As new generations grew up with work as the highest value, as parasites disappeared, as production continued to increase and poverty was eliminated, crime would also disappear. In a world where no one suffered, there would be no need for religion, which Marx believed was a tool to oppress the weak—if no one is weak, if no one is oppressed, religion is unnecessary. As this process spread throughout the world, and workers' states emerged, conflict would eventually die off, and the need for government would disappear. Eventually, governments would simply cease to exist or "wither away," and true communism would emerge. In this final stage of human history, human society would achieve perfection. In this highly industrialized, work-oriented world, the new motto would be "from each according to his ability, to each according to his needs." This new society would be one of abundance, so "needs" would be understood as whatever a person needs to realize their greatest happiness and potential.

From the vantage point of the twenty-first century, this formulation seems very naïve, but many people found this theory convincing and based not only their own lives but also government policy around it. First, it seems highly scientific—volume 1 of *Capital*, Marx and Engels's major work on this topic, is close to 1,000 pages of very dense text. It contains a systematic overview of European history from which Marx developed his theory. In addition, Marx and Engels, and subsequently many other people, wrote many more books based on this theory. The appeal to science was very strong in the nineteenth century. Second, working-class conditions were appalling, and this seemed like a logical answer to them. It seemed so logical, in fact, that it frightened wealthier and more powerful people into passing a lot of legislation to avoid the predicted revolution. Third, as a theory, historical materialism has a lot to recommend it. It is hard to argue with the idea that people are shaped by the environment in which they live or that economics forms at least a substantial part of any society's foundations.

RUSSIAN MARXISTS

The Russian radicals who adopted Marxism were faced with some significant challenges in making the theory work for Russia. Russia was clearly not highly industrialized; most of its population consisted of peasants, not workers. Russia was only beginning to engage in capitalism and had certainly not developed anything approaching a bourgeois democracy. In trying to figure out how Marxism could be applied to Russia, Russian Marxists split into several groups by the early twentieth century. One of the groups melded Marxism with Populism. Known as the Socialist Revolutionary Party (SRs), these revolutionaries believed that the Russian progression would be somewhat different from that of the rest of Europe. Adopting the Slavophile belief that Russia had a special destiny and that the Russian commune represented a uniquely Russian brand of communal life, the SRs believed that the peasants represented the revolutionary class in Russia. Joining with the industrial workers, the peasants would lead a revolution and establish a new kind of socialist utopia that would combine industrial communism with agrarian communalism to form a unique Russian utopia. Most of Russia would continue to live in the rural communes but would have the benefits of education and mechanization to improve their lives and to form a tie to the industrial centers where the workers would control their industries and their cities. The urban–rural nexus would provide all the necessities for a rich life without privileging one lifestyle above the other and would preserve the organic Russian peasant commune. By 1905, the SRs had become one of the largest political parties in Russia and had itself split into left, center, and right SRs, the left espousing the use of terror, the right insisting on a peaceful, gradual approach that would eventually result in the peasants leading the uprising themselves. Most SRs, of course, fell between these two extremes. As far as political parties went, the SRs appealed more than the others to the peasants, who recognized in the SR agenda a desire to maintain the peasant way of life.

The other Marxist party in Russia was called the Social Democratic Party (SDs). This party was led by Plekhanov but split in 1903 into two separate groups, the Bolsheviks and the Mensheviks. The Mensheviks, led by Iurii Martov, believed that the Russian party should be a mass workers' party. They espoused peaceful agitation among workers, working with unions to educate the working class and bring workers into the party. The Bolsheviks, led by Vladimir Lenin, believed that this type of party organization would not work in authoritarian Russia. Lenin argued that a mass-based, democratic party would result only in mass arrests. He further believed that the Russian workers were too backward to lead themselves and that unions in general tended to embrace short-term economic goals and ignore the larger goal of revolution. Lenin believed that the only way a Marxist revolution could occur in Russia was to keep the party small and underground; only professional revolutionaries, dedicated to revolution above all else, should be permitted into the party. These revolutionaries would work through unions and in the factories themselves to educate workers and push them toward revolution. In 1903 the SD party broke between these two groups, and over time, the differences between Bolsheviks and Mensheviks grew. By the time World War I broke out, the two parties had very different platforms, goals, and strategies, although both remained true to the belief that Russia would eventually travel the inevitable path to a workers' revolution, and ultimately Russia would become communist. Their differences were in their methods, not their ultimate goals.

The Bolsheviks and Mensheviks were, by definition, interested in the growing working class rather than the peasantry, and they directed their revolutionary efforts accordingly. Bolsheviks and Mensheviks both sent agents into factories to educate and mobilize the workers. In his memoir, Kanatchikov, who eventually became a Bolshevik, wrote about his first encounter with such a revolutionary (Savinov) and how different he was from the other skilled workers:

Merry, sociable, and thoroughly skilled in our trade, he quickly overcame the normal workshop hostility with which the old-timers always treat the newcomer. Whenever the foremen left the shop, people would gather around his workbench. Jokes and wisecracks would fly about, anecdotes would be told, and at times a loud, infectious burst of laughter would resounds. Obscenities were almost never heard.[4]

The revolutionary debated politics and religion with the older workers and impressed the younger workers with his ability to counter every argument logically and thoroughly. Although these discussions made him uncomfortable, Kanatchikov found himself ever more persuaded by the appealing young radical:

There were several times when I was deeply angered and pained by Savinov's words. Questions that I had long since resolved, so I thought, and which had raised no doubts in my mind would suddenly begin to drill themselves slowly and steadily in my brain, as if a piece of thin cold steel was being thrust into it.[5]

Savinov had traveled extensively in his efforts to enlighten the working class, and his experiences impressed Kanatchikov, who remembers Savinov saying: "I'll tell you one thing that's for sure: everywhere you go, life is just as bad for the worker, who always lives in pitch-dark blackness."[6] Eventually, Savinov gave Kanatchikov literature that further opened the young man's eyes and led to his joining the Bolshevik Party.

Savinov's experience with Kanatchikov was not common—most workers utterly rejected radical revolutionaries who repudiated all of the beliefs that Russians firmly held in the late nineteenth and early twentieth centuries; the workers feared the agitators' atheism and violent opposition to the tsar, still held by many if not most Russians to be the sacred ruler of Russia. The life of a worker simply did not lend itself to radical activity—the long hours they worked and the dire poverty in which most of them existed did not provide the leisure or the space to consider the long-term political agendas that revolutionaries emphasized. Workers were far more interested in day-to-day economic problems and were more responsive to agitators who appealed to their desires for better pay, job stability, and better working conditions than to calls to overthrow the entire government. But revolutionaries who began with economic issues often found it difficult to move the workers past those issues to the political agenda. Revolutionaries who posed as workers were also subject to the same harsh conditions and long hours as the workers themselves, which left little time for them to conduct their propaganda and educational work. Because many of the revolutionaries came from more privileged backgrounds, they found the long hours, dirt, noise, and physical labor to be far more physically debilitating than the workers and often had to stop their work for health reasons. Consequently, the revolutionaries who spent their lives trying to mobilize the workers were often terribly frustrated, and many gave up the struggle, concluding that revolution would have to come from above if it was to come at all.

Even with the legalization of political parties and unions after 1905, the government suppressed radical activity as much as it could, and most revolutionaries spent time in prison or Siberia or were forced to flee the country. Many communists lived in Zurich and maintained strong ties not only with Russian revolutionaries but also with communist parties in other parts of Europe. Thus, many of the leaders of the Russian revolutionary movement of the early twentieth century were even farther removed from the daily lives of the people they wanted to serve than the nineteenth-century Populists had been. From their vantage point of Zurich, the Bolshevik and Menshevik leaders wrote long treatises on how to conduct revolution, but they had little contact with the workers they claimed to represent.

ON THE EVE OF WAR

On the eve of World War I, Russia was slowly emerging into the modern period but retained many of her traditional features. Most of her population consisted of peasants who lived in the traditional communal fashion. The elite was fragmented and dependent on their government service, which prevented them from posing any real challenge to the autocracy. The emerging professional, industrial, and working classes were still very small portions of the overall population, and although they posed real challenges to the traditional order, they had not yet gained enough strength to force significant changes to the political or social structure. The Revolution of 1905 had shaken the autocracy but had not resulted in any real sharing of power—the emperor was still sovereign, and the Duma, such as it was, continued to be dominated by the elites. Russia was ruled by an emperor devoted to his position as divinely ordained autocrat and determined to maintain that position regardless of the changes occurring all around him. The industrial sector of the economy was growing but was severely hampered by the economic drag of peasant agriculture, which kept many potential workers in the countryside and did not produce enough to both feed the population and provide export grain for capital development, and showed little inclination to change. Revolutionary movements and liberal philosophy posed a challenge to the intellectual hegemony of Orthodoxy, but the vast majority of Russians knew little of these new ideas and heartily feared what they did know about them. Most Russians, both urban and rural, continued to adhere to Orthodoxy, and the Church continued to dominate in areas of family law and governance. For the vast majority of Russians, life had changed little since the days of Peter the Great, except perhaps to become more difficult as rising prices and an increasing population strained the subsistence economy of the countryside. When war broke out, nationalism surged in Russia as it did in all of the belligerent nations, but it did not last long in the face of an economic and

Coronation of Nicholas II. Eon Images.

political structure that was not prepared to deal with the terrific cost of modern warfare.

WORLD WAR I

World War I was by far the largest and bloodiest war that the world had yet seen, and Russia suffered greater casualties than any other belligerent. Over the course of the war, Russia mobilized 15,500,000 men, of which 1,650,000 were killed, 3,850,000 were wounded, and 2,410,000 were taken prisoner.[7] Russian ineptitude in the war is legendary: lack of supplies forced men into battle without weapons or boots—they were told to get supplies from dead soldiers on the battleground; the officer corps proved itself to be an old boys' club, led by incompetent men who did not understand modern warfare in the least; Nicholas himself made the worst mistakes of all, failing to harness the goodwill of the early months of the war, refusing to allow independent public organizations to assist, and most disastrously, taking command of the front himself and leaving the government in the hands of the empress and Rasputin.

Russia's failures in the war were largely due to poor management and infrastructure. The inadequacy of the railroad and road system meant that supplies could not get to the front or the cities reliably. The unplanned and virtually unmanaged influx of refugees from the western provinces overran the cities where resources were already depleted. Peasant agriculture continued to produce, but the low prices for grain and high prices of consumer goods meant that peasants did not sell their grain; they saved it or consumed it themselves, exacerbating the hunger problem in the cities. By 1916, rationing had begun in the cities. Paradoxically, life for the upper classes in the capitals remained relatively unchanged, and while working-class women lined up for inadequate bread rations, the elite continued to enjoy sumptuous dining in restaurants and at banquets. The contrast between the wealthy and the impoverished had never been more striking than it was in the last couple of years of the war.

The war upset cycles of daily life for all segments of the population. The huge mobilization meant that men of all classes left home and went to the front, leaving many households in the care of their wives. Women of the upper classes threw themselves into volunteer work as nurses both at home and at the front, sewed, knitted and rolled bandages for the troops, and tried to help the refugees that poured into the cities. Working-class women found new jobs opened to them as the men went off to war, and their involvement in the workforce went from 27 percent in 1914 to 43 percent in 1917. Several hundred women even joined the infantry.[8] Women also became far more politically active during the war as a result of the government's failure to deal with the problems at home. Soldatki rioted when the government failed to provide promised benefits, women workers went on strike as workdays were lengthened and salaries were eclipsed by rising inflation, and a significant movement for equalization of wages began. Women led bread riots and attacked merchants they suspected of price gouging or hoarding.[9] The government failed to respond to any of these problems.

REVOLUTION

On February 23, 1917, a bread riot broke out in St. Petersburg (renamed Petrograd during the war); as with most bread riots, this one was started by women who then marched around the city, gathering support from the factory workers. The riot continued for several days, and the authorities found it impossible to stop. The Petrograd garrison was called out to put down the riot, but the soldiers refused to fire on the crowds, and many of them joined the demonstration. Other naval and army units mutinied as well. After just one week, the Duma realized that the government could not control the demonstrators and advised Nicholas to abdicate, which he did on March 2. The Romanov dynasty and Imperial Russia had ended.

Although it is tempting to blame the war for the revolution, it is clear that the war only exacerbated and highlighted problems that had long existed in Russian society. The revolution was not caused by any single event or problem but developed out of the failure of the Romanov dynasty to address the myriad of social and economic problems that Russia had been struggling with for centuries, not the least of which were revealed in the problems of daily life experienced by the vast majority of Russians in the late nineteenth and early twentieth centuries. Over the last half-century, the quality of life in the countryside and the working-class sections of the cities had been in steady decline. The government's attempts to reverse the economic problems without making social and political concessions proved wholly inadequate and merely frustrated the vast majority of Russians. World War I made the existing problems worse and threw the inadequacies of the government, economy, and infrastructure into sharp relief. The fact that the revolution was started by the segment of society that had historically been one of the most passive—working-class women—highlights the magnitude of the autocracy's failure to deal with the problems of modernity as it developed in Imperial Russia.

NOTES

1. Information on radical lifestyles taken from Barbara Engels, *Mothers and Daughters: Women of the Intelligentsia in Nineteenth-Century Russia* (New York: Cambridge University Press, 1983), 180–184.

2. Nicholas Riasanovsky, *A History of Russia* (New York: Oxford University Press, 2000), 383.

3. Vera Broido, *Apostles into Terrorists: Women and the Revolutionary Movement in the Russia of Alexander II* (New York: The Viking Press, 1977), 205.

4. Reginald E. Zelnik, trans., ed., *A Radical Worker in Tsarist Russia: The Autobiography of Semen Ivanovich Kanatchikov* (Stanford: Stanford University Press, 1986), 29.

5. Zelnik, 31.

6. Zelnik, 33.

7. Riasanovsky, 454.

8. Catherine Evtuhov, David Goldfrank, Lindsey Hughes, and Richard Stites, *A History of Russia: Peoples, Legends, Events, Forces* (Boston: Houghton Mifflin Company, 2004), 579.

9. Barbara Engel, *Women in Russia, 1700–2000* (Cambridge: Cambridge University Press, 2004), 132–133.

Glossary

Barshchina—Labor dues that serfs owed their landlord.

Bol'shak—Male head of the Russian peasant household.

Duma—First national legislative body (1905–1917).

Khazars—Turkic peoples whose realm (800–920) encompassed the eastern Crimea, central Ukraine, and the Aral Sea. They developed Kiev as a regional outpost. The Khazar elite practiced the Jewish religion.

Kremlin—Fortified center of cities that enclosed the government offices, major churches, and arsenal for the city. The Kremlin, capitalized, refers to the center fortification of Moscow where the tsar's court was located.

Meshchanstvo—Term that replaced the earlier posadskie liudi to describe all those town dwellers, usually artisans, craftsmen, and lesser merchants, who were subject to the tiaglo.

Mestnichestvo—System of ranking for the elite based on clan, place in the clan, and length of service to the tsar that determined all social, political, and military precedence. Established by Ivan III and governed elite life until it was abolished in 1680.

Mir—The village commune, usually composed of the elders, which was in charge of overseeing all communal aspects of village life.

Nihilists—A radical group of the 1860's that advocated complete destruction of the Russian political and social system.

Obrok—Monetary dues that the serfs owed to their landlord.

Posad—Area between the kremlin and outer wall of a city where the residences and businesses of the inhabitants were located.

Posadskie liudi—Town dwellers subject to town taxes, conscription, and labor obligations.

Raznochintsy—A category of society encompassing those who did not fit into the other *soslovie,* translated as "people of various ranks."

Rus—Name used by the Scandinavian Vikings (Varangians) for themselves and later applied to the territory inhabited by Slavic, Finno-Ugrian, and Scandinavian peoples.

Slavs—Indo-European linguistic group that emerged in the area from the northern Carpathain Mountains to the Dniester River around 500. Today the language group includes three distinct Slavic language subgroups: western (Polish, Czech, and Slovak), southern (Slovenian, Serbo-Croatian, Bulgarian, and Macedonian), and eastern (Ukrainian, Belarusian, and Russian).

Soldatki—Soldiers' wives.

Soslovie—The categories or estates of Imperial Russian society, composed of the gentry, clergy, merchants, meshchanstvo, and peasants.

Streltsy—Musketeer regiments created by Ivan IV in 1550. They formed an essential part of the tsars' armies until they were disbanded by Peter I.

Terem—Women's quarters. In the Kievan period, these were limited to princely palaces but eventually became a part of the housing design for all of the upper class.

Tiaglo—Taxes and labor and conscription duties.

Varangians—Scandinavian Vikings who moved south for the fur trade as the Khazar kingdom weakened in the ninth century. They dominated the river and land routes for the north–south trade with Byzantium and founded Novgorod around 850.

Veche—Assembly of freemen in the major cities of Kievan Rus.

Zemskii sobor—Assembly of the land called first by Ivan IV in 1547, again at the end of the Time of Troubles in 1613 when it elected Mikhail Romanov to the throne, and thereafter whenever a tsar chose to call it; the last was called by Tsar Aleksei (1645–1676). It was usually composed of boyars, church officials, lesser nobles, and important merchants and sometimes included representatives from other groups. Except for the 1613 meeting, the assembly had no real authority and was used as a sounding board and advisory body for the tsar.

Zemstvo—District and provincial assemblies created in 1864 to govern the countryside in the wake of the emancipation of the serfs. The zemstva were elected by curia—gentry, townsmen, and peasantry—and after 1889, were thoroughly dominated by the upper classes.

Selected Bibliography

Alexander, John T. *Catherine the Great: Life and Legend.* New York: Oxford University Press, 1989.

Broido, Vera. *Apostles into Terrorists: Women and the Revolutionary Movement in the Russia of Alexander II.* New York: The Viking Press, 1977.

Bushkovitch, Paul. *Religion and Society in Russia in the Sixteenth and Seventeenth Centuries.* New York: Oxford University Press, 1992.

Cherniavsky, Michael. "Ívan the Terrible as Renaissance Prince." *Slavic Review* 27 (1968): 195–211.

Clements, Barbara Evans, Barbara Alpern Engel, and Christine D. Worobec, eds. *Russia's Women: Accommodation, Resistance, Transformation.* Berkeley: University of California Press, 1991.

Cracraft, James. *The Revolution of Peter the Great.* Cambridge: Harvard University Press, 2003.

Crummey, Robert O. *Aristocrats and Servitors: The Boyar Elite in Russia, 1613–1689.* Princeton: Princeton University Press, 1983.

———. *The Formation of Muscovy, 1304–1613.* London: Longman, 1987.

Engel, Barbara Alpern. *Between the Fields and the City: Women, Work and Family in Russia, 1861–1914.* New York: Cambridge University Press, 1996.

———. *Mothers and Daughters: Women of the Intelligentsia in Nineteenth Century Russia.* Evanston: Northwestern University Press, 1983.

———. *Women in Russia, 1700–2000.* Cambridge: Cambridge University Press, 2004.

Evtuhoff, Catherine, David Goldfrank, Lindsey Hughes, and Richard Stites. *A History of Russia: Peoples, Legends, Events, Forces.* Boston: Houghton Mifflin Company, 2004.

Frank, Stephen P., and Mark D. Steinberg, eds. *Cultures in Flux: Lower-Class Values, Practices and Resistance in Late Imperial Russia.* Princeton: Princeton University Press, 1994.

Frieden, Nancy M. "Child Care: Medical Reform in a Traditionalist Culture." In *The Family in Imperial Russia: New Lines of Historical Research* (pp. 236–259), ed. David L. Ransel. Urbana: University of Illinois Press, 1978.

Halperin, Charles J. *Russia and the Golden Horde: The Mongol Impact on Medieval Russian History.* Bloomington: Indiana University Press, 1985.

Hartley, Janet M. *A Social History of the Russian Empire, 1650–1825.* London: Longman, 1999.

Hittle, J. Michael. *The Service City: State and Townsmen in Russia. 1600–1800.* Cambridge: Harvard University Press, 1979.

Hughes, Lindsey. *Russia in the Age of Peter the Great.* New Haven: Yale University Press, 2000.

———. *Sophia: Regent of Russia 1657–1704.* New Haven: Yale University Press, 1990.

Kollmann, Nancy Shields. "The Seclusion of Elite Muscovite Women." *Russian History* 10, no. 2 (1983): 170–187.

Levin, Eve. "Childbirth in Pre-Petrine Russia: Canon Law and Popular Tradition." In *Russia's Women: Accommodation, Resistance, Transformation* (pp. 44–59), ed. Barbara Evans Clements, Barbara Alpern Engel, and Christine D. Worobec. Berkeley: University of California Press, 1991.

———. *Sex and the Society of the Orthodox Slavs, 900–1700.* Ithaca: Cornell University Press, 1989.

Lincoln, W. Bruce. *Nicholas I: Emperor and Autocrat of all the Russias.* Bloomington: Indiana University Press, 1978.

Madriaga, Isabella de. *Russia in the Age of Catherine the Great.* New Haven: Yale University Press, 1981.

Manning, Roberta Thompson. *The Crisis of the Old Order in Russia: Gentry and Government.* Princeton: Princeton University Press, 1982.

Marrese, Michelle Lamarche. *A Woman's Kingdom: Noblewomen and the Control of Property in Russia, 1700–1861.* Ithaca: Cornell University Press, 2000.

Martin, Janet. *Medieval Russia, 980–1584.* Cambridge: Cambridge University Press, 1995.

Moon, David. *The Russian Peasantry, 1600–1930: The World the Russian Peasants Made.* London: Longman, 1999.

Ostrowski, Donald. *Muscovy and the Mongols: Cross-Cultural Influences on the Steppe Frontier, 1304–1589.* Cambridge: Cambridge University Press, 1998.

Pavlov, Andrei, and Maureen Perrie. *Ivan the Terrible.* London: Pearson Education Ltd., 2003.

Platonov, S. F. *The Time of Troubles.* Translated by John T. Alexander. Lawrence: The University Press of Kansas. 1970.

Polunov, Alexander. *Russia in the Nineteenth Century: Autocracy, Reform, and Social Change, 1814–1914.* Translated by Marshall S. Shatz. Edited by Thomas C. Owen and Larissa Zakharova. Armonk: M. E. Sharpe, 2005.

Pouncy, Carolyn, trans., ed. *The Domostroi: Rules for Russian Households in the Time of Ivan the Terrible.* Ithaca, NY: Cornell University Press, 1994.

Pushkareva, Natalia. *Women in Russian History from the Tenth to the Twentieth Century.* Translated by Eve Levin. Armonk: M. E. Sharpe, 1997.

Raeff, Marc. *The Origins of the Russian Intelligentsia: The Eighteenth-Century Nobility.* New York: Harcourt, Brace & World, 1966.

———. *Understanding Imperial Russia.* New York: Columbia University Press, 1984.

Ransel, David L., ed. *The Family in Late Imperial Russia: New Lines of Research.* Urbana: University of Illinois Press, 1978.

Riasanovsky, Nicholas. *A History of Russia.* New York: Oxford University Press, 2000.

Riha, Thomas, ed. *Readings in Russian Civilization.* 2 vols. Chicago: University of Chicago Press, 1969.

Rowley, David G. *Exploring Russia's Past: Narrative, Sources, Images.* 2 vols. Upper Saddle River, NJ: Pearson Prentice Hall, 2006.

Smith, R. E. F., and David Christian. *Bread and Salt: A Social and Economic History of Food and Drink in Russia.* Cambridge: Cambridge University Press, 1984.

Thyret, Isolde. *Between God and Tsar: Religious Symbolism and the Royal Women of Muscovite Russia.* DeKalb: Northern Illinois University Press, 2001.

Vernadsky, George. *Kievan Russia.* New Haven: Yale University Press, 1973.

Wirtschafter, Elise Kimmerling. *The Structures of Society: Imperial Russia's "People of Various Ranks."* DeKalb: Northern Illinois University Press, 1994.

Worobec, Christine. "Death Ritual among Russian and Ukrainian Peasants: Linkages between the Living and the Dead." In *Cultures in Flux: Lower-Class Values, Practices and Resistance in Late Imperial Russia* (pp. 11–33), ed. Stephen P. Frank and Mark D. Steinberg. Princeton: Princeton University Press, 1994.

Zelnik, Reginald E., trans., ed. *A Radical Worker in Tsarist Russia: The Autobiography of Semen Ivanovich Kanatchikov.* Stanford: Stanford University Press, 1986.

INTERNET RESOURCES

Alexander Palace, http://www.alexanderpalace.org.

History of Russia, http://www.geographia.com/russia/rushis01.htm.

Historywiz, http://www.historywiz.com/russia.htm.

The Internet Public Library, http://www.ipl.org/.

Russian Links, http://www.hunter.cuny.edu/classics/russian/russian links/.

World Wide Web Virtual library, http://vlib.iue.it/hist-russia/topical.html.

Index

About the Author

GRETA BUCHER is Professor of History at the United States Military Academy. Her research interests include Russian, Soviet and East European history; Women's history; and early modern European history. She is author of *Women, the Bureaucracy and Daily Life in Postwar Moscow, 1945–1953* (2006) and has written and edited several chapters, articles and translated works.